UNAFRAID

UNAFRAID

JUST GETTING STARTED

KARI LAKE

Copyright to come

I dedicate this book to my fellow countrymen.
Benjamin Franklin once said,
"You've got a Republic, if you can keep it."
We are in the "if you can keep it" part.
Let's come together to save this great nation.

For we brought nothing into this world,
and it is certain we can take nothing out.
1 Timothy 6:7

CONTENTS

FOREWORD

by President Donald J. Trump

THOUSANDS AND THOUSANDS of patriotic Arizonans gathered in a packed auditorium in Phoenix on July 24, 2021. They had just lived through the greatest injustice ever inflicted on the Citizens of the United States: an Election that was Rigged and Stolen, and they were furious—and rightfully so! These wonderful people waited in the pouring rain for an entire day just to hear from their favorite President, yours truly, Donald J. Trump.

This occasion marked the first major speech I had given since our historic and patriotic Rally at the Ellipse on January 6th. Joe Biden, who had just been installed on Inauguration Day, was furiously fighting to censor anyone who dared to question the legitimacy of the 2020 Election. Americans from every corner of our magnificent Nation—myself included—were being censored and silenced. And for what? Exercising our God-given Right to Free Speech and, daring to speak about the Crime of the Century.

Amidst the total chaos and turmoil that the Democrats dragged our entire Nation through emerged a woman who was unafraid to stand up boldly and speak the TRUTH. That woman, of course, was my friend, Kari Lake.

During that Rally, I went down the list of Candidates who had joined us that day. As I was naming the various Arizona Gubernatorial Candidates, something truly remarkable happened. I said the words "Kari Lake," and the crowd went wild. Thunderous applause, quite literally, shook the room as thousands of Arizonans cheered, clapped, and screamed at the mere mention of Kari's name. For other Candidates also there, who were mentioned by me, this big auditorium remained virtually silent.

Kari's strength comes from her ability to tap into people's hearts. And there is no heart that beats bigger, better, and stronger than that of our great MAGA Movement, the Greatest Political Phenomenon in the History of the United States.

Our shared Movement to Make America Great Again threatens the evil among us. It threatens the Globalists, the Marxists, the Cartels, the Deep State, Drug Dealers, Human Traffickers, Big Tech Tyrants, the Chinese Communist Regime, and other Foreign Interests—these people are trying to destroy our great Country, and they know that the MAGA Movement, which always puts America First, is their biggest problem and threat.

Anti-American forces worked together to try and bring us down in 2020, and again in 2022. Once they got away with stealing in the dead of night, but actually over many days and many months, it was all too tempting for them to try it again in the light of day.

What happened to Kari Lake on November 8, 2022, is one of the most egregious cases of "highway robbery" in any State's History. As was proven in the findings of an Election Report, Arizona Elections are rotten to the core. When it wasn't enough to pull out the usual tricks, they sabotaged Election Day, with a large percentage of Election Day polling locations experiencing "technical problems," but almost entirely in Republican areas. They had to take Kari to a deep blue Democrat area, where the machines worked, so she could vote. People in Republican areas were not so lucky. Thousands of Patriots, who waited patiently for many months to cast their vote for Kari on November 8th, were turned away at the voting booth. Many of them drove from place to place, simply looking for a place to vote. No American should be forced to drive around from location to location or wait in line for half a day to cast their sacred vote.

In a situation like this, many Candidates, too weak to fight, throw their hands up and accept this horrible and very unfair situation. But not Kari Lake. She has a great big heart, but is as strong a fighter as there is. Kari knows we have no choice but to win, because they are destroying our Country. Kari Lake's story does not end in a defeat, because she is just getting started!

UNAFRAID

Crash Landing

"WE ARE GOING DOWN."

I was sitting in the back of a tiny charter plane somewhere over Arizona, bundled up in a wool jacket and multiple blankets—this tiny plane didn't even have a heater. A deep sleep came to an abrupt end when the smooth plane ride turned into what felt like the world's most aggressive game of bumper cars. I was 11,000 feet in the air with two of my closest confidantes, Lisa Dale and Colton Duncan. Normally, any bit of turbulence is enough to make Lisa panic. But Colton isn't the kind of guy to lose his cool, especially during tense situations. I could see his eyes moving to the windscreen of the plane, which was completely covered with ice.

We seemed to be losing altitude quickly, and the pilot's visibility wasn't any more than a few inches in front of him from a tiny 3-inch spot in the otherwise frosted-over window. All we could hear was the engine and the sound of ice hitting the plane. I should have known this flight was doomed when we took off and the co-pilot's door flew open just above the airport forcing us to quickly turn around and land in order to shut the door before taking off again. That was a bad omen. This, however, turned into a bigger omen: *I'm not supposed to get to where I am going tonight.* God had put us on a detour.

I looked over at Lisa, who was one of my oldest and dearest friends. A few months earlier, I had shocked her when I told her I was running for governor of Arizona and persuaded her into giving up her comfortable life, to help me start up a grassroots campaign. In the twenty-seven years since Lisa and I had first met working at the NBC affiliate in Arizona, I had learned two things about her: first, she was always up for a good adventure; and second, that if that adventure included the one thing she feared—flying—she was going to be a nervous wreck. Somehow, on this night, I convinced her that taking a charter plane was a safe idea. Even I got a little nervous when I saw the size of this plane as we boarded it. It was *tiny*. Colton, my right-hand man, didn't seem phased by any of it. He put on his eye-mask and was already sleeping before take-off.

From underneath the huge blanket that I was sharing with Lisa, I leaned over and assured her this was all perfectly normal, and we were all going to be just fine. I wasn't sure I even believed that myself, seeing as how every single window on this plane was covered in ice. But I thought it would provide a nice counterbalance to Colton's frenzied declaration that the three of us were about to plummet to our deaths. My words seemed to calm everyone down, at least for a moment.

As we sat in silence, jumping at every bump in the air and howl of the wind outside, I closed my eyes and prayed. This is something that I've done for years, since I was a young girl in Iowa. Thank God, my mom and grandma taught all nine of us kids to pray. I often don't even realize that I'm talking to God until I'm already feeling comforted by Him.

God, if this is how I have to go, I'm ready. But I would really love to stick around for my family, and to become the next governor of Arizona. I know there are people counting on me.

I opened my eyes and scanned the cabin again. There were no signs of improvement. If anything, our situation has grown worse. The windscreen was still completely obscured. We didn't dare ask the pilots any questions as we knew every ounce of their concentration was required to bring this flying icicle safely to the ground. I found myself hoping that if the plane did go down in spectacular fashion, that Colton and Lisa would be able to limp away from the wreck. They could do great things someday, even if I was about to become an *in memoriam* segment on Newsmax.

I also thought about the irony of our situation. All the fun trips Lisa and I took together with our families. The adventures, road trips, and all the risks you take in your youth and think "Wow! Thank God we survived." I thought about the hundreds of flights Colton said he had taken working in politics in his twenty-six short years. In all of those years, in all of those miles, in all of those flights, we had all managed to survive unscathed. Maybe our luck was running out.

I didn't even know what state we were about to crash in. We had left Phoenix and headed to Orlando. We were told it would take us all night to get there and require a few stops for fuel. We'd have to fly at a lower elevation because the cabin was not pressurized and it would be too cold and dangerous to fly any higher. What we didn't know was that the rain coming down when we took off from Phoenix was going to turn to ice within minutes.

We were all wide awake wondering exactly *how* and *when* this plane would crash. Would it be a ball of flames or something we could walk or crawl away from? I wondered if from the ground anyone looking up could tell our plane was in trouble—or did it look like a small, twinkling star in the sky?

———

Once, when I was about ten years old, I spotted a plane above as I was lying in the grass in our yard in the wide-open country in Iowa. It was one of those days when my parents had told me to "get out of the house and go outside and play and don't come back in until dinner," which was common back then. I had lots of good ol' boring time outside. Running around, climbing trees, exploring, riding bikes, getting into trouble with the neighbor kids. But on that day, I had laid down in the brown grass for a little bit of serenity. Looking up, I spotted a white speck moving across the sky—a plane flying over. Not many planes landed anywhere near my home in the middle of rural Scott County. As I tracked it, I wondered what it was like being on a plane. *Could they see me? Could they see my house?* I thought, *Someday I'm going to be on a plane going somewhere.* At that moment the most calming, beautiful feeling came over me—I recognized it now: God had enveloped me, reaching out with a message for me—one that stayed with me all these decades later. He said, *Yes, you are. You are going to be on a plane. And you ARE going places.* This was definitive. This was *declared.* This wasn't a choice; it was going to happen. That is how powerful that God-moment was. I wanted that feeling to last. But just as powerful and real as it came upon me, the feeling went away, leaving behind a sense of certainty and confidence that got me through a lot of difficulty and insecurity while I was growing up.

That moment was powerful. I *knew* God had something exciting planned for me. And as this plane was struggling to stay in the air, I thought, *Well, He did give me an exciting life. Didn't think it would be THIS short but . . .*

I always knew God would protect me and watch over me, but at this moment we were dealing with physics, an ice storm, a plane that should *never* have taken off in the first place, and two pilots who would need more than just skill to avert a disaster. We would need a miracle.

In the freezing plane, I saw my breath and Colton's and hoped these wouldn't be our last breaths. Was this God's plan? I hoped that it was.

The running for governor part—*not* the plane *crashing* part.

Maybe I should explain how and why I was running for governor and on this frigid plane in the first place . . .

CHAPTER 1

The Red Pill Generation

IN THE MOVIE *The Matrix*, John Anderson, who would later become Neo, was given the choice between a blue pill and a red pill. The blue pill enables you to live an artificial life controlled by a machine—the Matrix. The red pill allows you to break free of the Matrix and see the world as it really is. The "Uniparty" system is not unlike the Matrix, but more on that later.

My dad was a high school history and government teacher and a well-liked and highly respected football coach. I know he never planned to have nine children, eight girls and one boy, but that's how life works sometimes. Mom, who was an only child, loved all the chaos and commotion that came with having a big family.

Dad worked incredibly hard to provide for us, but we never had much food in the house when I was little. Often at dinner, it felt like I was fighting for scraps. We'd make do. Having eight siblings meant I had eight different role models. And frankly, eight different competitors. The youngest in big families are always trying to keep up with their older siblings. That competition motivated me.

With eight older sisters, the hand-me-down clothes I inherited probably made me look about a decade out of style. But it never bothered me all that much. No one ever told us we were poor; back in the '70s and early '80s everyone had some sort of struggle.

I've never envied others or felt jealous of people's success. Instead, I was curious as to how they made it, and what were their secrets to becoming successful. Success stories fascinated me. A TV show called *Lifestyles of the Rich and Famous* was popular back in the '80s—that may have been the first time I ever saw Donald Trump. His skyscrapers in New York City and luxurious life, beautiful wife and family. This guy was truly living the American Dream. Hard work and ingenuity paid off for him. He had what so many people wanted. I could have never imagined someday I'd be in that skyscraper featured on that TV show with a man the world was just getting to know named Donald Trump. I could have never imagined that we'd be friends. And I could have never imagined the fantastical journey that led me from rural Iowa to the life I have now. God works in amazing ways.

I was raised that if you work hard, you can get ahead. Conversely, if you don't work hard, life will be difficult and you will struggle. It's your choice. Our parents gave us life. It's our job to take that gift of life and do something with it. There is no one to bail you out or save you. It is sink or swim. That was the environment I grew up in. We weren't the Waltons. I had a childhood that was a mix of hard knocks, chaos, dysfunction, love, and struggle and I wouldn't change one darn thing about it. Seeing what kids are dealing with today in this crazy world, my childhood—warts and all—was downright idyllic.

During my early childhood, Jimmy Carter was the president— a weak president, to put it mildly. Under his watch, he set off one of the worst recessions in our nation's history. He left America in an ash heap. Ronald Reagan inherited the mess. Thank God for Reagan; he was perfect for the job—and a perfect leader for the time. Ronald Reagan guided a nation that had lost its confidence through a difficult, dark time—restoring our economy and our national mojo.

Times were tough. Almost all of my friends back in junior high and high school had dads who had lost their jobs during those years. Families struggled. That was one of my first real wake-up calls about the destructive nature of "progressive" (more accurately "regressive") policies.

I remember being baffled about the Iran Hostage Crisis. Fifty-two Americans were held for 444 days by a group of radical college students, while our so-called Commander-in-Chief peanut farmer impotently twiddled his thumbs in the Oval Office.[1] Calling him a farmer is actually an insult to hard-working farmers who were my neighbors and friends growing up. They'd never show that much weakness. America was being embarrassed on the national stage. Carter made America *weak*. But it's always darkest before dawn. And out of the gloom of the Carter-era came the morning: Ronald Reagan.

The Carter-era arose from the Watergate scandal and the downfall of Richard Nixon. After the fall of Nixon, Conservatism was adrift, the Grand Old Party needed a new direction. Ironically, that new direction was found in the past. After his nomination to GOP Presidential candidate in 1964, Barry Goldwater had famously stated "I would remind you that extremism in the defense of liberty is no vice. And let me remind you also that moderation in the pursuit of justice is no virtue!"[2]

Speaking in support of Goldwater that year, Reagan said, "You and I are told increasingly we have to choose between a left or right. Well I'd like to suggest there is no such thing as a left or right. There is only an up or down. [UP] to man's age-old dream—the ultimate in individual freedom consistent with law and order—or DOWN to the ant heap of totalitarianism."[3]

The media and Goldwater's Democratic opponent Lyndon B. Johnson managed to successfully paint Goldwater as a lunatic, turning the slogan, "In your heart, you know he's right" into, "In your guts, you know he's nuts."[4] But Reagan emerged from the Goldwater-era as the party's rising star.

Decades later, Reagan was able to repackage the Barry Goldwater ethos and present it to the American public. Ronald Reagan became the working-class hero of the 1980s. And this country felt ALIVE again. Reagan, always the Great Communicator, brought the country a sense of optimism that broke this country free from the Jimmy Carter malaise.

Maybe I'm looking back at my past with Red, White, and Blue colored glasses, but during my childhood and young life there was a constant sense of patriotism all around me. My generation may not have always trusted the government, but we LOVED our country.

In sixth grade at John Glenn Elementary School in Donohue, Iowa, Mr. Ragona, our principal and neighbor, started the day gathering the entire student body for announcements, the Pledge of Allegiance, followed by the singing of three or four patriotic songs. After that we went to our classrooms to learn math, science, grammar, and history—oh how we need to return to something similar to that now, and fast! Sadly for our children and our society, our public schools have fallen so far—they prioritize insane ideologies meant to harm our kids, like gender confusion, CRT, and victim mentality. They have been teaching our children to hate America. Telling them their motherland is evil and racist. It's tragic.

Every single parent I met on the campaign trail—including gay moms and dads and parents who were Black or Hispanic—told me they wanted this stuff *out* of their children's classrooms. Thankfully I didn't have to endure that type of "education." Thankfully the Iowa schools were doing a good job preparing students for real life back then. But also, *real life* in rural America was teaching kids to be prepared for the future. We can't expect schools to teach our kids everything. Families, neighborhoods, and culture is where we truly learn. So we must ask: In those areas are we doing our best to raise-up the next generation? Right now, I think we can all agree, we must do better.

From education to pop culture, we had it made growing up in the '80s. Some of the most significant movies of my youth were reflections of the qualities that made America great.

In *Top Gun*, Maverick's unwavering belief in his own exceptionalism, coupled with his love of country, led him to heroically shoot down three enemy MIGs and save his countrymen from the looming threat of an unnamed (Russia?) foreign adversary.

In the *Right Stuff*, good old-fashioned American ingenuity sent seven brave military pilots on a historic mission toward the stars to win the Space Race.

In *Rocky IV*, Rocky Balboa, the working-class Philadelphia hero, punched Communist stooge Ivan Drago so hard that he ENDED the Cold War.

To top it off, life imitates art. The American Olympic hockey team, a group of collegians, dramatically defeated perennial champion, the Soviet Union, in the 1980 Winter Olympics—the "Miracle on Ice."

Good defeats evil. America defeats the Soviets. It was all so simple and clean.

As comedian Yakov Smirnoff would say, "What a country!"

I consider myself a child of the Red Pill generation. We didn't need to be "red pilled" into waking up to the brutality of Communism and Globalism. Society was churning out good, red-blooded, America-loving people who wanted to work hard and achieve the American Dream. I was incredibly lucky to grow up during a time where the country was united around the understanding that national pride was a way to unify a melting pot of all kinds of people, and was nothing to be ashamed of.

Like me, Ronald Reagan was a Midwestern kid, who grew up in a blue-collar family, with deep faith and a love of country. I greatly admired him. There was something about his energy. There was a calmness to him. And kindness and happiness he exuded. He was an incredible communicator. His folksy oratory, his corny jokes, that twinkle in his eyes, it was like Santa Claus was in the Oval Office telling the boys and girls of America that everything would be alright. And telling lots of adults that too.

Reagan was coming of age when the Great Depression was underway—he knew tough times, he also knew they were temporary. And that with hard work, optimism, American values, and God, better days would lie ahead.

I felt a deep kinship with him. I think everyone who was alive during his presidency who is honest with themselves would say the same thing. To know him was to love him. We ALL felt like we knew him.

We grew up in hometowns about an hour away, but obviously many decades apart. He too must have had a God-moment. Some divine inspiration that led him on the path from small-town Dixon, Illinois, to Davenport, Iowa, where he took his first sports announcer job at WOC radio (it eventually became KWQC TV where I got my first job in television news) and then to WHO radio in Des Moines where he was radio announcer for the Chicago Cubs. That foray in announcing took him to California for Spring Training, which led him to Hollywood, and the rest was big-screen history.

Over the course of a few decades, Ronald Reagan had gone from doing broadcasts, to headlining big screen pictures, to leading the United States of America.

What a country!

My career path was also non-linear. One of my first real jobs was mopping floors as a janitor in a drug treatment center. What was so interesting about being a janitor was that it is rewarding work. You can see your success. You start your shift with a mess and through your efforts you start to restore order. I'd clean rooms for the day where people would later meet for rehab counseling trying to bring order back to their lives. I encountered a lot of troubled people, many bound for jail or there to avoid jail by agreeing to go through treatment. Often I wondered what led them, at such young ages, or in the prime of life to be so destructive to themselves. It struck me that the 12-step-program that so many treatment centers relied on at that time, brought GOD back into the lives of these broken people.

While I worked, I found myself building a storyline about the people I encountered while they were going through rehab and I was cleaning. I'd imagine the who, what, where, when, and why of how they ended up there. And I always made the ending of their story (since I got to choose it) successful. My desire to listen to or read about others' success stories made me realize we all had a winning story inside just waiting to unfold. Imagining the people in this treatment center getting better and going out to conquer the world. Visualizing their success in my mind. Because of privacy and confidentiality, I couldn't talk to them. But I wish I could have told them what I envisioned they would do. Instead, I prayed for them. It is so important in the midst of difficulty to see a positive outcome, to see a way toward better days.

I loved coming up with those stories while I worked. That love for storytelling led me to my first "real" news job at KWQC-TV in Davenport. It was cool to think about the Gipper having walked the halls. I was following in the footsteps of Giants, walking down the path toward that American Dream. Of course, I had no real idea where it would take me, but I was going somewhere.

My desire to be that "success story" led me to want to tell other people's stories. I didn't care if I was forecasting the weather, doing a human-interest piece, or delivering hard-hitting news. All that mattered was that I had a clear line of communication into American families' homes.

I felt a great sense of responsibility doing the news. I was an ever-present figure in people's lives. They trusted me, and I made a solemn vow to never breach that trust. My job was to give people the news straight and without bias. When you're a journalist, you do the research on a story, write it out, and then present the story in a clear and concise manner. My job was to tell *all* sides of the story (sometimes there are more than two sides) and leave my opinion out. You let the viewer reach their own conclusion. Boy, times have changed!

Now, so-called journalists in the corporate media wear their bias on their sleeves. They revel in their ability to manipulate the American public. They don't tell stories anymore. They sell a narrative. I truly believe that the modern media is the most dangerous institution in America and in the world. And it isn't so much *what* they're telling us. It's what they're *not* telling us. There is a "look here, not there" agenda in the corrupt corporate news.

For three decades, I watched newsrooms change around me. I watched good newspeople leave to be replaced by young ideologues. You could hire three newbies fresh out of the indoctrination training centers called Journalism School for the price of an experienced, seasoned journalist who had roots in the market. I watched the so-called Fourth Estate abandon all editorial standards and become nothing more than Progressive Pravda.

And it saddened me. Reagan once said, "I didn't leave the Democratic Party. The Democratic Party left me."[5] My experience with the news industry was much the same. One day, during Covid, I lifted my nose up off the grindstone of a career—a job I worked incredibly hard to succeed at—only to look around and not even recognize my profession any more.

I never stopped being a journalist. The news industry simply stopped doing journalism. And the Reagan-less Republican Party was a bystander in all this.

It was all so tedious. The Republican Party would offer some milquetoast country-club candidate, and the media would pick up their pitchforks and chase them around like they were Frankenstein's Monster. And we, the children of the Red Pill Generation, were expected to defend these mediocre candidates under some sort of obligation to the party of old. We were going through the motions. Reagan's departure from the political arena left so many of us chasing that patriotic feeling we'd all grown up with.

The Bushes couldn't replicate it. By the time Mitt Romney and John McCain were dumped on us, the Republican Party had hollowed out Reaganism and rendered it meaningless, cowardly, and stale. It seemed like the Democrats were picking the Republican Presidential candidates for us—the "Uniparty."

We longed for a leader who put the interests of the family room before those of the boardroom. We were looking for a new beginning, a fresh start. A leader who could return the Republican Party to those populist and patriotic roots. One who could form a unique connection directly with working-class America.

2016 seemed like it would be the final nail in the coffin. A third Bush, this one from Florida, had been selected to preserve the political status quo that spoke to no one but the out-of-touch ruling class.

The Red Pill Generation longed for someone who would fight for the little guy. Who placed domestic interests over foreign affairs. Someone who, unlike Barack Obama, would make *no* apologies for American Exceptionalism. Someone who understood the art of the deal.

In 1987 a New York real estate mogul named Donald J. Trump—that same guy I'd seen on *Lifestyles of the Rich and Famous*—released a memoir/business book called *The Art of the Deal*. It sold like gangbusters. It rejected the cynical Wall Street notion of "Greed Is Good" and demonstrated how with bravado, integrity, and ingenuity, any American can thrive under our capitalist system and achieve the American Dream. And Trump? He was the archetype: his swagger, his confidence, were not unlike Reagan, but uniquely Trump. These qualities, having been missing in recent Republican leaders, were universally American.

Americans learned a valuable lesson from the *Art of the Deal*. We are all provided opportunities to thrive in this great country. What truly matters is what we do with opportunities when they present themselves before us. Trump would give the American public "Reaganism on steroids." And Donald J. Trump—the man who had helped build skyscrapers and whose story first impressed me as a kid in the '80s—became the man who would redefine Conservatism and reinvigorate a Republican Party that was on life support.

When Donald Trump came down that escalator, dormant Reaganism rose from the grave, reformed into something different, but still recognizable. Right then a hero was born for Americans from all walks of life who just wanted a shot at the American Dream. That's when the Red Pill generation put on their red MAGA hats and began the work to Make America Great Again.

CHAPTER 2

A Modern-Day Persecution

CANCEL CULTURE IS REAL. Ask any American who's been canceled. It sucks. Cancel Culture is run like a mob mentality. It's base emotion. Innate in human nature. A desire to destroy, to humiliate another human, while still being able to tell yourself that you're serving the greater good. It's justified cruelty. This is the same mentality that led to the Salem Witch Trials, to the lynchings. You dehumanize someone to justify doing harm to them physically, emotionally, or politically. Thankfully, we've replaced sticks and stones with simple words. And if you refuse to let them hurt you, it can make you a stronger person.

I refuse to be a victim. But I can't deny that the constant venom being spit in my direction used to really get to me. Now that I see it for what it is—a spasm of panic—it rolls off me like water off a duck.

The worst cancellation I ever experienced was on July 15, 2019. My co-anchor John Hook and I were getting ready to tape some promotional spots for our newscast later in the night. It was all routine stuff. John and I would be in our places making small talk waiting for the production staff to get in our ears and tell us we were ready to tape.

Here's what they didn't tell us. We were already live and our private conversations, unbeknownst to us, were going out in real-time over the station's website.

A few weeks before my cancellation, I had announced that I was going to be joining the new social media platform, Parler. Parler was marketing itself as Twitter without the censorship. It would be a space where people could engage in their God-given First Amendment rights without having to walk on eggshells fearing a block or a ban, or having your account be buried so no one could see your posts.

Naturally, Orwell-worshiping Leftists in the Fake News decided it was a playground for Nazis and racists. That's what they said about any platforms they did not approve of. They wanted everyone trapped on Twitter where users could be silenced and canceled.

At first my new profile page on Parler didn't even make a splash. But out of the blue, it became a problem. I didn't get it. I had just come back to work after taking a few days off to tend to a sick family member. And when I returned, a young social activist running the social media accounts told me I had to shut down my account. I was perplexed that someone, who works in the media and relies on the First Amendment, would want to censor anyone.

I was sharing that opinion with Hook as we spoke privately about it while we we're waiting to record some promos.

JOHN HOOK: "Oh, they don't want you tied into anything like that where you're going to get blowback from the *Phoenix New Times*."

KARI LAKE: "F**k that. They're just a bunch of twenty-year-old dopes. And it's a rag for selling marijuana and it used to be a rag for selling sex."[1]

For context, I should tell you about the *Phoenix New Times*. The *New Times* was formed in 1970 by a group of leftist Arizona State students who wanted to make a publication that spoke to the anti-war crowd. Over the ensuing decades, not much has changed. This paper is a leftist rag that combines Marxist screeds with restaurant reviews and blurbs on the latest concerts. For years they infamously used the *New Times* to act like a real paper, but it was really a front, a vehicle, to push Backpage.com—a classified-ad type listing for sex trafficking, including the sex trafficking of children. The Justice Department shut down Backpage about fifteen years too late, but they finally shuttered it.[2] The *Phoenix New Times*, separated from that ugly chapter, evolved a bit and now they hawk marijuana products to a readership chasing a high instead of sex. Alright, back to my story.

HOOK: "I know, but they're in a position where they've got to explain it."

ME: "I'm reaching people."

I mean, how stupid. Having to explain to the *New Times* that I like free speech. Duh. I was perplexed why wouldn't every media outlet want their reporters and staff reaching *more* people in the market? More people, more readers, more advertising money. Seems like a good business model. Were they not interested in people who were on to the BS, who were seeking freedom and the truth from other outlets outside of the Fake News? Still baffles my mind to this day.

Twitter, Facebook, Parler. All of these were avenues for me to share the news with the widest audience possible. Why are we limiting our audience? If a journalist is doing their job, they are sharing information. But you see, it's reciprocal. What pro-censorship people fear is the feedback. They fear truth-tellers, like me, reaching people. They fear the *Truth* reaching the people.

Modern journalists live in a bubble. They think their journalism degree gives them the moral standing to decide what everyday Americans living throughout the country have the right to know. They refuse to challenge themselves. They hold fast to their preconceived notions. They wanted to push out into the public that the idea of going to Parler was like attending a Hitler rally. The idea of simply communicating and observing, rather than interpreting, never even crossed their minds. It's completely antithetical to what journalism was supposed to be. And that's the point I was trying to make to John. For the record, I don't believe for one second most of the people pushing this agenda really believe it. They push it to scare others from waking up, branching out to platforms that the government and other censors have no control over. They push it to scare people from practicing free thought and free speech.

John and I had been working together for decades. He was my "work-husband" and he was a great sounding board. He was playing devil's advocate here. But he knew where I was coming from.

We got the signal that we were ready to go live and we wrapped up our conversion and did our jobs.

A couple of hours later while we were on the set doing the news, during a commercial break, a coworker texted me that one of us could be heard using the F-word and the phones were ringing at the news desk about it. Then another text, the conversation we had had a few hours later somehow got looped and has been playing on the station's main webpage where people clicked to watch our newscasts! We were told an engineer at the station had "accidentally" recorded my conversation with John. Company admitted they goofed. Fine. This stuff happens. Except it wasn't that simple.

That clip had been put on a loop on the station's homepage and suddenly, it didn't feel like much of an accident. But I was willing to give the network I loved the benefit of the doubt. This must have been a mistake. No one at the station was out to get me. Why would they be? We were a working family. With the storm brewing, the mob starting to form. The leftists over at the *New Times* and the "Arizona Repugnant" (everyone stopped calling it the *Arizona Republic* when they filled their ranks with social justice activists and fired true journalists with depth and understanding of Arizona) picked up the story and tried to topple me since I didn't play along with their leftist narrative and bias. I was unable to respond. Company policy was: don't talk to the press. I know . . . a media company that doesn't talk to the media. Kind of funny.

I went to the higher-ups and asked them to put out a simple statement explaining what happened since the local media was infatuated with the non-story of me pointing out simple truths about a local rag of a publication. The national media had picked up on it too. A simple statement by the station would have cleared up the numerous errors in the reporting and would have put the story to rest. An honest mistake and a statement would have shown they had my back as I was being attacked for their mistake and was muzzled and not able to respond, per company policy.

I was waiting for someone to come to my defense and explain what had happened, but they never did. The station refused to say a damn thing in my defense. Twenty years of being an exemplary employee. Twenty years of dedication to my craft, my state, my colleagues, management—and crickets.

I was angry. I had never felt so betrayed in my life. The silence of the station and forced silence of me would make doing my job impossible as this ridiculous non-story suddenly had turned into the biggest story in America. I hunkered down at home to weather the storm with my family.

Naturally, rumors circulated that the network had suspended me. Colleagues who wanted to come to my defense couldn't.

Decades of hard work were crashing down because a private conversation got recorded and sent out across the globe—and the people
who had promised to have my back had abandoned me.

Looking back with the benefit of hindsight, the cancellation was
one of the best things that ever happened to me, because it reconnected me to my faith.

As the jackals in the leftist Fake News were circling, and turning this story into something way bigger while trying to destroy
my reputation along the way—like so many people who've been
canceled—I feared I would be fired, lose the career I had worked so
hard for, lose everything. The second night when this stupid story
had spun into BS levels that mimicked an international crisis, my
kids were being asked if their mom got fired, the trolls on Twitter
(before I knew they were not even real people) were attacking me
non-stop, threatening me and harassing me with no signs it would
end. I thought about the vitriol and it pained me that our children
are growing up with this kind of hatred online. I begged God to
intervene, *Please God. Get me through this. This is so hard. Don't let my
whole world fall apart over this.*

Thankfully I had faith in God. Before that, I didn't feel the need
to lean on God all that much. When things fell apart, I grasped for
Him; other times I went silent. That was my stance on faith. Use it
sparingly when needed. But at that very moment, I NEEDED God.

I feared the Cancel Cult would harass me right out of my job. I
feared they would harass me into ruin. How would I ever recover?

*God, I know I'm just a flawed human being. And I only come to You
when I need You. But I need You right now. The pain is too much for me
and I don't know what to do. I need You. Please show me You are with me.
Please show up for me. I know You are out there.*

If it seems like a drastic reaction, this was back when so many
were being canceled and losing everything. Now I look back years

later and almost laugh. Getting canceled? Who cares! It is a rite of passage in this upside-down world. But at that time, it felt like the end of the world personally. Very few of my friends in the newsroom had even reached out to check in. As if someone in the middle of being canceled was somehow contagious and simple communication with the canceled individual would infect them.

I experienced a tremendous sense of existential guilt right then and there. Who was I to ask God to jump in and help now when I had strayed so far from His path? But I prayed anyway. And I went to bed that night dreading the next day, but also hoping that a new morning would bring me the answers I needed.

And it did. God DID hear me. And it was incredible! Because I woke up the next morning and the cavalry had arrived. I checked my phone and it was hot to the touch. Notifications and messages had poured in overnight. The Conservatives, common-sense folks, freedom-loving Americans had rallied around me. The TV station was getting inundated with phone calls and emails to get Kari back on the air. The messages and emails coming my way were powerful. Viewers telling me they had my back and wouldn't watch if I didn't return. You hear so much about how the Conservative movement hates the media. But when my life went into freefall, the Conservative movement was there to catch me. So as I lay in bed looking at my phone, I felt God's embrace. He heard my prayers. I knew that I was no longer alone. People who heard and saw the pile-on of the Cancel Club rejected it, and embraced and supported me.

I couldn't stop smiling. My family, who was so attuned with what I was going through, immediately recognized the change in me.

One morning, my daughter, Ruby, came to me and said, "I want you to wear this for protection." She opened her hand to reveal a cross. I've worn a cross every day ever since.

Returning to work the next week, my renewed faith was like a suit of armor. God showed me He was with me the entire time. I had been through metaphorical hell and I had come out on the other side stronger for it. Despite the armor, things had changed at the station during my absence.

During my self-imposed exile, the cancel-happy liberals at work must have felt emboldened. The alleged "suspension" of Kari Lake must have felt like quite the scalp. I was no longer "respected journalist Kari Lake," to them I was "that Conservative woman who needed to be closely monitored." Even though nothing in our recorded conversation showed my political affiliation, 95 percent of the media is liberal and they knew I was not drinking their Kool-Aid.

———

A lot had changed since I first walked into a newsroom. Journalism schools have moved away from teaching journalism—telling both sides of the story, keeping your opinion out of it and using critical thinking skills, while questioning the government talking points and flushing out corruption. They've replaced all of that with liberal indoctrination and training students to be social justice warriors. I hoped to lead by example and help teach the younger staff to think for themselves. But brainwashing is a hard spell to break.

Things came to a head in January of 2020, when the first case of Covid surfaced in Arizona. We never learned his or her name. All we knew was that the infected person was tied to ASU-Tempe, lived in Maricopa County, and had just returned from a trip to Wuhan, China. Putting the pieces together, it seemed very likely the infected person was one of the exchange students ASU had allowed to come into this country from Communist China, to take part in something at Arizona State University called The Confucius Institute. The Confucius Institute was supposed to open up channels for American and Chinese citizens to communicate with each other. It mostly ended up being a vehicle for Communist spies to get a foothold on our college campuses, and, as it turns out, help usher a pandemic into this country.

The newsroom was in hysterics. The mysterious Wuhan virus causing people to collapse from a full standing position—toppling like trees in a forest—had arrived at our front door right here in Arizona. People felt like it was the end of the world. I was even caught up in the madness at first. With an asthmatic child at home, knowing that allergies or a simple cold or flu bug would land him in the hospital in critical condition, my mama bear protective mode kicked in.

One day, with the pandemic starting up, the network divided us up and sent most of the staff to work from home. I set up a studio in my small home office and started broadcasting the news from home. I did not miss a beat. My initial thought when the government told us we had just two weeks to slow the spread was that two weeks didn't sound that bad. Except it wasn't two weeks. It was never intended to be two weeks.

This gradual realization set in while I was watching the nearly daily Fauci press conferences hoping he would announce this Covid madness would soon end. But every time that little man opened his mouth, my finely-tuned BS Meter would go crazy. Everything he said was either nonsensical or contradictory.[3] I spent a lot of these conferences just studying the others speaking in the White House Press Room, like The Scarf Lady Deborah Birx and others pumping out fear. It was all starting to sound suspect. At the time I didn't know President Donald Trump (other than I had interviewed him twice) and reading his facial expressions made me wonder if he, too, thought these so-called government "health experts" were full of garbage. I could tell his Spidey Senses were going off too.

While nothing Fauci was saying was making sense, the corporate media treated his words like gospel. And they acted like it was their sacred duty to proselytize for him.

Being a newscaster, part of my job was to be the last line of defense in preventing nonsense or factual errors or bias from making it on the air. That anything that came out of my mouth was something I had control over. But as the pandemic wore on, it became harder and harder to escape the fact I was having a REALLY hard time reading the news. In the world of the corrupt news media Covid Fear and racial division were the theme du jour. Balance, common sense, and stories that calmed people's fears were of zero interest.

Pitch a story on someone who had Covid and recovered with few symptoms—no interest. Pitch a story of hydroxychloroquine helping with symptoms—no interest.

The Covid narrative didn't make sense. How was I supposed to be true to myself when I wasn't buying what I was supposed to be selling?

More and more, during the Covid craziness, I found myself leaving the signing off for the night as the newscast ended feeling sick to my stomach. Had I compromised my integrity? I was telling people what was going on, but it was only PART of the story, the other part was missing. These were half-truths and the good people of Arizona deserved the full truth. At the end of the day, a half-truth is just a dressed-up lie.

It was during that time at home, where disheartened by the state of the world around me, I turned much deeper to my faith. I know I wasn't alone. Many in this confusing time found solace in God.

I come from a middle-of-the-road religious family. My father was a Lutheran and my mother was a serious Catholic. So devoutly

Catholic was my maternal grandfather, that he actually disowned my mother for six years for marrying outside the church.

So I was raised a little bit Lutheran and a little bit Catholic. We went to church and Sunday school every week as kids. As I got older, I fell into being a lapsed or lazy Catholic. But Covid changed all that. With my at-home TV studio setup, I spotted a dusty Bible I had sitting on my home office desk, blew the dust off of it, and plopped it open. I started re-reading the Bible again, but this time with fifty-plus years of life experience under my belt. The words had *so much more* impact than when I last read the good book in Sunday school.

In any newsroom in the country, having a Bible open at your desk is not something you would ever see. My home news studio setup was awesome. I had a computer and a camera right in front of it and an iPad loaded with the latest news scripts on the left, and my Bible to my right. No teleprompter, but I prefer ad-libbing anyway, so that wasn't a big deal.

I'd read the news, then during the commercial breaks, I'd read the Bible. Back and forth, I went from news script to Bible, Bible to news, and then one day it hit me.

I looked to the Bible: this was the TRUTH.

I looked at the news script: these were the lies.

My husband, Jeff, was my sounding board nightly after I'd finished the newscast. He saw my frustration with the Corporate News' bogus push to scare people. I could barely stomach reading this garbage to the viewers at home. If I was finding it vapid, meaningless, or even dangerous, surely the viewers felt the same way. I told Jeff I wanted to quit, but I knew that my paycheck was not easily replaced. Few people in the country made the kind of money I was making. And those who did, wouldn't willingly walk away. But here I was, wanting to do just that at a time when the economy was sketchy at best, or on the verge of disaster, at worst.

Jeff was supportive of me leaving. He could see and hear my frustration with my profession. He told me not to worry about the money. But I did. I'm not a materialistic person, but I'm also reasonable. And no reasonable person would give up such a big salary. I knew the job had gone from being personally and financially rewarding, to unethical and biased. It now felt simply immoral. If I continued doing it, that would make me an immoral person. And I'd have to answer to God for that.

One night in November of 2020 I simply asked God to give me a sign. I told Him I was sure leaving the job was the right thing to do, but I didn't want to be filled with regret for leaving such a lucrative career. So I flipped open the Bible and dropped my index finger down on the page and read the first passage I saw. I couldn't believe my eyes:

> For we brought nothing into this world, and it is certain we can carry nothing out. (1 Timothy 6:7)

Whoa! I got the message. Loud and clear. I call it direct communication from God's lips to my ears. That was the passage that changed my life and gave me a punch of courage.

During Covid I felt a real tug at my heart to get my butt back to church. Slight problem: churches were closed down. The church we belonged to was open "by appointment only." I found that notion ridiculous, unconstitutional, and just plain wrong. People needed God more than ever. Why was the government putting barriers between us and God? Why were they so quick to cast aside our very first liberty—religious liberty? And moreover, WHY were churches and churchgoers willing to *allow* the government to do this??

I shared that grievance with everyone who listened. It was my best friend, Lisa Dale, who suggested that I attend her Bible church that Sunday.

"Isn't that one of those megachurches?" I asked. "That's kind of weird, isn't it?"

"Not at all. Just come and see for yourself," she replied.

On the way to the church, I told her that I was giving serious consideration to quitting my job. She looked at me like I was insane, but she was too kind to put it into those exact words. "Kare, you're just having a bad week, don't quit."

She was right about the church. I had a life-changing moment when stepping inside. The music, the worship was so powerful that the first three times I went, I found myself weeping tears of joy during the service. It was powerful. I felt a connection with Jesus Christ I'd never felt before. I felt the Holy Spirit.

The pastor's sermon spoke to me—like he knew exactly what my mind was wrestling with. As if he knew I was about to walk out on my thirty-year career and step into the great unknown. My mind was racing—was this pastor reading my mind? I turned to Lisa to see if we were on the same page.

"Holy crap!" she said in wonderment, "he's talking to you!"

The next Sunday was the same thing. Once again, the sermon resonated with me deeply. It was on that second Sunday when Lisa was convinced and said what I knew deep in my heart, "Yeah, you need to quit your job."

On the evening of December 25, 2020, I read the news for the last time. And closed the chapter on my wonderful, long, and successful career. I kept my decision a secret. Not even my "work-husband" knew.

As the newscast came to an end, I felt my heart race and a lump forming in my throat. Knowing this was my last time anchoring a show with my work partner was filling me with emotion. We were the longest-lasting, most successful news duo in the entire country. Twenty-two years together. Almost all of it spent at number one in the ratings. We finished each other's sentences. Made each other laugh, a lot. Sometimes we irritated each other. We got married around the same time, had kids around the same time. Our kids were friends and so were we. This was heavy. This was a goodbye that only one of us knew about.

We "signed off" at 10:35 p.m. that night. "Merry Christmas, Kari," John Hook said as we closed the broadcast.

"Merry Christmas, John," I replied, tears about ready to fill my eyes.

"I'll see you next year," he said. I was scheduled to take a week off for vacation and return in January of 2021. The news music came up, they cut our mics, I powered down my equipment in my home-studio, and dabbed the tears rolling down my cheeks. I closed the chapter that had been the last three decades of my life.

Actually, I didn't just end a chapter. I closed a book. Little did I know what God had in store for me would require a whole new book. That this next book would be an action-adventure, history and political saga, suspense-thriller and true-crime story all wrapped up in one with too many twists and turns to imagine.

I had officially handed my life over to God 100 percent in the past year. Not 50 percent. Not 75 percent. One hundred percent. I told Him, *I'm Yours. You lead me where You want me to go.*

I guessed that would lead me to working behind the scenes somewhere. After spending my entire adult life in the limelight, in front of the camera, I was ready to retreat to a slower pace. I never craved the attention or fame; it was just something that came with the job and I was ready to live a more private life. I was actually really looking forward to it.

The day we celebrate Christ's birth—two years after an attempt of my personal and political cancellation—resulted in a Christian rebirth. Little did I know it prepared me for what would lie ahead; I was about to be catapulted into the center of the political world, start a movement, and not even *wince* being canceled daily by members of my former profession and the corrupt political elite.

Everything that had happened in my life up to that point was preparation for what was to come. And with God now 100 percent in charge now, I was 100 percent UNAFRAID.

CHAPTER 3

Take This Job and Shove It

MY DECISION TO walk away from a three-decade career in the news industry was the hardest choice I ever had to make. But after I did it, I didn't regret it for an instant. I was uncaged and liberated. No longer serving under the direction of network guidelines, I promised myself that I'd take the opportunity to speak my mind.

And I had a LOT to talk about. America was a little over a year into the Covid pandemic and our freedoms were under assault. A small government Conservative at heart, I watched in horror as the government swelled in size and power and began to meddle in almost every aspect of people's lives. The government shut down our churches. It closed our schools. It chained off our playgrounds. It shuttered our gyms. They effectively locked people in their homes. To justify this, they invented one of the most Orwellian terms I had ever heard of: "social distancing," a happy spin on denying human beings the basic social comfort they needed to survive.

I had friends who ran small businesses. These were hard-working people who put their blood, sweat, and tears into their projects and were only just reaping the rewards of years of their labor thanks to a strong Trump economy. I watched as those lifelong dreams were snuffed out in a matter of weeks by an uncaring government monolith that saw no problem with people shopping at Walmart, but drew the line at the local mom-and-pop shop.

Maybe the worst of it were the stories that emerged from the hospitals. Human beings were left to die alone in hospital beds, while hospitals prevented loved ones from saying goodbye. And then to add further insult to injury, those same bereaved family members were forced to watch their loved one's haphazard funeral proceedings, broadcast on tablets and computer screens, and performed by overworked funeral staff.

"This was for the collective good," the government would tell us. But I didn't see the greater good in ANY of this. People *need* people. To isolate them to this degree struck me as less of a plan to protect people, than it was to control them.

For the most part, people complied. Good-natured Americans locked themselves in their homes because they were told to. But the hits kept coming.

People swallowed this indignity, turned on their TVs, and were greeted by the sight of Black Lives Matter and Antifa rioting and looting in Chicago, Portland, New York, and Scottsdale in "protest" over the death of George Floyd.

And George Floyd got to have multiple funerals. Thousands were allowed to attend. This was the new normal. Commemorating the life of a family member? Way too dangerous. But celebrating the life and the sudden death of a hardened criminal? That was somehow fair game? "Shut up," Big Government said. "Social justice outweighs all other concerns."

The hypocrisy was infuriating.

The American people were being told to trust the science, but the science was constantly changing without rhyme or reason. New edicts and guidelines came out at a fast pace. The top government virology and public health "experts" were telling President Trump he would be responsible for the deaths of millions of Americans if he didn't immediately shut down the economy and the country for a couple of weeks. Trump is a businessman, a marketing genius, a Patriot, and a strong leader. He is not a medical doctor. He is not an expert in deadly viruses or vaccines. He had to rely on the so-called experts who were at the time considered "world-renowned" in their field. Only later did we all figure out these "experts" are complete and total frauds.

The man in charge of charting the medical future for the American people was an imp named Anthony Fauci. Fauci, most famous for failing to solve the AIDS epidemic, was a government lifer.[1] But this was his moment and he knew it. Fauci seemed to revel in his new-found messianic power, as he began to dictate what medical alternatives the American people could be "allowed" to have.

Hydroxychloroquine? An inexpensive drug with a 65-year record of safety and effectiveness, even with pregnant women. "It's not proven!" he said.

Ivermectin? "Horse paste!" he shouted, refusing to explain how an award-winning drug was suddenly for animals only.

But these vaccines? You HAD to have these vaccines. These vaccines were now of critical importance to the survival of the human race—per Anthony Fauci. "Show us the medical efficacy of the vaccines. Prove they are safe for adults, children, pregnant women, and babies," we asked. Their response was that you can either take them, or else.

One of the worst things about the Covid hysteria and the vaccine rollout were the commercials. The phony kumbaya ads sponsored by Big Pharma. The media was officially bought and paid for by Pharma—that meant no newsroom would ever cover the stories of deadly and debilitating side effects of the shots. Instead, the news anchors and reporters were telling us the shots were safe and coaxing the public to get the jab.

And while the American people were forced to choose between injecting some unknown substance into their body, or losing their jobs, access to their favorite store, or the ability to travel, Anthony Fauci and his benefactors in Big Pharma became rich beyond their wildest dreams.

They didn't care how many other people's dreams they shattered along the way.

If people wouldn't comply, they would be made to comply. I watched as mandates in defiance of our Founding Fathers' wishes were imposed on an increasingly isolated American populace.

Businesses were raided. People were beaten. Our economy cratered. And our cities burned. A further humiliation was the masks. The idea that a thin piece of cloth that sealed off neither my mouth or nose offered some magical resistance to a virus seemed ridiculous to me.

It didn't help matters that Anthony Fauci had begun the pandemic by saying that masks were useless, only to change his mind without explanation just a few months later.

But what bothered me the most were the mandates. I believe that people have every right to get a shot or wear a mask, but it had to be their choice. The idea that the government had the right to control people's medical decisions wasn't just a slippery slope, it was a straight-out plummet toward fascism. That's not the constitutional republic that our Founding Fathers promised us.

But that was how it worked in Covid America. The government told us to jump, and expected us to ask "How high?" That wasn't my style. I preferred to keep my feet firmly rooted to the ground.

One of the consequences of Covid-hysteria and the government making it almost impossible for you to leave your house, was the introduction of mass mail-in balloting to our election system.

Couldn't leave your house? Send a ballot.

Didn't know where your polling place was? Send a ballot.

Are you mentally incapacitated or infirm? Someone will come collect and send your ballot for you.

Are you dead? We'll send a ballot for you anyway.

Are you a fan of Joe Biden? Send multiple ballots.

I'm being tongue-in-cheek, but only slightly. There's no denying this simple truth that the Covid restrictions allowed for the unconstitutional loosening of our election procedures, resulting in an influx of ballots coming from every direction, with no discernible source.

And then there was the matter of Hunter Biden's laptop. Hunter's laptop—or the laptop from hell, as President Trump called it—was an old laptop that Joe Biden's tire-fire of a son, Hunter, had dropped off at a computer repair shop in Delaware, and promptly forgotten about.

While doing a basic diagnostic of the machine, the shop owner had discovered the laptop's contents were the motherlode of personal depravity and political corruption.

We're talking about business dealings with foreign leaders, where Hunter clearly leveraged the family name to make money, sex tapes with prostitutes, hard drug use, and what looked disturbingly like sex crimes against children.

But perhaps most noteworthy was a series of emails between Hunter, Jim Biden (Joe's brother) and a business partner (Tony Bobulinski), where they laid out what was clearly a quid pro quo. An arrangement where Hunter would exploit the Biden name in shady business deals and potentially treasonous activities, and Joe the "Big Guy" Biden would receive 10 percent of the profits.

Pretty damning, right?

This laptop was turned over to the FBI, before the 2020 election, only for the FBI to sit on the information for months. Finally, the laptop surfaced ending up in the hands of the *New York Post* who set about airing the dirty Biden laundry to the world.[2]

This material suggested that the Biden family was compromised by foreign interests. It was a giant red flag. And the whole country deserved to know of its existence before making the choice of who would be the next leader of the free world between Joe Biden and Donald Trump.

But the intelligence community and the Fake News didn't see it that way.

Through a coordinated effort by Big Tech between Big Government, a disinformation campaign was waged painting the contents of the laptop as Russian disinformation. Former intel officials wrote letters, newscasters rolled their eyes, all in an effort to discredit this very legitimate evidence of Biden Family corruption.

In an attempt to strangle this story in its infancy, Big Tech arranged a complete media blackout and censorship campaign, deplatforming and blacklisting anyone who attempted to share the story.

What resulted was an uninformed public, an unholy alliance between Big Tech and Big Government, all of which resulted in a disastrous presidential election, where the "winning" candidate somehow came out on top despite generating no public enthusiasm, not running a campaign, and not answering any questions from his subservient press.

I remember on election night (November 3, 2020) I was doing live election coverage for Fox10 in Arizona. I can still recall the moment when my producer got in my ear, and told me that Bret Baier from Fox News had just called Arizona for Joe Biden.

I allowed myself a glimpse at the clock. It was 9:20 p.m.

Arizona polls had closed just an hour and twenty minutes before; there were reports that Arizonans were still standing in line waiting to vote, and Fox News was saying that it was already over. What was the rush?

It didn't feel right. I said as much on TV three times during our election night broadcast. I expressed my concern about that early call, but all I could do was talk, I couldn't change anything. I wrapped up the election coverage with my co-anchor John Hook like this:

> ME: I've been watching the numbers and we've gotten so few additional votes since that first batch came in. I am seeing ever so slightly Biden's numbers come down and ever so slightly Trump's going up. Who knows where it goes.
>
> The problem with calling this when you still have 900,000 possibly upwards of 1 million votes out there is that voters get it in their mind when they go to bed that one person won and the other one didn't and when they wake up tomorrow or two days later and it flips—there's distrust in the system. The people who feel like their candidate maybe was robbed because at one point they were told the candidate won and now the votes are counted and the candidate didn't. It's just with the powder keg situation we're in. It's just kind of dangerous.
>
> JOHN HOOK: Well we're taking our cues from FOX, the mothership, that's kind of what we do, so right now they've called it for Joe Biden so there's really not—ya know, we can speculate, but we just have to go with what they've told us so far.[3]

I was appalled that "the mothership" as Hook called it, was trying to influence this election. This was absurd and wrong. For the next week, the world watched as President Trump ate into Joe Biden's lead.

We all expected Trump to somehow pull it off. But this was a corrupted election system set on delivering the White House to Biden. The people were for Trump, but the corrupt rot at the heart of Maricopa County Elections was not. Eventually, the rest of the networks began to join Fox News in calling Arizona for Joe Biden. At the end, according to their bogus results, a margin of just 10,457 votes separated the two candidates.

This result seemed . . . unlikely. As long as I'd lived here, Arizona had been a red state.

Hell, Arizona was so red that Joe Biden had become the first Democrat to "win" Maricopa County since Harry Truman. What were the chances that out of all of the Democratic candidates to make these historical gains, it was the old pervert who never left his basement, couldn't draw a crowd, and had no ties to Arizona?

And besides, Arizona was MAGA Country. You could feel it, you could *see* it.

Driving around the Valley, you would encounter Trump rallies on random street corners, trains of cars miles long, enthusiastic flag parades, the red MAGA hat joining the cowboy hat as an Arizona fashion accessory.

Whenever Donald Trump came to Arizona, he would draw record crowds. The one week Joe Biden stopped by he drew about six people to a bus tour stop in Flagstaff.

Yet we were supposed to believe that all that meant nothing? That there was some secret underground base of Joe Biden supporters that took an entire state by surprise?

The people wanted answers.

It started on election night, when thousands of people swarmed the Maricopa County Election Tabulation Center for a spontaneous "Stop the Steal" rally. These were people of every race, age, and gender out protesting for a more transparent "democracy." And unlike the Left, with "their mostly peaceful protests," these citizens weren't destroying property, or burning flags—far from it. They were praying.

It was beautiful. But the mainstream media didn't see it that way. I watched as the Radical Left and the media began to paint their insurrectionist narrative LONG before January 6.

In the month that followed, grassroots Arizonans repeatedly called upon their (supposedly) Republican governor to call a special session to investigate the election. Instead Governor Doug Ducey went radio silent.

Undeterred, people petitioned the Maricopa County Board of Supervisors to delay their canvas to give investigators more time to do their work prior to certification. But Maricopa County seemed desperate to sweep the entire process under the rug.

On November 30, it seemed like people's prayers were answered. Representative Mark Finchem, and a group of Arizona legislators, hosted a hearing that gave President Trump's attorneys and eye-witnesses the opportunity to present evidence and testimony about the irregularities on Election Day. In an incredibly selfless move, Finchem paid to rent a conference room with his own money so that this testimony could get out. It was incredibly compelling. But I'll never forget what happened about halfway through this event.

While one of the witnesses gave testimony, someone entered the room, approached the lawyers table, and whispered something to one of Trump's attorneys. It didn't take long for the news to spread: despite knowing that the proceedings were ongoing, evidence was finally being shared that Governor Doug Ducey, Attorney General Mark Brnovich, and Secretary of State Katie Hobbs had secreted away and certified the election under all of our noses.

To add insult to injury, President Trump had tried to call Ducey during the certification ceremony. Ducey took out the phone, smirked as the ringtone "Hail to the Chief" echoed through the room. Ducey looked at that phone and then jammed a pudgy finger into the mute button.

It was the ultimate betrayal. But defeat is not in Arizona's nature. We were down, but we certainly were not out.

Over the next few months, grassroots Arizonans continued to pressure their legislators until finally an independent audit of the 2020 election was announced. The Arizona audit, Senate leaders Karen Fann and Warren Petersen announced, would provide skeptical voters the transparency that the election did not. Independent auditors would be allowed to sift through the ballots, examine their integrity, and then collect their findings into a report that would then be turned over to the Attorney General for future "action."

The biggest hurdle the audit faced was that the whole process was quite literally unprecedented. There was no professional election auditing company. So when the Senate hired a group of forensic investigators called the Cyber Ninjas, they were immediately met with skepticism and derision by the partisan press. To help answer some of these concerns, the Senate appointed three liaisons to help oversee the audit.

It was a thrilling time to be in Arizona. After the gut punch of the 2020 election, Arizonans felt like they were on their way to getting the truth to the nagging questions surrounding Joe Biden's "victory."

And so that was the environment I found myself in during the days following my decision to leave the media industry.

I guess we should get into that. Why did Kari Lake walk away from the media industry after thirty years of delivering the news to the people of Arizona? To make a LONG story short: my decision to leave my job was because journalism was replaced with propaganda, and I wasn't interested in lying to my fellow citizens.

When Covid started to ramp up, the network forced me to work from home. And it was from the comfort of my own living room that

I witnessed the corporate media pushing fear and an agenda that I felt was meant to divide us.

Covid was bad. But the news was making it out to be apocalyptic. Every hour filled with all terrible news, the climbing death counter next to their chyron, a macabre reminder of constant loss and impending doom. Except there was no context to it. Yes, Covid was spreading like wildfire, but the vast majority of people who caught it, not only survived, but emerged from the virus with a natural immunity. While the loss of life was tragic, the people the virus hurt the most were people with pre-existing conditions and the elderly. In short, the virus was acting like a virus. If you were particularly susceptible to it, you were going to get it. I understood that accommodations needed to be made and protections needed to be provided, but at the expense of our children? Our families? Our freedoms? This was a trade-off the American people never agreed to make. The choice was made *for* them.

I wanted to tell the stories of the survivors, of those who were persevering in the midst of the restrictions and insanity. The people who had encountered disease and successfully fought it. I wanted to learn what they had learned from the experience. Those able to keep their businesses afloat. Those showing the American spirit. There was no interest in stories that would calm people's nerves, reduce their fear, and set us on course to recover and move forward. There's no incentive to sell hope when the profit comes from fear.

I left the news because I saw a rejection of commonsense stories that would help bring people together. I witnessed a calculated decision to ignore any potential solutions to the health problems that ran the risk of infringing on Big Pharma's profits.

It was also during this time at home that I reconnected with my faith and our God. And it was with the Lord's blessing that I left my career in search of a new beginning.

When I announced my resignation via a video, I had no political ambitions. I just wanted to tell the public my reasons for quitting my job. To my surprise, the video went viral. And almost immediately people started to reach out to me to ask me if I would consider running for office.

Dozens of people were messaging me every day, encouraging me to run for office. "We need someone we trust," many said. "We need someone with courage, who understands us."

What the hell is wrong with you? I thought. *We just had the election stolen. Why would I ever want to be part of that? And why would I go from the corrupt media into the even more corrupt world of politics??* But for all my protestations, I was starting to warm to the idea. I love Arizona, and whatever my next career step would be, I knew I wanted to be in a position to help make the state better.

So I reached out to Jan Brewer to pick her brain about the idea. She texted me to say maybe I should consider it. Jan Brewer had been the 22nd Governor of Arizona. She served Arizonans well in that capacity from 2009 to 2015. While she scored some policy victories, the highpoint of her gubernatorial tenure was a testy exchange she shared with Barack Obama on the tarmac of Phoenix-Mesa Gateway Airport during the president's January 25, 2012 visit to Arizona.

You've probably seen the photograph. Obama leaning over the governor as if to intimidate her, Brewer standing her ground and wagging a finger in his face. It's a wonderful image. An image that Jan would use in the ensuing years to paint herself as a stalwart conservative warrior. This bit of self-mythologizing left out the fact that Jan had run to the press the day following the incident to claim she "was not hostile" in the meeting, but who can begrudge her the good story?

Regardless, while Jan was partially responsible for the codification of Obamacare, and vetoed some very conservative legislation, she remained a respected figure in Arizona conservative circles. So for her to say that she thought I had a future in politics meant a lot.

We met on a Friday afternoon in March of 2021, a few days after my resignation had been made public at Zipps Sports Grill on the west side of Phoenix. Covid was still an ongoing concern. I remember how surreal it was walking into this restaurant and seeing the tables spaced out like chess pieces on a board, as if there was a certain amount of overlap (six feet?) that separated you, your table, and certain death. But I walked past the chess match over to the corner of the restaurant and spotted the familiar blond hair and big smile of Jan Brewer. I took a seat across the booth from the former governor of Arizona.

I covered Jan during my journalist days. I took it as a sign of pride that she considered me a "fair" journalist. We had become a little more friendly after her term in the 9th Floor was over. Jan would occasionally text me during difficult times, when she felt like I needed encouragement.

When I sat down with Jan, I expected nothing more than our usual friendly chat. And for a while it was exactly that. We ordered our drinks and Jan asked me to explain why I had chosen to leave the news. I told her and we began to reminisce about the less insane Arizona that we both knew and loved.

Our conversation was interrupted by a pair of construction workers who came to our table looking particularly excitable. "Are you Kari Lake?" one asked. I confirmed that I was indeed. He continued, "I want to thank you for your courage and integrity. It took some balls to walk away from your job like that." I smiled. And his companion stepped forward. "You are our freaking hero! You are a freaking rock star! And I just want you to know that I picked up your tab." Flattered, I thanked them profusely. A few more people came to our table over the course of my conversation with former Governor Brewer. It was a sign of what was to come for me. People appreciate courage and a fighter. That's what we need. Though they did not recognize Brewer, I made sure to introduce her to those who approached out of respect for her.

We resumed pleasantries.

We talked about my husband, Jeff.

We talked about my children, Ruby and Leo.

My interest in politics . . . tentative.

Covid . . . let's end this nonsense.

The state of the county . . . ominous.

"Joe Biden is really hurting this country," I said. Jan nodded in agreement. I continued, "I'm hoping for the best, but I expect the worst. We just gotta keep fighting. That election was a nightmare. It's so wrong what happened."

Jan tilted her head.

"Thank God that Karen Fann got us the forensic audit. I guess we'll see what that turns up."

Very bubbly and kind up until that moment, Jan stared over at me and with a disapproving tone, balked at *any* notion of looking into the 2020 election, or even questioning it. It was a visceral reaction that, frankly, shocked me. She shot me down for supporting an audit as if I was a school girl who stepped out of line and needed to be disciplined.

Jan quickly changed the subject to God-knows-what, I couldn't even hear what she was saying or remember because my mind was trying to understand *why* she would so vehemently oppose simply "checking under the hood" of the botched 2020 election to alleviate voters' concerns and make corrections to areas in our election process that needed improvement. As Jan continued talking, I racked my brain wondering *why*.

My take at the time was, the more the Maricopa County Recorder and Board of Supervisors protest, the more they must be hiding. It's not conspiracy talk. We all saw how they used Covid to shut down the places we used to vote: churches and schools. They ended small precinct voting where fraud is easier to detect and forced massive Voting Centers on us. They flooded Maricopa County with ballots. And I don't think it made anyone feel any better when Maricopa County's response to good faith questions was to stonewall our voters and their state legislators.

It angered me to see how the media treated people who had questions about the election. We are *supposed* to question our government and call out corruption. So is the media; that's their job. There were normal people with perfectly reasonable doubts about an election process that seemed designed to be intentionally nontransparent. All they wanted was for their representatives to answer their questions and help them put aside their fears. And it wasn't like allegations of this type were new to Arizona. People had voiced similar concerns in 2018 when many Republicans were winning on election night, only to see the lead disappear overnight for Democrats to be declared the winners in the following day or two. Kyrsten Sinema had emerged victorious after a week-long counting process and credible rumors were reported of misplaced ballots being found at the side of the road or in people's trunks.

I could understand why people had doubts. I shared them too. My mind wandered from all of that Covid undermining of elections to the reason our former Republican governor was so *triggered* about an election audit. My mind came back to the oversized booth at the sports bar, the two beers at the table, and our lunches we were both still picking at and the sound of Jan launching into another story.

I wish I had recorded it because the story she told means a hell of a lot more to me *now* than the first time I heard it.

On January 21, 2009, Democrat Governor Janet Napolitano resigned from her position to join the Obama administration.

Secretary of State Jan Brewer was next in the line of succession and was sworn in to take her place. Jan barely had time to measure the drapes in the 9th Floor before being thrown into the 2010 Republican Gubernatorial Primary, which she won, and then a General Election contest against the Democratic Attorney General Terry Goddard.

On September 2, 2010, Jan debated her opponents on local PBS television station. To call her performance a *disaster* would be an understatement. It may be one of the worst debate performances in the history of debates. Here was Jan's opening statement:

"Thank you, Ted, and it's great to be here with Larry, Barry, and Terry and thank you all for watching this tonight. I have . . . ah . . ."

A look of panic in her eyes, Jan shook her head back and forth and looked down in a long painful pause.

". . . done so much . . . and I just cannot believe that we have changed everything since I become your governor."

More panic. Jan froze like a deer in headlights. She paused for a painfully long time.

"We've cut the budget, we have balanced the budget, and we are moving forward. We have done everything that we could possibly do."

Jan froze again. She looked down at the desk and began to laugh nervously. It took her NINE excruciating seconds to collect her thoughts. An *eternity* of silence on live TV. She finally started to speak again.

". . . We have did what was right for Arizona. I will tell you that I have really did the very best that anyone could do. We have . . ."[4]

You get the gist, right? Jan Brewer *tanked* the debate. Upon leaving the stage post-debate, Jan described being swarmed by a group of freaked-out staffers. They begged her not to debate again. They told her what had happened on stage was almost political suicide. Jan told me that she turned to her staff with a big grin and said, *Don't worry.*

I'm going to win. She told me she was 100 percent sure of that. She wasn't worried one bit.

Jan didn't elaborate. She didn't lay out a change in strategy, a new approach to campaigning. She didn't even have a triumphant comeback performance in the next debate. No, Jan just *knew* she was going to win. And she did.

Hmm. Seemed strange to me.

Maybe the reason Jan didn't want this forensic audit is because she had a strong suspicion of what people would find when they cracked open the voting machines and closely examined the ballots. Jan Brewer knew a lot about elections. She used to be Secretary of State—overseeing the elections in Arizona.

After finishing her story, Jan took a few more sips from her beer and we spent the next few moments in small talk. The rest of our meal was polite. A few more people came up when they saw me and told me how much they appreciated me "taking a stand" against the Fake News and how they appreciated my courage. After thanking Jan for her time and saying goodbye, we parted ways. I didn't know it would be one of the last conversions the former governor and I would have.

Later, after announcing my candidacy, Jan Brewer decided she hated me. She co-chaired the campaign of one of my RINO primary opponents, and spent the rest of the election cycle bashing me every chance she got—calling me an "election denier." Even *after* I won the primary, she went on radio, continuing to disparage me and said she would not support me as the Republican nominee unless I would meet with her and tell her I was lying about my concerns about the 2020 election—and tell her that I made it all up just to get elected.[5] This was *crazy* talk. Of course I was *not* lying.

I believed *then* and *now* that 2020 was rigged and I was proven right when they went above and beyond what they did in 2020 to steal another election on November 8, 2022, in order to stop me and our movement.

Jan Brewer wasn't the stalwart conservative we thought she was. And she is certainly not interested in election integrity. She's a member of the Uniparty; she's not interested in bringing the Republican Party together. But that's okay—I will continue working to solve our problems and improve everyone's shot at the American Dream. And I continue to invite the RINOs out there to start loving America again, and join us in putting America First.

CHAPTER 4

The Ride to the Big Stage: CPAC

AFTER WALKING AWAY from my career because the news business became too corrupt to be salvageable, I *somehow* ended up in the even *more* corrupt world of politics!

In 2021, I began campaigning to become the next governor of the greatest state in America: Arizona. And I had a feeling deep in my bones I was going to win. The excitement I saw in the towns and communities I visited along the way was like nothing I'd ever experienced before in my life. I was famous in Arizona because of my TV news persona, but this was different. This was a deep connection to the people. It was an Arizona version of what I'd observed in campaigns like that of Donald J. Trump and even Bernie Sanders. Populism. People connecting through ideas, policy, and trust.

Together, my campaign staff and I had been to house meet-and-greets, backyard barbecues, and coffee shops all over the state. We held rallies where thousands of Arizonans showed up. We gained the support of hundreds of thousands of people, all eager to give a big middle finger to the political elite and out-of-touch Establishment in *both* political parties—people sick of the typical politician who stopped working for the "We the People" in order to work for special interests. Arizonans were tired of elected officials acting like tyranical rulers—ordering the people around and forgetting the oath they took to uphold the Constitution.

Arizonans were tired of shady, shoddy elections, a wide-open border with millions of people pouring across, drug cartels and narco-terrorists funneling poisonous drugs through our state and skyrocketing crime in our neighborhoods. Papa Bears and Mama Bears, like me, were tired of the garbage being pushed on our kids at school. What I was witnessing on the campaign trail was a Mama Bear Revolution that included dads, grandparents, and even students. Fed-up Arizonans saw in me a candidate they trusted—a friend who had been in their homes for nearly three decades for hours each day, giving them the straight scoop. In me they knew they had a candidate who would work *for* them, listen *to* them, and keep my promises.

Almost as soon as I announced my campaign June 1, 2021, I knew things were going to be special. Within hours of the announcement, someone had texted me a photo from a roadside rally where a twenty-ish-year-old woman was waving a homemade sign around. It said: Kari Lake for Arizona Governor. I had only been an announced candidate for about ten hours, and a young woman was so thrilled by the prospect of me being governor that she took the time to craft a homemade sign and wave it on the side of a busy road. That sign was a VERY good sign.

Three weeks later something else incredible happened. We gathered enough signatures to make it onto the ballot. Being new to politics (other than covering politics) I didn't realize it normally took candidates eight or nine months to gather enough signatures to get on the ballot, and usually that meant hiring signature gatherers and paying for those signatures. We were able to get thousands of the required signatures in three weeks—a state record. Something special was happening in Arizona politics and I found myself smack-dab in the middle of it.

Campaigning came easy to me because even though I didn't personally *know* everyone I was meeting on the campaign trail, I had covered the people of the 48th state for so long that I *felt* like I knew them—and they all knew me. I didn't have to go into a room and introduce myself and hope they'd remember me and my name. They already knew it. I was practically part of their family. What a blessing that was for me as a candidate!

———

Fast-forward to February 2022, and my rag-tag campaign propelled by The People had become a sensation. There were no high-priced flacks, no career-political consultants running the show. I found it disingenuous to have Washington, D.C. consultants come into Arizona to tell me what issues to avoid and what issues to talk about, what to say while campaigning. They didn't know the people like I did. So I decided to become my own campaign manager. I had benefited from the extremely high name recognition I had earned during my thirty years in broadcasting to wage all-out war on establishment Republicans during the primary, and that hard work was paying off. I noticed about five months earlier the corrupt corporate media and even the international news started covering my campaign. It was the perfect storm: a Trump endorsement, some great viral video clips, and most importantly, incredible, common-sense policy. When I jumped into the race, I had 85 percent name ID in Arizona. That means 85 percent of the state knew me, and about 65 percent had a very positive image of me.[1] That's the kind of name ID that you can't buy with a million consultants. I was running against a "Karen" named Karrin, whose consultants were salivating to get their hands on her elderly husband's billions and they knew they could string her along and make her think if she would just put "another million dollars in this week, and another million in next week . . . she could be governor." That kind of "consulting" made them a killing, stroked her ego, and left Ed Robson, her ninety-three-year-old second husband $30 million poorer. That kind of mercenary consulting is what is killing our country.

Karrin Taylor Robson was an open-borders, pro-mask, pro-Covid lockdown "Republican" who was ready to spend her new husband's endless supply of cash to try to buy the governor's office. In her quest to win, she poured more money than ever seen in a primary race in Arizona into trying to tear me down in the most despicable attack ads imaginable. She failed. My Name ID had skyrocketed to 99 percent,[2] but some people believed the lies she told and the Fake News parroted. That's the downside of the politics of personal destruction.

A month earlier I had delivered a rousing speech at President Trump's first rally of 2022 in Florence, Arizona, to a crowd of 50,000 people. It was magical. The wind howled, the flags flapped, and the people were filled with love as I took the stage to the most rapturous applause I'd ever received in my life. That speech opened the country and the world's eyes to the fed-up mom running for governor in Arizona: Kari Lake.

Seeing my rising popularity, CPAC (Conservative Political Action Conference), the most famous political convention in politics, took notice. I had met the President of CPAC, Matt Schlapp, and his incredible wife, Mercedes, on a couple of occasions and asked advice from them from time to time on political issues. After hearing about the great reaction I was getting at events, the organizers offered me a coveted spot to give a speech in Orlando, Florida. All the heavyweights in Conservative politics had spoken on the CPAC stage over the decades, so this was truly a YOU'VE FINALLY MADE IT moment.

I accepted with pleasure.

For years, CPAC has been the beating heart of the Conservative movement in the United States. A few times a year, figures from all over the Republican Party come together to give speeches, talk policy, and attend the occasional party with like-minded Patriots. During the worst of the Covid-19 pandemic, when local liberal officials began enforcing mask mandates with totalitarian glee, these gatherings became especially important for Americans who cared about their freedom.

Even before I was a candidate, I had attended CPAC in 2020. I was struck by the joy with which all these Republicans were walking around and greeting one another. They seemed happy and *fun* in a way that the Democratic-Party-of-today couldn't even understand. And frankly, Democrats could never draw a crowd like they do at CPAC.

My speaking slot was the first day of the convention, Thursday afternoon during something called the "Power Hour"—a back-to-back-to-back slate of speakers that happens just as the four-day event opens. This was a good slot, but not a great one. And speaking for four minutes is hardly enough time to get the crowd going. Still, it was a great opportunity. Of course, I dreamed I'd land one of the highly coveted spots on Saturday night or when President Trump was scheduled to speak. But heck, this was my *first* speaking gig at CPAC so I was elated. Given the size of my campaign and the noise we were making in the national press, I knew I could have brought down the house in one of the primetime spots. Someday I would get that spot, but not this time.

I didn't have a stump speech, which is a memorized speech that politicians give over and over again, to the point they could recite it in their sleep. Usually a consultant or a team of them will write the speech for the candidate—after spending $150,000 on polls and focus groups to figure out what they should say. The candidate then regurgitates it every day on the trail. In short, a "stump speech" is your "sales pitch" to the voter. I usually spoke off-the-cuff, ad-libbing (I'm not good at memorizing) and talking about what was on my mind that day or issues voters in the room asked me about. But for a big event like CPAC or Turning Point USA, I preferred a locked-down, prepared speech just in case I "blanked-out" or found myself at a loss of words. Thankfully that has never happened. But there's always a first time and I certainly did *not* want it to be on one of the biggest stages in *all* of politics.

For the next few days, I worked on a speech that would introduce my campaign to the massive audience gathered at CPAC. I'm sure most of them knew who I was and what the movement stood for, but I saw this as a way to really get their attention and announce that I was the leader of the next generation of America First candidates. I planned on taking Trump's incredible policies and mission to put the needs of Americans first, to a state level and restore Arizona to a safe state where you can afford to live, raise a family, get a great, affordable education, and most importantly kick out the cartels and prevent our Arizona from becoming California. My opponent at the time was trying to turn Arizona into a purple state with squishy Republicans in charge who pushed a liberal agenda while telling voters she was a "lifelong conservative." I, on the other hand, wanted to secure our border, reform the corrupt elections to restore faith and transparency in our sacred vote, push back on the Fake News agenda, and end Covid restrictions and mandates that killed our small businesses, destroyed our health, masked our children, and forced experimental shots on people if they wanted to make a living and feed their families. So I put all those concepts into my speech.

Because of the packed CPAC schedule, my small team—Colton, Lisa, my husband, Jeff, and I—were going to fly into Orlando overnight, arriving a few hours before the event, freshen up and drive to the event with little time to spare. We'd booked a commercial flight out of Phoenix that left in the early evening. Knowing how important the event was, I had even dragged everyone to the airport early (something I rarely do under normal circumstances).

As a result, we found ourselves standing around at the gate around dinnertime without having eaten. I am not the world's best public speaker, but I can tell you that hitting a stage in front of millions of people watching, both in person and online, would be disastrous if I was *both* sleep *and* food deprived. So Lisa and I decided to head back to an airport restaurant we'd seen on the way and sit for an hour before the flight began boarding. Jeff said he would head to the gate and let us know when they started boarding. About twenty minutes later, Jeff texted that the flight was boarding! We decided to finish eating and board toward the end. We were a three-minute walk to the gate and knew as long as we made it there with ten mins to spare, we were fine.

By this time Colton had walked up from security as we were leaving the restaurant. From down the terminal I could see something was wrong. The gate was empty, and there was a well-groomed, terse gate attendant standing behind the desk. We smiled as we handed him our boarding passes. "Hi." He didn't respond until he gave me a second look.

"I'm sorry," he said, in a not-sorry-at-all tone, raising his eyebrows and smiling. "But the doors are closed." Lisa, Colton, and I looked over at the door, it was wide open. "The boarding is over and we have given away your seats." I said, "The door is open." He nodded to his coworker and she shut the door. We had arrived fourteen minutes prior to the flight. I've flown this airline for decades, ten minutes has always been the cut-off time, I told him.

"The boarding process now ends *fifteen* minutes prior to takeoff," he snapped in a catty tone. During this time I texted my husband, Jeff, who was already on board.

They shut the door and gave our seats away!

He texted back a photo of our two empty seats: *No they didn't.*

My suspicion: this was a liberal gate agent who wanted to make things difficult. I was tempted to lose it, but took a deep breath. The agent shoved a boarding pass in our faces. He pointed to the words in tiny print: BOARDING STOPS 15 MINUTES PRIOR TO TAKEOFF. Apparently, during Covid the airline changed the rules. "You are one minute late," he said with a smirk.

Yeah, right, I thought. I showed him the photo my husband sent me and I told him that he had not given our seats away. They were still empty. He looked at the photo then grabbed the microphone with his fist and called out two names on stand-by and gave our seats away while staring us in the eye. We had a nasty man on our hands. "God," I prayed, "please give me patience. Give me love for this man." A man who, unbeknownst to me, was about to set us off on an odyssey that put our lives at risk.

There wasn't much I could do. The power-hungry gatekeeper was relishing in the fact that the Trump-endorsed candidate for governor was under his thumb, and he enacted his own personal retribution. Lisa, Colton, and I were stuck waiting in the airport with less than twenty-four hours to go until one of the biggest speeches of the campaign. Absolutely NO flights available to get us there in time. I tried one more time to get my new *friend* to make an exception, but he informed me that our seats had now been given away to passengers from the standby list.

There was, he informed us with a sick smile, absolutely nothing he could do.

For the next hour, I sat with Colton and Lisa in the terminal while the plane we were supposed to be on sat on the tarmac due to the fact that the plane didn't have pilots to fly it and due to a brutal storm working its way across the country. A polar vortex had just ripped through the northern US mixed with a cold front.

So much for global warming . . .

I could hardly believe how absurd the whole situation was. The plane was sitting there. Our seats were given away, and this gate agent would not let us on. While Colton searched for flights, I texted CPAC President Matt Schlapp and explained our situation. I asked if he could find another speaking slot for me.

Very tough, he texted back.

Well, I thought, *that's it. Either we get a flight out of here and make it to Orlando by tomorrow afternoon, or the biggest speaking opportunity in politics would be a no-go.* At that moment, if it were possible to drive from Phoenix to Orlando and make it in time, we would have done it. (We did the calculations and it was not possible.)

For the next two hours, we ran into roadblock after roadblock. We called everyone we knew with a plane and everyone we knew who might have had a friend with a plane. It seemed—as it often would in the months to come—all hope was gone. My choice to grab a bite to eat at the airport cost me a speaking opportunity at CPAC. I was kicking myself.

Just then, we managed to get someone on the phone who could help. There was this guy, he said, who knew a guy who knew another guy who had a small, private plane and could find a couple of pilots, and they could maybe get us out of Phoenix if we flew all night on a small plane. By "small plane" I assumed it meant a private jet where we could spread out and sleep through the night until we got to Orlando. I had NO idea it meant a single-engine plane that could fit people and one backpack as long as the backpack was not too heavy.

"You'll have to make a few stops," he said, "but it'll definitely get you there. What do you think?"

I thought about the speech we'd written and the thousands of people waiting to hear it, the incredible reach and power of CPAC and I didn't hesitate.

"Let's do it."

———

The plane (remember the scary plane in the prologue?) turned out to be slightly less luxurious than the words "chartered" and "private" would have suggested. No one would ever take a photo on this aircraft and post it to Instagram to "brag" they were "flying private." As I boarded with Colton and Lisa, I heard the pilot ask me to stop and make sure that Colton's backpack was placed across from one of us and not moved as it would be "balancing out the weight." (Yikes.)

I felt good knowing we didn't have to worry about getting to CPAC. That I would make my speech. But man plans and God laughs.

Instead, I awakened to a freezing cabin, full of my favorite people who honestly believed we might be going down. For the next few minutes, I huddled close to Lisa and Colton while the pilot radioed around using every bit of his training to find a place to try to land.

What felt like an eternity, happened in mere minutes. It all ended with a very hard *boom* as our iced-over plane hit hard against an icy, flat surface. We slid down a dark runway. I had no idea where we were. Had we made it as far as Texas? We all thanked God. And praised the pilots. I can still remember the collective sigh of relief that came out of our mouths at that moment. It felt good to be alive.

Stepping off the plane, I could have sworn I was back in rural Iowa in February. The night air was howling. My frozen cheeks felt the sting of snow that felt like miniscule shards of ice cutting into them. There was nothing in sight other than a small building that looked like an original one-room Old West house you'd see in *Little House on the Prairie*. A small wooden sign painted with the words Airport Terminal nailed onto the small overhang. Where in the hell were we? Was this Texas? I wanted to ask the pilots but they were inspecting the plane. Colton had to check his iPhone to find out that we'd landed in Wilcox, Cochise County, a Wild West rural area of Arizona that sits just 150 miles south of where we'd taken off.

I was amazed. We'd been sleeping so heavily during the first few minutes of the flight that we'd all assumed we had made it at least halfway to Florida already. Now here we were. We took off from Phoenix, and Mother Nature decided we were not going to go far. Turns out we were in the air an hour, at most. If we had taken off from our houses on bicycles instead of heading to the airport earlier that day, we probably could have ended up closer to Orlando than we were right now.

I looked around at the five of us standing on the tarmac. Clearly, God was trying to tell me something, and I was pretty sure it wasn't, *"Keep heading to Florida, Kari! I really want you there tonight!"*

Still. God HAD got us safely back down on the ground and for that I said a prayer of thanks. I sent a text to CPAC about our emergency landing and let them know they could give away my speaking slot. I told him that I'd really appreciate it if he could find me another opportunity to speak later in the weekend, but that God did not seem to want me traveling any farther this evening. To which CPAC replied: *Thank God you are okay! Don't worry. We will make something work.*

After spending the night crammed together in a roadside motel in Wilcox, Arizona, the next morning Lisa said, "Kare, if you had any doubt at all, you now *know* that God is with us. We *should* have died last night. He protected us. He wants us alive and on this path." She was so right.

It also occurred to me that the whole time we were in the air—even when it seemed like we were definitely going to go down—God had been watching over us. For some reason, I realized, we were *not* supposed to get to CPAC on time.

Two days later, after we made our way to Orlando on a regular, uneventful commercial flight, I learned what that reason was.

After hearing about the crash landing and everything else we'd endured to make it down to Florida on time, CPAC had arranged for me to speak Saturday morning. We arrived at the convention and after seeing the huge reaction the crowd was giving me in the event hall, CPAC organizers called me Friday night and told me they were scheduling me in an even better spot—the *best* spot—the speaking slot on Saturday afternoon, *right before* the main event: a speech from President Trump.

To put it mildly, I was thrilled! Not only was this a bigger crowd—everyone would be in their seats waiting to see the President—it was also a bigger platform to spread the America First message that I had been working so hard to bring to Arizona.

At every stage of the campaign, this pattern would repeat itself. My team and I would find ourselves met with what seemed like a huge setback, wondering how on earth we were going to make it out. Then, just when it seemed that all hope had faded, we would realize that *everything*—from minor setbacks to near plane crashes—were part of the plan that God set out for us. The same plan I had sensed when I was a little girl looking up at the sky in my yard in rural Iowa.

God always makes things work out. Not according to our plan—according to His plan. And His plan is *always* better.

————

On the afternoon of the CPAC speech, I was blown away by the size of the crowd. More than five thousand people were packed into the convention hall in Orlando to hear me speak. Just before I was scheduled to go on, we did our usual prayer huddle backstage. Colton, Lisa, Jeff, and I wrapped arms and asked God to fill my mouth with words and my heart and mind with the Holy Spirit. I prayed that we win over the hearts and minds of anyone who hears it. Then I was ushered just inches away from the stage where I stood on a piece of tape that said HOLD. Looking down at my black, patent leather pumps—butterflies buzzing around in my stomach—I wondered *how* in the *world* this kid from Iowa got here? How did I end up in the center of the world of politics? At such a pivotal time?? Then I heard the announcer say my name.

"Ladies and Gentlemen, please welcome Kari Lake!"

The CPAC hall erupted in cheers and applause. It was so loud when I stepped out on stage that the music that played as I walked down the catwalk to the podium got drowned out. The massive event room was packed. That was the beauty of speaking directly before President Trump. Even with thousands of people there, I recognized faces in the crowd. As I strode onto the stage, the applause grew even louder. This crowd was incredible.

"Hello, Patriots!!" I said over the applause.

I launched into my speech. I talked about the lawlessness Arizona was experiencing that had been ushered in when Joe Biden, on day one, came into office and stripped back President Trump's effective

Border Policies. I warned that this country—Arizona, in particular—was being invaded by Narco-terrorists, and that the Biden administration was doing nothing to stop it. I declared that the Canadian truckers protesting for their right not to get a vaccine were not terrorists, they were heroes, and that parents who wanted a say in the education of their children were not terrorists either—all despite the far Left's assertions to the contrary.

The clip that got the most attention was when I directly called out the Fake News. It had been almost exactly a year since I resigned from my job out of disgust over what the news business had become.

The crowd was rapt with attention as I explained my reasons for walking away from a hugely successful career and a massive paycheck. I laid it all out: "Because journalism had been replaced with propaganda—and I refuse to lie to the people of Arizona and that's exactly what's going on in the news today. I thought I worked for the good guys, but there are no good guys in corporate news. Here's proof . . ." The crowd seemed to lean in. Most of them had stopped watching the news or had drastically changed how they were getting information, fully aware of the bias, lies, and agenda being forced on the good people of this country. I went on, "They would rather cover Covid death stats than tell you about treatment that works—ivermectin and HCQ." The crowd started to cheer. "They didn't want to talk about the risks with the Covid shot. They went mum on that."[3]

My blood pressure started rising at the thought of that. Imagine, the media intentionally keeping information that could have saved lives away from people. Disgusting. "And they refuse to be honest about our rigged election of 2020." The crowd went wild. Cheering at me for calling out the corruption in our elections. "I'm talking to you guys. Right back there." I pointed at the press up on their risers. Several people in the crowd, who by now were on their feet cheering for me, spun around to look at the propagandists. The cheers transformed into a roar as I pointed with my arm straight out in their direction. And stared-down at the press. I felt defiance rising up in me as I stepped away from the podium toward the media stopping just short of the edge of the stage. The roar from the audience got louder as I threw up my hands in a what-in-the-hell-is-the-matter-with-you-guys gesture. I could hear a few people gasp, wondering what I was up to.

"I have a question for you," I asked the media in a heartfelt tone. "Why won't you be honest with the people of this country?!"

The crowd ERUPTED. They turned to look at the media and loved that I was pinning them down publicly. Shaming them for their disgusting lies.

"Why won't you tell us the truth about the 2020 election?!" I stood. Unflinching. Unafraid.

"You owe it to the people of this country to be honest about what happened." By this time the production team had flipped the house lights on exposing the press riser. "We know what happened." I walked back to the podium, knowing that the press had lost so much of their reach and power, but irritated that more of them didn't have love for their country, or courage to leave a corrupt industry where their corporate bosses forced them to lie for a paycheck.

"Hopefully we've turned them off." I smiled at the crowd and looked back one more time at the propagandists. "Forget what your bosses say—and tell the truth."

Unlike the lying media, the Patriots in that room were willing to do the right thing.

Holding nothing back, I punctuated my speech with a few more fiery lines. The crowd was up on their feet and ready to take the energy from this venue back home to make a difference in their states and neighborhoods. Maybe it's my years in television, but I like to deliver speeches as if I'm talking directly to the crowd, often asking them questions. If I'd had more than a few minutes to speak, I could have gone on for hours—about the major issues plaguing our country and get into what my policies would do to fix them, but I was given just five minutes to speak, and by now I'd taken about ten. (Sorry, Matt. Sorry, Mercy.)

Walking off the stage, I felt more energized than I had felt in a long time. I had just aced my first CPAC speech. I felt a renewed assurance that running for governor of Arizona was a purpose that God was guiding me toward—that it was, in fact, the very thing He had in mind when He spoke to me all those years ago as a child. I felt that sense of amazement and wonder; God is the only explanation to how I had gone from that yard in the middle of rural Iowa—ten miles to the nearest tiny town (a town with just 270 people)—to the center of the political world at such a pivotal time in our history. I had become friends with some of the most incredible patriotic people in our country, including a man who had given up so much for America, President Donald J. Trump. A man who took the stage moments later, called me by name, and shared kind words.

One month later CPAC endorsed me.

Though I had a shaky route to the big stage, it was a moment that would propel me into a campaign and a movement that God had been preparing me for all along.

CHAPTER 5

The Californication of America

ONE OF THE major messages I repeatedly returned to on the campaign trail was, "Don't California my Arizona."

My mission is to see Arizona remain a great symbol of the American West. I don't want to see it become some homogenized, unrecognizable state—like California's cousin. California is the "Progressive Utopia" in action. They have long since stamped out the last embers of the Conservative fire that Nixon and Reagan spent forty years building and let it die out into smoldering ruins. That's the only natural outcome after decades of one-party Democrat control.

And what does that realized Utopian dream look like? In other words, what is the future for these red states where the Uniparty Swamp is corrupting elections and turning blue.

It looks a lot like San Francisco. What used to be the "Paris of the West," one of the most beautiful cities in the world, now looks like a scene out of a zombie apocalypse.

That's what a decade of Gavin Newsom's Progressive Democrat leadership will do to you.

It's discarded needles on the streets, tent cities, and homeless encampments. It's broken windows and cracked sidewalks. Closed-down businesses. It's multigenerational reliance on government handouts and the end of self-reliance. It's rampant crime perpetrated by an increasingly lawless younger generation, a generation that has been taught the only way to not be victims themselves is to victimize others. And the crimes they commit are begrudgingly tolerated by neutered law enforcement agencies that are now too afraid of the public derision they will receive if they make a misstep in doing their jobs.

The list of Progressive policies that have failed is as long as Hunter Biden's rap sheet. They've used "Vision Zero" to implement their green agenda and deliberately tie traffic into knots, all to make driving so inconvenient to force people to throw away their keys, take the bus, or go "green." They've used "Criminal Justice Reform" to let criminals loose on the population, elect activist judges to eliminate bail and reduce sentencing, and turned a blind eye as criminals continue to commit their crimes knowing they will never see any real consequence to their actions.

Their version of "Housing Equity" has made it so costly and impossible to build new housing that they've created an artificial housing crisis and tens of thousands of newly homeless people. Their homelessness policies are an abject failure and have actively enabled long-term street homelessness, vagrancy, and public drug use.

The Left's taxes, regulations, and wasteful spending are causing skyrocketing inflation, driving businesses and jobs away at a record pace and preventing new ones from getting off the ground.

Normal Americans don't want any of this garbage. Mama Bears know this is a disaster for our families—our children.

That's why Democrats want us to "embrace the weird."

In the past, it would have been weird to have a withered old creep in the Oval Office (Joe Biden), but not anymore.

It would have been odd to have someone who can't form intelligent sentences and has a questionable path into power to be second-in-line behind the President (Kamala Harris), but not anymore. Meritocracy is dead in the modern-day Democrat Party.

It would have been unheard of to tap someone who couldn't even fix the potholes in South Bend, Indiana, to be the United States Transportation Secretary just because he was gay (Pete Buttigieg), but not anymore.

It would have been ludicrous to put an overweight, middle-aged pediatrician in charge of the United States Public Health Service Commissioned Corps because he decided he wanted to be a girl (Richard "Rachel" Levine), but not anymore.

It would have been silly to put a gender-fluid, kleptomaniac with a dog fetish in charge of our country's nuclear arsenal (Sam Brinton), but not anymore.[1]

It would have been asinine to put a woman who can't string a sentence together in charge of briefing the American people on behalf of the President, just because she's a black lesbian (Karine Jean-Pierre), but not anymore.

It would have been absurd to think that a flat-out Socialist, who changed his name to run for office, left his wife while she was nine-months pregnant, cyber-bullied randos on Twitter, and has the emotional maturity of a five-year-old, should run to represent Arizona in the Senate (Ruben Gallego), but not anymore.

AOC, Rashida Tlaib, Ilhan Omar, Ayanna Pressley, Katie Hobbs, Mark Kelly, John Fetterman. Candidate quality for the Democrat party doesn't matter anymore, because these people serve an ideology, not a constituency. And they know better than to step out of line. They got elected promising to be different, and the moment they were sworn into office, they marched this country lockstep toward a direction that only leads off a cliff.

This is a cast of fundamentally unserious people being tasked to lead our country through serious times. AND they are failing at it. Of course they are. They're incompetent. If you elect clowns, you're going to get a circus. That's why the ringmaster has taken control of our elections.

When the coward Katie Hobbs followed the example of Joe Biden and spent the three-month general election cycle hiding from the public and refusing to debate, she robbed the people of Arizona of the opportunity to see a clear contrast between the two candidates running for governor.

I believe this was always the plan. For one, as I've already discussed, the fix was clearly in. For another, it would have been an absolute takedown. It would have been like, as country music legend, Patriot, and my friend John Rich described it, a chainsaw versus a birthday cake. The results of that debate would have left even the most hardened of Katie Hobbs's supporters with no doubt in their mind this was a race she could not (and should not) win.

This wasn't about personality—although under her leadership, a woman of color had been fired, successfully sued, and won twice in a court of law, costing the taxpayer millions of dollars due to discrimination. No, it was a matter of policy—a matter of my common-sense solutions versus her absolute batshit insanity plans.

My America First policies would benefit every single Arizonan. The thing about common-sense solutions is that they are not race, or age, or religion-specific. No, they work for *everyone*. I was applying for a job for ALL Arizonans. Not just the ones who voted for me. I believe America First is the most inclusive political ideology in the history of this country. Talk about a big tent . . .

And what did Katie offer? Nonsensical word salad, open borders, promises of handouts, a racial reckoning, and access to unrestricted abortion including infanticide, basically, the same Hunter

Biden Crack Pipe dreams that all modern-day Progressives offer an electorate they're desperately trying to manipulate: empty prxomises, boundless spending, fear-mongering, and racial division. All with a healthy amount of demonizing their opposition (proud election denier over here!) thrown in the mix. In truth, the modern Left has nothing tangible to offer the American people but panic.

History has shown time and time again that dividing people along racial lines never leads to equitable solutions. It leads to genocide, like Rwanda or apartheid, like South Africa. In America we are not divided by religion, skin color, and the hundreds of other ways the Left tries to separate us. We can have our differences, but it's our patriotism and love for our country and our Constitution that brings us all together.

Equity is just clumsily packaged consultant jargon for Communism. The end game of that is redistribution of wealth, property, and destruction of the middle class while consolidating power in a privileged, self-serving oligarchy. The goal is to make people completely dependent on the federal government for survival. It's simple, by depriving people of choice, by breaking down civilized society under the pretense of breaking barriers, you give people NO choice but to obey.

Their priority isn't to advance the working class but to expand the welfare class. Big Government knows that if you depend on them to address your day-to-day needs, you will never be able to break free from them. That's how we get liberal debacles like Obamacare, affirmative action, DACA, and the Green New Deal.

The purpose of these programs is two-fold: First to make the majority of people dependent on the government for basic services. Second, to replace the remaining self-reliant holdouts with people willing to be dependent on the government for basic services.

Demographics ARE destiny, after all.

I have never met a single American who wants an open border. And I believe most Democrat voters care about a secure border as well. These Democrats don't want the cartels in control of our border. They don't want fentanyl pouring in, killing our young people. But more and more, we're seeing Democrat leaders are on the side of the cartels, and not the American people.

Why is that?

Because the Democrat leaders have reached a sick, cynical peace with the fact that alongside the drugs, the weapons, the traffickers and thugs, many potential new Democratic voters will be coming to America as well. They did the math and it's more politically expedient for them to let our next generation of American youth be poisoned by fentanyl, if that also comes with the understanding that the next wave of immigrants will vote blue.

I don't think that's a fair trade—not even close. I don't think any sane American who can see the emerging future does, and that's the problem: the modern Left has gone insane.

I never thought declaring there were only two genders while on the campaign trail would be an applause line. I didn't think a nominee for Supreme Court Justice (Ketanji Brown Jackson) would be unable or unwilling to define a woman. But that's just a sign of the times we live in.

This new self-identification of gender phase is just the Progressive Globalist ideology taken to a transhumanist form. They've already concluded our borders mean nothing. Why not add basic human biology to the mix? If boys can be girls and girls can be boys, then we lack meaning. We are not humanity, but an amorphous blob of malleable flesh. Does it sound like Orwell's *1984* newspeak to you?

And the Left wants that. Because they know if they can take away your self-worth, your individuality, tell you that they are different in a way only THEY can understand, then they have power over you.

It's political grooming, and it works. We've seen this for years in our education system. We've watched as our universities went from educating the best and brightest to indoctrinating them and turning students against their parents. Instead of scientists or builders, we have Gender Studies majors and Critical Race theorists, ready to take their grievances out into the American workforce and make us suffer for it.

So how do we fight back? I believe it starts at home. They're called "kitchen table issues" for a reason. Mama Bears and Papa Bears need to understand that they are raising the next generation of Patriots. That's an incredible responsibility, especially with every institution, and almost every education system seemingly designed to brainwash their children and alienate kids from their parents.

Parents, we must uphold traditional family values while at home. We must be the role models that our children are deprived of in our culture and the classroom.

The political Left fears an aspirational, motivated, and politically active American youth. They do not want that unleashed upon this nation or the world. They want your kids either looting a building, mutilating their genitals, or scrolling mindlessly through their smartphones, simply unaware of, and apathetic to the world burning around them.

We need to give our little ones an actually patriotic, God-fearing alternative amidst all that hate and propaganda. Because a God-fearing, patriotic next generation of Americans scares the hell out of the woke mob. That's why we are so blessed to have organizations like Charlie Kirk's Turning Point USA to help undo some of the damage indoctrination has done to our young people.

We know what the Left's vision is, and it sucks. It's oppression. It's dependency. It's division. Their whole arsenal of ideas is completely morally and intellectually bankrupt. California is the epitome of this, but it's spreading. We're seeing this poisonous doctrine in practice all over in America. It's there in plain sight.

Covid brought this into stark clarity. Big Government shuttered the small mom-and-pop shops and let the big boxes stay open.[2] They let you drive through for fast food, but they prevented you from going to that little neighborhood eatery you love.[3] They forced people to wear masks while walking on the beach, for crying out loud.[4] They actually told people to stop singing at church, stop worshipping God at church.[5] But if you wanted to burn a city block to the ground, you were golden.[6] The Left turned criminals loose and gave their bad behavior a hall pass.[7]

They let a mob try to murder Kyle Rittenhouse and then tried to put him in prison for defending his life.[8]

They call unarmed January 6 Capitol demonstrators "insurrectionists" and jail them without benefit of a trial[9]—while killers, arsonists, and looters across our major American cities are hailed as "mostly peaceful" protestors, bailed out, and released by Progressive activists (including Kamala Harris).[10] And they called that "equity."

Despite what the radicals peddling their indoctrination say, the United States was not, and is not built on a foundation of racism. We do not need to, and must not view all outcomes as a result of race. Teaching our students that they are either oppressors or oppressed based on the color of their skin is deeply evil. We can't tolerate it. We need to eradicate this hateful indoctrination, root and branch.

And, like I said, we as Conservatives, need to provide people with a better alternative.

We need to bring God back into the mix. We need to bring family values into the equation. We need to stay rooted in the values and traditions that made this country great. So when Obama says, "You didn't build that," we say: "Oh, YES WE DID!"

For the benefit of our children, think less TikTok and more time together. We must win the culture war at home. That's where the battlefield is. MAGA helps. The iconography, the attitude. It's transformational. It's actually countercultural in this culture of globalist rot.

By simply not being boring, and actually showing that we care, the America First/Family First Conservative movement has an opportunity to attract a new generation of young voters. It's not a tall order, but this young generation is ready. That's why they were so involved in my campaign. They recognized who was locking them down, masking them up, and taking away their graduation ceremonies they should have been having. They knew the career politicians were behind that madness.

What does that mean for us? It means asking the old guard to step aside and let new young people, new to politics come into the party. We can all work together. We must. It means leaving the country club and working directly alongside the people. It means spending more time in people's family rooms than in corporate boardrooms. It means pushing back against the Left's relentless assault on our freedoms. It means remembering the principles this country was founded on that make it so special.

It's not rocket science. It's America First. This is about waking people up. And sometimes you can't just tell me how bad the system is; you have to show them. In some ways, Joe Biden's incompetence has been the ultimate red pill.

During my run for governor, every single day, I had people come up and say they're either Independents who voted for Biden or Democrats, and they would tell me, "I'm voting for you. It's the first time I voted Republican. I can't believe what's happening in this country. We're losing so much of our freedom. I'm afraid of what's next." Truth is, I am too! That's why I'm fighting like hell every single day. We can't give up or give in. Too much is on the line for our kids' future.

Joe Biden and his Marxist ideology is driving people away from the Democrat Party. People are watching these horrible policies erode their freedoms and their prosperity and they are rebelling against them. I wish we didn't have to go through this pain for people to wake up to what's really happening, but I truly believe we are heading somewhere good.

And whether you're waking up today or you woke up twenty years ago, or you wake up tomorrow, we welcome you. We want you in the new Republican Party, the America First Republican Party, and we can promise you that party will bring forth ideas that will make our economy strong, our family strong, our businesses strong, and our states strong. If we keep allowing the federal government to control us, we will lose this country.

We ALL must take our rights back. That means everyone, no matter how uncomfortable it makes them, must be active participants in the political arena. We ALL must push back against the institutions and educate people on where the leftist dogma inevitably leads. We ALL must reject the Californication of this country and expose leftist lunacy for the world to see—before we are a failed nation of fifty "Californias."

CHAPTER 6

America First

IT'S ALMOST IRONIC. That America First, an inherently non-interventionist political ideology is leading that charge against Globalism. We are locked in an existential battle for the soul of our nation. And this is a conflict we MUST win.

America First is the New Republican Party. It's the party of We the People. Globalism, on the other hand, is just a fancy word for Communism. Globalists believe in a New World Order. Where a centralized ruling body dictates the direction of the world over. America First believes in individual freedoms and placing the needs of the American citizen over some monolithic "collective good."

America is supposed to be the Shining City on a Hill. She is the standard bearer, she's the straw that stirs the drink, she sets the example that the rest of the world follows. Our best leaders understood that a thriving America leads from a position of strength.

The Founding Fathers showed the world our independent fighting spirit. They decoupled from the world's great superpower. In a way, they broke free from an earlier form of Globalism. Vanquished the British monarchy militarily and then set about creating the greatest system of governance in the history of the world.

Theodore Roosevelt fortified our Navy and helped give America the dominant stronghold along our seas.

Richard Nixon went to China and reminded the growing Communist threat that America was still the dominant player in town.

Ronald Reagan's savvy diplomacy and utilization of American strength shattered the Soviet Union.

And Donald Trump's sheer unpredictability, coupled with his master negotiation skills—plus skill at fighting for the American worker and building up the economy—kept America as the premier force on the world stage without having to fire a shot. Peace through strength. Emphasis on *world peace*.

America First is inherently a non-interventionist movement. We believe in placing domestic interests over foreign interests. We have our own problems at home. Why don't we prioritize fixing the very real problems here?

Seemed like my entire life the United States had been at war or getting involved in war somewhere around the world. That needed to end. That's one of the reasons why I was so taken with Ronald Reagan. The man who brought down the Berlin Wall, and got East and West Germany to wield the sledgehammers to do it. But the Republican Party learned the wrong lessons from that triumph of diplomacy. It decided that proactive meddling in foreign affairs was the way forward. We championed "Democracy" while we created quagmires. American blood mixed with sand and washed away on foreign shores. And for what?

So George W. Bush could pursue a vendetta left over from his father's time in office?

So Barack Obama could win a merit badge in droning innocent citizens?

It was all so pointless. Human life is not some infinite resource meant to be sent to feed the war machine—the Military Industrial Complex.

For a while I saw no end in sight to this waste of humanity. I remember on April 19, 2007, John McCain, at a campaign stop in South Carolina during his disastrous run for the presidency, was asked about whether he would take military action against Iran.

"That old, eh, that old Beach Boys song, Bomb Iran," he chuckled. "Bomb, bomb, bomb, bomb, anyway, ah . . ."[1] And the room laughed. I guess I didn't get the joke.

See, while John McCain was amused at the idea of even MORE armed conflict in the Middle East, I was starting a family in Arizona. And I figured this guy's insatiable desire to start more wars did nothing to protect America and would only mean my children's generation would be required to fight. I am fully on board with protecting our homeland—unfortunately that was not the priority of our government with McCain and the Uniparty in power.

Starting wars in the Middle East and destabilizing countries around the globe, the GOP seemed a hell of a lot more interested in fighting wars abroad than in fighting to solve America's problems at home. Two bad choices. McCain and Obama. I voted against McCain. Then along came Romney. Another foreign intervention-loving neoconservative. And honestly, when it came down to it, he wasn't so different in policy than Obama himself. The Uniparty was on full display. Both sides were rotten.

It was around then the American people started to wake up. They started to notice that seemingly no matter what letter was beside a politician's name, R or D, they all seemed to belong to the same entrenched ruling class—the Uniparty. A group that looked out for the interests of the wealthy, elitist political class while leaving working-class, ordinary Americans struggling in the wake behind them.

That's why in the fight upon us, it is clear, it is not about Democrat vs. Republican, it is Globalism (the corporate name for worldwide Communism) vs. America (We the People).

John McCain was the patron saint of the Uniparty. He placed the priorities of the military industrial complex over his constituents in Arizona. For decades it was always the same, John would come home for six months every six years and throw out some empty red meat to the voters—"Complete the Danged Fence!"[2] "Repeal Obamacare"— and then he would promptly return to Washington upon his reelection to champion a foreign war, or speak on the need to import more foreign workers to take American jobs.

There was a mythology built around him. He served the political machine, never met a potential war he didn't like: Afghanistan, Iraq, Iran, and he tried to foment an anti-Russian uprising in the Ukraine. He got involved in toppling a duly-elected president there that ultimately led to Zelensky, and $100s of billions of US taxpayer money being funneled into Ukraine, money badly needed here at home.

Everyone has a mean McCain story. From bullying staff to holding decades-long grudges toward dear family friends. He was generally loathed by his constituents for the duration of his tenure in Washington.

When Donald Trump bulldozed through that McCain facade in 2015, he was applauded by Arizonans. And what did John do in response? Showed his vengeance by voting down the best chance this country will EVER have to get rid of Obamacare. He then refused to resign despite his terminal brain cancer diagnosis—knowing that the uncertainty would leave the Arizona GOP paralyzed upon his passing. We lost that Senate seat. What McCain did wasn't in the best interests of Arizona. And Arizonans are tired of pretending that it was.

But this isn't about McCain. It never was. It was about the neoconservative ideology he championed. One that led to foreign conflict and crippling national debt. When you're offering the American people two sides of the same coin, you can't be surprised when they pocket the coin and go home.

By 2016, America was embroiled in multiple wars, and mired in the second term of Barack Obama. Obama was a race-baiting, weak politician, who spent the duration of two miserable terms apologizing for America's "mistakes" on the world stage,[3] and relentlessly demonizing Americans as "Bitter Clingers" who held onto their Bibles and guns.[4] He stoked racial tension for political gain, when he had an opportunity to heal.

Americans wanted a leader who didn't hold them in contempt. And then, along came Donald J. Trump to remind them that America is exceptional and how they are an important part of that.

Make America Great Again. Say what you want about Donald Trump, the man knows how to sell a brand. It was a hell of a pitch. This country was once great and it can be great, again. It was a political shot in the arm. Especially, compared to the third term of Bill Clinton, the Democratic Party was pitching an exhausted public.

Donald Trump spoke to the common man. As a political outsider, an independently wealthy man, he was free from the shackles of the Uniparty. He could not be bought or co-opted to serve the politician machine. He was liberated to speak the unspoken things that the Republican electorate had been dying to hear.

And the best part of the Trump experience was he didn't have to grow into it. No. From the moment he came down that elevator on June 16, 2015, to announce his run for President, Donald Trump was fully formed. The speech he delivered that day may be the best encapsulation of America First policies ever delivered. It caught me flat-footed. I had never before heard a more perfect summation of the problems plaguing America. And there had never been a more perfect messenger. Donald Trump had reached the summit of that Shining City on a Hill. He had reached the American Dream, and here he was telling the American people that it was a rigged game that only he knew how to play and we were all on his team.

"The American Dream is dead . . . I will bring it back bigger and better and stronger than ever before."[5]

That speech is the Rosetta Stone for America First. An America First Republican believes in a secure southern border, healthcare for our veterans and their families, a rebuilt military to achieve Reagan's peace through strength. They believe in keeping the promises we made to our senior citizens through Social Security, Medicare, and Medicaid. We believe that Obamacare should be repealed and replaced with something that actually works. We believe that by simplifying our tax code, we *can* revive our middle class. We believe it's time to stop exporting American jobs, American lives, and American money to foreign countries. We believe in returning the ultimate power over a child's education to that child's parent. We believe in supporting our allies and putting the fear of God into our enemies. To put it simply, we're tired of being taken advantage of. It's time to start winning for a change.

Donald Trump had packaged *The Art of the Deal* into the most dynamic series of political proposals Americans had heard in decades.

President Trump proved during his first four years in the Oval Office that these policies worked. We decoupled ourselves from foreign entanglements, both militarily and financially, and ushered in an unprecedented era of American prosperity.

America was respected again. Our middle class was thriving. We know these policies work and they will work again. Then The Steal happened and Joe Biden was installed into office. Still, America First is very much alive. But that doesn't mean it doesn't need to change.

It's up to us to make sure the America First movement doesn't just become a marketing gimmick. Anyone can slap on a Red Hat and tell a forgotten part of the electorate that they want to "Make

America Great Again." But it needs to mean something. It needs true Patriots leading it and great policy. Absent that, America First is just another slogan that can be co-opted by the Uniparty establishment in order to herd us all back in line behind a candidate they choose who may even try to *act* like they are America First when they are *actually* a Globalist's dream come true. That would be a disaster, one we must not let happen.

At its core: America First is a movement of common-sense solutions. A populist movement that places the needs of its constituents over the consultants or the entrenched ruling class. America First seeks to empower people to live the American Dream. It creates a great economy, and the government does its job to make sure our streets are safe and our border is secure. And then every American can thrive.

Fundamentally, America First is a return to basic law as laid out in our Constitution. While writing the Constitution, our Founding fathers knew that as our country grew and the population spread out, the federal government would struggle to address the needs of the populace. This ongoing concern birthed the concept of Federalism—a model of government that allows individual states to be principally responsible for looking after its citizenry's domestic and personal interests.

I believe that a return to federalism is the answer to most of our problems. Since our nation's inception, the federal government has bloated in size. It has created a never-ending series of departments and organizations meant to impose burdensome regulations on states. Whether it's the ATF, the FBI, the DOJ, the CIA, EPA, the Department of Education, this is government red tape and it's strangling the life out of us.

People are really tired of the federal government pretending they run the show. We run the show. We the people run the show. And our Founding Fathers gave us the tools to fight back.

So when I ran for governor of Arizona, I sat down and hammered out an agenda that focused on America First solutions to improve the lives of hardworking Arizonans. I approached every issue with that federalist-oriented mindset. I was uniquely attuned to the issues that concerned Arizonans the most. And number one on that list was our wide-open southern border. The policy we ended up crafting is probably my favorite policy from the entire campaign—the centerpiece. The issue I addressed the most. The issue I *forced* the other Republican candidates to address and share their opinions about. And they and the Swamp hated me for it. Because they *want* the border open, illegal aliens coming in and drugs pouring across. They want the cartel's control and cartel's racket to continue. Makes you wonder if these politicians are somehow part of it.

I read an article from the America First Policy Institute about constitutional remedies to our open border. I was fascinated by it so I reached out to Russ Vought and told him I wanted to do that—AND go even further. I wanted the most bold, aggressive, effective border policy this country has ever seen. I wanted it to stun the cartels and restore Arizona's sovereignty. What we ended up crafting had its origins explicitly tied to the United State Constitution.

It was based on the rights states have to protect their border when there is an invasion. The federal government guarantees protection to the state under Article IV, Section 4, of the U.S. Constitution–also known as the Guarantee Clause. Under Joe Biden, the federal government was unlawfully dictating what states could and could not do. So Arizona would lead a coalition of like-minded states in drafting an interstate compact to secure our southern border. Under Article 1, Section 10 of the U.S. Constitution, Arizona would invoke its inherent power, call for a Declaration of Invasion, and focus its resources on solving the problem without the express approval of the federal government. We didn't need it. Arizona could exercise its state sovereignty to safeguard its communities and restore sanity and security to our open border.

Donald Trump said, "A nation without borders is not a nation."[6] And he was 100 percent correct. By allowing the uninterrupted flow of illegal immigrants into our country, we are ceding control to the Mexican drug cartels and enriching the Communists in China who are supplying the cartels with the ingredients needed to help manufacture their poison.

Inaction is complicity. I refused to sit around and do nothing while Joe Biden facilitated the great mass migration in our nation's history. Reporters would ask me what I intended to do if Joe Biden tried to stop me. I told them I'd do it anyway.

"What are they going to do?" I'd reply. "Arrest a sitting governor?"

I'm UNAFRAID of Joe Biden. But I can guarantee you he was terrified at the notion of dealing with me.

Almost every problem facing Arizona was flowing like a stream directly from that open border—street crime, sex trafficking, human trafficking, crimes with guns, drugs, And in order to save the state, I would have to turn off the tap. The devastating impact on our people wasn't hard to see.

When I was working in the news industry, I had to drive through the heart of Phoenix to get to the station. Over the years, I watched with growing horror as our homelessness crisis exploded. What had started as a few isolated individuals on the streets had mushroomed, by the time of my run for governor, into burgeoning tent cities. These people, many in the throes of drug addiction, are being met with a homeless *industry* that in many ways enables drug abuse. And I knew if we concentrate less on keeping the homelessness industry going and put more effort into rehab, tough-love, and reform, we could turn these folks' lives around and make them contributing members of society.

Chronic street homelessness is not an easy fix. I needed to consult the experts. And no one had more knowledge of the problems plaguing cities like Phoenix, and the innovative policy solutions that were necessary to help turn them around, than Sam Stone, whom I made my campaign policy director.

Looking back on it now, Sam Stone was probably an unlikely pick to be my policy guru. He was an aide to the Phoenix City Councilman Sal DiCiccio. DiCiccio was an absolute bulldog. On a city council filled with raving lunatics, Sal was the lone voice of sanity. When I was working as a reporter, it was Sal's office that I would contact to get insight on the inner workings of the City of Phoenix. And Sam Stone was the guy who answered those calls. Sam was sick and tired of watching solutions get ignored. I provided him the platform to use his brilliant mind to not only help solve Phoenix's problems, but the rest of the state's as well. And Sam more than rose to the occasion.

Our city streets were beginning to look like something out of a zombie movie Once-promising young minds shuffling around garbage-strewn streets desperately looking for their next fix. And I truly believe God did not envision any of us living on the street with a needle in their arm.

My plan sought to provide our homeless population with innovative treatment designed to get them clean and ready to return to productive society. But this would come with some conditions.

We would ban urban camping while expanding shelters. And if they declined treatment, they would be politely encouraged to move on. We can have compassion for the homeless, but it cannot be at the expense of everyone else.

Americans work hard for their money. They pay their taxes and they want their streets back. They want to be able to take their kids to the park after work, without the fear of stepping on used needles.

They want to walk the sidewalks to grab a dinner downtown or a game and not fear being accosted or hurt by a drugged-out individual. They don't want their property value to go down to zero because a homeless encampment has been set up on their front lawn. There's no compassion in the way we're handling homelessness right now. No compassion for the homeless person, and zero compassion and respect for the hardworking, taxpaying citizen who is doing everything right and watching their community get destroyed by this problem. It was time to stop being enablers and provide our chronically homeless the tough love they needed to get healthy and get their lives back on track.

My homeless policy went hand-in-hand with my border policy. We have to stop the drugs from coming in through our southern border. There's no use in working to keep people off drugs on the street if there's a constant flow of new product and new temptation coming in from the border.

My next goal was to provide Arizonans much-needed economic relief. Thanks to the disastrous fiscal policies of Joe Biden, Arizonans were (and as of this writing still are) suffering through the highest rate of inflation in the entire country. The liberal tax-and-spend agenda was having a disastrous impact on the average Arizonan family and driving up the cost of basic household goods. My goal was to ease the burden on the people of Arizona.

To start, I promised to eliminate all taxes on groceries and rent in the State of Arizona. My team and I calculated this would put half a billion dollars back into the pockets of Arizona families. I planned to cut taxes every year I was in office. Starting with the sales taxes and then moving on to our onerous property taxes. In order to do this, I planned to identify and roll back any cumbersome and unnecessary regulations that made it harder for businesses to do their work in Arizona.

The goal was to incentivize companies to come to Arizona and set down roots. And the best way to do this was to move the government out of the way and let the people do what they do best: create, explore, and thrive.

I believe all of these common-sense policies would have helped Arizona build one of the most competitive and prosperous economies in the country. I still do. Our movement, called Karizona, became the greatest grassroots movement in the history of the state. Republicans, Democrats, and Independents all flocked to the America First banner because they knew this ideology wasn't necessarily right or left. It was just about common sense.

Americans aren't stupid. Every day more and more of them are waking up in droves to the lies of the Democratic Party. And guess what? They're running toward us. And we need to be there to embrace them. America First is the most inclusive movement in the history of this country. It sells itself. Do you want freedom? Do you love your country? Dynamite. Welcome aboard. America is great. But WE can make it even greater. And we want YOU to be a part of it!

I trust the average American citizen a hell of a lot more than I trust some government bureaucrat, some international conglomerate, or some league of nations.

If you empower people to pursue those dreams and get the government out of the way, there's no limit to what people can accomplish. The American Dream can be revived. It *must* be revived. The American experiment is a glorious thing. Fifty individual states all under one flag. There's no other country like this. Why would we aspire to be anything else?

For decades now, we've been outsourcing American jobs under the misconception that we are also outsourcing American ideals. This is a fantastical notion. The American experience is uniquely

American. Absent of those experiences, all other countries receive is a pale imitation.

We saw it in Vietnam, we saw it in Afghanistan, we saw it in Iraq. You can lead a horse to water. But that doesn't mean the horse is going to stand for our National Anthem. The best way to improve the lives of people across the globe is to rebuild America, empower our people to enjoy their God-given freedoms, pursue prosperity, and lead by example. Every other person on earth will want to replicate that.

It's time to put domestic affairs before all else. America doesn't need to sacrifice anything. It doesn't need to apologize for anything. It must be a shining example on the world stage. And if the rest of the world wants to, they can copy our notes and our Constitution. Our singular focus should be on perfecting an already exquisite product.

Like I said, America is great. And with America First policies, it can be even greater.

CHAPTER 7

Inside the Fake News

FROM THE MOMENT I started broadcasting I loved the work, and the work seemed to love me back. That is, until the era of Fake News took hold across news organizations nationwide.

For almost three decades I got up early and got home late, and my day was spent researching, confirming, and writing stories so I could deliver the unbiased news of the day to the people of Arizona.

I was diligent in my work. I checked sources, I crossed the t's and dotted the i's. I was blessed to work with another professional journalist named John Hook for the bulk of my career. Together we formed an incredible team, a tandem that achieved high ratings and earned the trust of hundreds of thousands of viewers across the state of Arizona. We also made Fox News a fortune in their flagship Arizona station—a market critical to political advertising and powerful beyond belief since the station's signal reached almost the entire state.

Our job was simple. We did our due diligence, assembled the facts, and provided the information the viewers needed at home to form their own opinions and draw their own conclusions. We respected our audience and didn't feel it was our jobs to tell them how to think.

I covered stories around Arizona, around the country and even around the world. My job took me to Cambodia. I've been to the White House a couple of times. I've interviewed sitting presidents. Covered the biggest Hollywood stars. So it was a great career. A fun career. I really enjoyed it, for the most part.

But the job that used to be so rewarding to me, seemed to slowly be taking a piece of my soul.

I was raised in eastern Iowa, part of the Quad Cities, a community that straddles the Mississippi River. As a kid I barely watched television. Only in my early twenties did I start watching the news. I remember watching *The Today Show* and Tom Brokaw, and thinking this was interesting, important, and was a job I would like to do.

Working for the number one station in my hometown, I started behind the scenes. Then one day someone said to me, "I think I see you as a news anchor someday." I thought, *Really? Oh, that would be cool.*

When I moved to Phoenix, I was working with such a great group of professionals, seasoned journalists. You had all age groups represented. All political ideologies. When I arrived I was an anomaly—only twenty-four years old and about to take a job at a number one NBC affiliate in the nation's 20th TV market. Thanks to my strong work ethic and ability to do news reporting, weather, and news anchoring, I catapulted from the 96th TV market to the 20th. That was almost unheard of in 1994.

Now it's common for newsrooms to be filled with grads coming straight out of journalism school lacking work and life experience, with no exposure to different political points-of-view. Most are young, childless, and liberal and—like it or not—that affects how they see the world. The average TV viewer now is 45+, has a family, has lived in the community and has a right-of-center worldview. But with liberals deciding what stories fill the newscasts, the viewers are being served a biased helping of propaganda.

It's really not the fault of these young "journalists." Think about it, since the time they are five years old and enter kindergarten, they've been brainwashed and indoctrinated into liberal/progressive ideology at school. A young producer, fresh out of journalism school, has a different perspective on life and the stories they choose for a newscast than someone who learned how to do old-school journalism, where you tell both sides of the story and keep your opinion out of it. As the anchor, I am the last line of defense before the news reaches the viewer. I found myself seeing more and more liberals slant and wokism being pushed into the news. Anti-Second Amendment, pro-choice, anti-police, open-borders . . . *Where is the balance here? Where is the parity?* I would wonder as I tried to ad-lib some fairness into the stories.

Other than through words, and story selection, there are many ways you can manipulate a story to place your opinion in it. You frame the person with whom you agree so they look more attractive. You interview the person with whom you disagree in the middle of a parking lot at high noon. Cast terrible shadows on them. You illustrate a disagreeable point of view by interviewing someone who looks or sounds ridiculous or "uncool," to make their entire stance seem preposterous. Or lately, I've noticed news outlets just stop seeing "the other sides" stance and they will just plain ignore it all together. They refuse to interview candidates whom the corporate bosses are not supporting, while filling the airwaves with the globalist candidates the bosses do support.

It's fake news, whether it's intentional or accidental manipulation, or just people who are so entrenched in their liberal ideology that they don't even realize there's another possible point-of-view.

Too many in today's newsroom think the conservative side of a story is so reprehensible that it should not even be presented to the audience. Instead of management stepping in and correcting this, biased "journalists" are rewarded.

Thankfully there are many independent journalists doing good work. And the ranks of these modern-day heroes continue to grow. But the legacy media characterizes them as right-wingers. Fair journalism seems like it's right-wing to them because they themselves have strayed so far from fair journalism and so far to the Left, everything else seems radical.

I think I first noticed this dramatic change in political coverage during the presidency of George W. Bush. "Dubya" was a weak man, not articulate or particularly bright, but he seemed well-intentioned and likable enough. But the media didn't see him that way. After all, he had "cheated" their man, Al Gore, out of the presidency he had earned. Somehow Gore was never called an election-denier though, imagine that.

They took every "W" stumble, every inarticulate word he uttered and used it to turn him into a caricature, a laughingstock. Most disturbing were the attacks on his character, calling him a warmonger and a racist—a foreshadowing to today's journalism where everyone who doesn't tow the leftist line is called racist. Yes, you could possibly say the man was a warmonger, because he got the country into the Iraq War based on lies that there were WMDs inside Iraq. But a racist? A bigot? These claims were never sourced or supported with facts by the journalists who communicated them. They were treated like facts and repeated until they simply became accepted as true. There were times when the nightly broadcast was indistinguishable in tone from *The Daily Show with Jon Stewart*.

There was a growing, troubling aspect to this where the media seemed to coordinate these attacks across multiple media and outlets.

And the tactics worked as George W. Bush became one of the least popular presidents of all time. To the frustration of most Republicans, George Bush was simply incapable of defending himself. He took all of this on the chin and he had a glass jaw.

The end of his presidency saw the complete and catastrophic collapse of the Republican Party leading to a Democrat president and record gains by the Democrats during the 2008 election. One Barack Hussein Obama, a man with a mysterious past and virtually no accomplishments on his résumé, ascended to the presidency.

The media turned Barack Obama into a rockstar, giving him hagiographic depictions, apologizing for or simply not reporting any of his stumbles (e.g., the 57 United States[1]), and swarming any independent journalist who attempted to give the man the proper vetting.

How did the Republican Party counter? Poorly, of course. They found one of the most boring, go-along-to-get-along RINO candidates in John McCain, a man who had been the media darling among Republicans, hoping the media would be far more generous to him than they were to George W. Bush. This was not to be the case. As soon as he became the Republican nominee, opposing Barack Obama, albeit weakly, the media turned on him.

Four years later, another RINO candidate, Mitt Romney, was portrayed as a cold, calculating businessman who strapped puppies to the roof of his car and would push your ailing grandmother off a cliff.

Let me make this clear. I'm not offering apologies or excuses for the quality of these Republican candidates. John McCain was an absolute disaster, completely incapable of putting up a fight. He couldn't handle any criticism. He spent more time attacking critics of Barack Obama than actually criticizing the man he was supposedly trying to defeat. He very likely ended up voting for him. And Mitt Romney? Mitt Romney's presidential campaign effectively ended after the second 2012 presidential debate where he spent more time unsuccessfully debating the moderator Candy Crowley than Obama, his Democratic opponent.

Near the end of Obama's second term, on May 2, 2016, I had the opportunity to travel with a group of reporters to the White House and observed the kid gloves treatment by which the president was treated by my companions in the White House Press Corps.

I can still remember the softball questions the reporters asked when it was their time to question the leader of the Free World. "What is the most difficult part of your job?" "How have you managed to work with those Republicans in Congress?" "What enchants you the most about being president??"

Do these sound more like the questions of a professional journalist or a fawning middle schooler? It was outrageous to witness this. Journalists were supposed to be the Fourth Estate; they're supposed to speak truth to power, not give it a tongue bath.

When I was given my five minutes with the president, I can honestly say I think I gave him the most challenging interview he ever received, asking about the Supreme Court nomination process and Arizona Governor Jan Brewer's confrontation with him at Phoenix Sky Harbor Airport, and forcing him to answer a question about his least favorite person on the planet, Donald Trump, who by then had nearly bulldozed through the crowded field of Republican opponents. The day after my Obama interview, the last of Trump's eighteen GOP opponents, Senator Ted Cruz, dropped out making Trump the nominee.

Fast-forward six years later. I'm no longer a working journalist, I'm the gubernatorial candidate. And Obama, who is no longer president, has lost all his swagger and, frankly, looks nervous every time he is in front of the camera, comes to Arizona to stump for my opponent, Katie Hobbs. To my amusement, he recalled that interview I did with him in what might have been the most tepid display of support for Hobbs ever seen. You can't blame Obama for that, Hobbs was one of the weakest and worst Democrat candidates this country has ever seen.

With nothing to attack me over, the Left had started going after me for being an effective communicator, for presenting myself well and looking good on camera. You can't make this stuff up! Obama, in front of a small rally crowd in a high school gymnasium in Phoenix, starts into his *attack* on me. And in typical Obama fashion, it was weak:

> OBAMA: "She's good in front of the camera because she's been doing it for a long time. Some people don't know this but apparently Kari Lake actually interviewed me back in 2016 when I was president. She was a local news anchor. She was doing her job."

Okaaaay. I'm listening to this thinking maybe he's supporting me.

> OBAMA: "I have to admit. I don't have a clear memory of the interview. It was a little fuzzy. I do know this. I don't remember at the time thinking that she was the type of person who would push debunked Covid remedies, or promise to issue a Declaration of Invasion at our border, or claim without any evidence that the 2020 election was stolen."[2]

Knowing I was living rent-free in Obama's mind was one of the highlights of the campaign. Especially when he went on to say I looked good on camera and followed up with the lackluster introduction of my opponent, Hobbs:

> OBAMA: "Katie, she may not be flashy. She could've been, she just chooses not to be."

This made me laugh hard. The Saint of the Fake News came to town and gave the Fake News almost *nothing* to work with in the waning days of the campaign as they wrote their puff-pieces about their choice for governor, Basement Hobbs.

It dawned on me that my first and only encounter with Obama back in 2016 ended with his prediction, *"I don't think Donald Trump is gonna end up being president."*

Fast-forward almost exactly a year later, May 2017. I find myself back in Washington, D.C., and golly gee, guess who's president? The Press Pool in the Trump White House all had a raging case of Trump Derangement Syndrome (TDS). Their behavior was the polar opposite when it came to their treatment of the new administration. They were hostile and rude. My photographer, Jon Noetzel, and I were stunned. We listened as the media talked out in the open to each other about how much they hated Trump. It is outrageously unprofessional for any reporter, camera person, media employee working the Press Pool at the White House to have those discussions and especially shocking those conversations were happening in the press room just adjacent to the West Wing.

It was a night-and-day contrast, completely adversarial. I wouldn't be surprised if suspected terrorists received fairer treatment during their enhanced interrogations at Guantanamo Bay than the 45th President received from the bloodthirsty press. And the press endeavored to use the information they gleaned from these interrogations to take the president down. The reporters had their knives out and each of them was looking to exact a pound of flesh to create a negative-slanted fake news story.

But unlike Republican presidents of the past, President Donald J. Trump was ready for them. He refused to accept their false premises. He brought his gun to every knife fight. Donald Trump was the first Conservative leader to push back against the lies, the smears, and the absolute falsehoods propagated by the partisan press.

While the term had been used in previous generations, President Trump popularized the term "Fake News." The press was outraged when Donald Trump turned the tables on them and called them Fake News, describing them as the enemy of the people, because for the first time their status as an advocate of liberal progressive philosophy and an arm of the Democrat Party was exposed for the world to see.

The press conferences Donald Trump would frequently hold in the White House briefing room were a must-watch, because the president told it like it was. Trump would tell them exactly how he felt about their questions, and if he didn't particularly care for a reporter personally, well he would tell them that too.

By some strange coincidence, I was in the White House the day the press released the most egregious piece of fake news in U.S. political history: Russiagate.

Russiagate was a hoax perpetrated on the American people by the Hillary Clinton campaign in 2016 through the creation of a phony dossier claiming that Donald Trump was a compromised asset of Vladimir Putin and the Communist regime in Russia.[3]

These were explosive claims deserving of a thorough investigation before publishing, but the media didn't have time to let facts get in the way of a good story—one that supported that Trump was unworthy of the presidency. Hell, they didn't care about facts. They were colluding with the Swamp to bring down a popular, duly-elected president.

Truth didn't matter. Instead, they continued to publish unsubstantiated and ludicrous leaks about anyone surrounding Trump and his inner circle. These allegations were enough to force the resignation of National Security Advisor Michael Flynn three weeks into the new administration, and would continue to be used as a pretext for an all-out smear campaign against anyone in Trump's orbit.

It was a feeding frenzy for the news media, and even my own news organization wanted a seat at the buffet.

Years later, we would find out that BOTH Barack Obama's Justice Department and the Democrat nominee Hillary Clinton were actively spying on Trump's campaign and the beginning months of his administration. This scandal was worse than Watergate. Watergate compared to Russiagate was like a parking ticket compared to a mass murder. It's tough for me to think of anything as bad as the media colluding with the Democratic party and the Swamp Uniparty in an attempt to bring down the sitting president of the United States. What could be more treasonous?

But the media neither investigated nor apologized for this, never had their day of reckoning, never even returned the Pulitzer Prizes they awarded themselves for their bullshit coverage.

No. They ignored all the emerging exculpatory evidence brought forward by people like Devin Nunes and Kash Patel, and simply moved on. Found something else to cover. Again, I always say, *It's not what they cover, it's what they don't cover that should make you think.*

Disclosure and repetition of this damaging information had distracted the new administration from the job of governing and could have handcuffed Donald Trump's ability to fulfill his campaign promises. Just what the media and Democrats wanted. Thankfully, President Trump carried out his presidential duties and was vindicated by the investigations that followed, albeit much later than desired.

Covid was really a moment of truth for the country and for me. Pre-Covid I had a neighbor who was the most beautiful, vivacious ninety-year-old woman I'd ever seen. She's in a walker now, Covid restrictions had permanently set her back over the course of the pandemic. She never caught the virus, but she wasn't able to do her daily walking and swimming and socializing because Covid scared everybody into their homes. And forced them to stay there.

The Deep State conspired with the media to keep up the fear of Covid in an attempt to oust Donald Trump from the White House and gain more control of Americans' lives. And to finally usher in their globalist agenda.

Fearmongering on TV meant that an hour-long news show had forty-five minutes of Covid-panic coverage. Somebody who's on a ventilator, a family that got wiped out from Covid . . . And while these were horrible stories—I'm not discounting that—there were also thousands of stories of people who got it, maybe didn't even know they had it or had very mild symptoms, or had a cold or flu and they got over it. How many times did the news cover those stories? The news put out nonstop coverage that was making things worse. I felt physically ill reading the news. And it felt wrong, unethical, and immoral to me.

———

As a candidate in the lead-up to the 2022 election, I had my own personal experiences with the Fake News. I am a fast learner. Early on in the campaign I saw how reporters would ask me the nastiest question to elicit a strong response from me. Then they would go back and edit out their utterly ridiculous, rude, or ignorant questions to try to make me look unhinged and them look good. So I turned the tables on them. With the help of my amazing husband, Jeff, who was by my side during the entire campaign and who is an incredible professional videographer, we started recording *all* of my interviews and I told the reporters if they weren't fair I would simply release the footage showing how intentionally biased the reporter was. Eventually the media started to change their approach.

By the end of the race, the embarrassment of being called-out so skillfully by me, led many of the Fake News "journalists" to behave differently. Fewer stupid, nasty questions, because they knew *they* were being recorded by *me*, and I was looking forward to making them the star of their very own viral news clip.

They even started to ask some decent questions. I felt proud of the crash course in ethical journalism that I was able to provide them. Hopefully, one day they'll thank me for this.

I read a study by the Media Research Center toward the end of the primary campaign that said 87 percent of the stories on Republican candidates during the election were negative in nature.[4] But they noted that one candidate got 100 percent negative coverage by the Fake News. That candidate was yours truly. And believe me, I had sensed it for myself. Local papers like the *AZCentral/Arizona Republic* (a paper originally owned by former vice president Dan Quayle's grandfather), better known as the "Arizona Repugnant" would compare me to the anti-Christ.

A Soros-funded rag called the *Arizona Mirror* never stopped throwing unsubstantiated attacks and vitriol my way. But like Trump, I wasn't willing to take this lying down. Over the course of my campaign, I wasn't just running against my Democrat opponent Katie Hobbs. I was running against the media—the LEAST popular institution in America. American hated Congress and folks like Nancy Pelosi, but they hated the News Media even more. The TV news media has a 7% approval rating and it's still dropping.[5]

It often seemed like the media joined with the Arizona Democratic Party to destroy the Arizona First ticket that I headed. They called us election deniers, threats to democracy, and warned everybody that if any of us were to win we would set the Grand Canyon State into a new Dark Age. One of the worst instances of conspiracy between the Fake News and my Democrat opponent occurred on October 26, 2022, three weeks before Election Day, when Katie Hobbs accused my staff of committing a Watergate-style break-in of her Phoenix campaign office.[6]

In retrospect, it almost seems orchestrated. On October 24, a young man was caught on camera breaking into one of Katie Hobbs's offices and walking away with a keyboard, a camera, and a few miscellaneous items. Two days later the Hobbs campaign issued a press release accusing my campaign of inciting this violence based on my rhetoric. They wanted to make me look extreme. Their whole pitch to voters was chaos versus sanity, and the hacks in the local media, like the national press who spread the Russiagate story, couldn't let facts get in the way of a good story.

They amplified and repeated Hobbs's claims, pounding our movement with allegations of extremism and coddling of violent elements. But only two days later the truth came out. The man who broke into the office was a mentally unwell illegal immigrant who had been living on the streets and had stumbled onto Katie Hobbs's office completely by accident. He was now in jail, having been arrested the day before on a *separate* burglary charge.[7]

The truth couldn't have worked out more perfectly for me. All of the policies I championed about fighting crime and about stopping the flow of opioids into this country, about providing help to the homeless, all of these were solutions that could have prevented this man from breaking into Hobbs's office in the first place. My staff and I knew we had to get the truth out in the most public way possible and we wanted to shame the media while doing it. So we called together an impromptu press conference outside my campaign office and invited Arizona Republican Attorney General candidate, Abe Hamadeh, to speak alongside me.

One of our favorite tactics was employing humor and props to illustrate a point. So my staff printed out a poster board where we assembled a few of the vitriolic headlines written about Katie Hobbs's false allegations and spread around the globe in twenty-four hours' time. And side-by-side we announced that we *too* had been victims of a break-in by someone from the opposing party, then I added I had photographic evidence that supported my belief that the perpetrator was Katie Hobbs herself! So on that billboard we put a large picture of a campaign staffer dressed in a chicken suit portraying the perpetrator of the break-in. After all, Katie Hobbs had been cowardly, ducking debates and public forums with me. She really was just a chicken. We made a mockery of both her and those hacks in the press. I spent the entire press conference ripping into each and every one of them demanding they vet a story for the truth before sending lies around the globe.[8]

That press conference was seen by millions on social media. We put it out live on Rumble and it brought in a huge live audience. Weeks later Rumble CEO, Chris Pavlovski, told me it was one of their most successful livestreams to date. Our campaign was now a phenomenon *outside* of Arizona.

We, the people, *do* deserve better from the press. An uninformed populace is a compliant populace. And maybe that's the end goal of all of the Fake News that we've been seeing over the last few decades. The media doesn't want people to challenge authority. They want them to bow down to it.

The truth has a pesky way of coming out. In 2022, Elon Musk purchased Twitter and began to expose collusion between Big Tech, the Democratic Party, and our increasingly partisan intelligence agencies to censor information they believed challenged the Left's narratives on elections, vaccines, crime statistics. Anything that challenged this radical agenda would be buried, deplatformed, and censored.

At about the same time, Mark Zuckerberg, the founder of Facebook, divulged in a podcast interview with Joe Rogan that Facebook had been directed by the FBI to bury the Hunter Biden laptop story, and all it implied about the Biden Crime Family, as

Russian disinformation.[9] These acts were blatant instances of election interference and cannot be allowed to continue.

This censorship extended to Arizona as well: then-Secretary of State Katie Hobbs and Maricopa County Recorder Stephen Richer worked with members of the federal government to censor anything they considered to be election denial. Sometimes I think about how far the media has fallen to serve the regime like this. And I wonder that perhaps George Orwell was not merely a writer, but rather he was prophetic.

I don't think even Nostradamus could have predicted my future back in 2021, when I sat down with my husband, Jeff, and I said, "I can't do this anymore." I worked thirty years in broadcasting. I had a wonderful career, but things had changed so much in the media that it was just unrecognizable. I really value the truth and honesty, and I didn't feel the media was interested in that anymore.

My "official" resignation came on March 1, 2021, but the people who welcomed me into their homes for nearly three decades didn't know that yet. So late on the 1st, my husband helped me create a video explaining why I was leaving. I'd been with the people of Arizona since 1994. I was making a personal sacrifice to walk away from my career and I wanted the viewers to know why.

Here's what I said straight to camera as my husband recorded:

"Hi everybody. I've got some news I want to share with you since so many of you have sent me messages while I've been on leave asking me how I'm doing or when I'll be back. Many of you left kind messages telling me that you miss me. I appreciate all of the messages and I miss you too. This time away from work has given me a chance to reflect on my work. Twenty-two years ago Fox10 hired me and paired me up with John Hook to bring you the news every night.

Shortly after becoming a team, we jumped in the ratings and we've held the number one spot for almost all of our time together. Anyone who's worked in TV news can tell you that is not an easy feat and it's one I'm extremely proud of and I thank you for that—for tuning in and inviting us into your homes.

Sadly journalism has changed a lot since I first stepped into a newsroom and I'll be honest, I don't like the direction it's going. The media needs more balance in coverage and a wider range of viewpoints represented in every newsroom, at every level and in each position. In the past few years, I haven't felt proud to be a member of the media. I'm sure there are other journalists out there who feel the same way. I found myself reading news copy that I didn't believe was fully truthful, or only told part of the story, and I began to feel that I was contributing to the fear and division in this country by continuing on in this profession. It's been a serious struggle for me, and I no longer want to do this job anymore.

So I decided the time is right to do something else and I'm leaving Fox10. I thank Fox for their understanding as I've come to this decision and I am grateful for the opportunity they provided for me to cover so many big stories over the years. As I close this chapter of my career, there will probably be some hit pieces written about me; not everyone is dedicated to telling the truth, but thankfully, many of you have figured that out. I promise you if you hear it from my lips, it will be truthful. It is scary walking away from a good job and a successful career especially in difficult times. I know God has my back and will guide me to work that aligns with my values. I feel such a deep connection to all of the wonderful Fox10 viewers here in Arizona and those I've met and interviewed over the years. Thank you so much for your trust and friendship, all these years. I will keep in touch, and I hope you will do the same."[10]

I opened a Rumble account and uploaded the video. I went to bed and I woke up the next day and my phone was blowing up with messages, emails, text messages, DMs, and my inbox was full. It was *all* positive.

"Thank you for standing up."

"We thought something's been going on with the news. You kind of confirmed it's just a bunch of lies."

"My relatives thought I was crazy when I was saying the news isn't always being honest with us. Thank you for confirming that."

Hopefully, I gave others the courage to just talk to that person at work who's been a real loud mouth and tell them you don't share their opinion. Dammit, you're entitled to your own opinion. It's called FREE SPEECH. Let's use it while we still have it.

If you see somebody speaking out, you need to support them. If you see somebody getting canceled or doxxed on Twitter or otherwise, step in and have the courage to say, "Hey, I support you." It will make a big difference if people start to see that.

I believe much of the media wants us to obey our liberal globalist leaders like sheep. They wish to make us afraid and angry. Don't just sit at home feeling fear and anger and just keep watching TV. Put the phone down, turn the TV off, and go out and live a little bit of life. That's where you're going to learn. Get your facts only from people who have earned your trust, and don't be afraid to question them and their motives as well. Form your own opinions.

Not too long after I left, journalists Ivory Hecker and April Moss walked away. Both told me that my exit inspired them to do the right thing. We have become friends since then. They are both *more successful* than ever before and *free* from the lies of the Fake News. I'm so proud of every honest journalist out there. Everyone that walked away from a paycheck and security because it was the right thing to do. And I will never stop working to expose the dishonest journalists who continue to lie and divide our country.

CHAPTER 8

Flipping the Script on the Enemy of the People

I ANNOUNCED MY run for governor with the motto, "Truth Matters." I believed that the people of Arizona deserved a politician willing to tell them the unvarnished truth, warts and all. I would be taking the muzzle off. I would be telling my own story.

The question was to whom?

I knew better than anyone the importance of narrative. And I knew the rot at the heart of the Arizona media. By walking away from that life, I had placed a giant target on my back. The modern media is a bit like the mob. They have their own omertà—a code of silence—they close ranks, and you're either with them or against them. And you don't just get to walk away intact.

So I decided to make myself the smallest target possible. I would shut out the media entirely. No interviews, no Q and A's—I had YouTube, Rumble, Twitter. I could set my own narrative. I didn't

NEED them. If you deny fire oxygen, it will burn itself out, so why should I set the match? They'd never be fair and I don't need them.

My video announcing my run for governor went viral.

And at first, it was exactly as I'd hoped it would be. The story was about Kari Lake: the woman who walked away from the media, the woman who understands Arizona and had some great common-sense solutions to the problems we face. Within hours of my campaign's launch, I was inundated with messages from friends, former colleagues, and regular everyday people, and I could tell that honesty resonated with people.

I found that idea to be both humbling and sad. People were so used to being lied to that someone speaking God's honest truth to them felt like a revelation. The shift in energy was palpable. People who had first treated my candidacy like a novelty, realized that I was in this thing to win it. Not only that, but people began to realize I COULD win it.

The first poll following my announcement was staggering: in a race with a field of experienced establishment candidates, the insurgent ex-reporter was lapping the field. By refusing to censor myself, and actually talk about the issues on peoples' minds rather than what political consultants want, I had separated myself from the rest of the candidates in the gubernatorial pack. Suddenly, for the first time in my life, I wasn't telling the news, I *was* the news.

And with all that attention, it was only a matter of time before the sharks in the media came to try to take a bite.

The goal of a political campaign is to win. The way to win is to get your message out across as many rooms and to as many people as possible. I knew getting into the race that my three decades of media training, and my coverage of Arizona, had given me a unique ability to connect with the people.

Accordingly, my team and I arranged a relentless schedule, taking me all across the state for eighteen months, leaving no stone unturned and no voter unreached. The media could follow me, but they would never come in between me and the people of Arizona. I was effectively cutting out the middleman.

As my momentum grew, the media requests poured. I put my Communications Director Ross Trumble in charge of fielding them. His job was to acknowledge their requests, set up interviews with some of the fair, alternative media, and weed out the Fake News requests and then tell them in the politest way possible to buzz off.

"They're not my intended audience," I'd say, "the people of Arizona are."

"You're going to have to talk to these guys *eventually*," Ross would respond.

As the weeks went by, I softened. I was encouraged by the energy I was feeling in front of the crowds. The people certainly thought the newswoman-turned-politician was a hell of a story, so why wouldn't the press?

So a month into my campaign when Ross floated the idea of breaking my radio silence, and sitting down for an interview with Dennis Welch of Arizona's Family, a local conglomerate that that airs its propaganda on two television stations including the Phoenix CBS affiliate, I gave it some thought and prayer, and finally relented. While Dennis's political persuasion was always obvious, he struck me as a man willing to put those biases aside in favor of a good story.

With Covid-mania in full swing, the media refused to let me make in-studio appearances without showing proof of vaccine status. That was a non-starter. After some negotiation, it was agreed that we would do the interview over Zoom. Dennis would do his side of the interview from what appeared to be an AZ's Family janitor's closet.

And I would do mine from the living room of my house. I loved that idea. My father was a football coach. He told me the importance of a home field advantage.

The battle lines were drawn.

On June 15, 2021, I sat down in front of my computer camera for the Dennis Welch interview.[1]

I did a mic check.

Took a sip of water.

Said hi to Dennis.

Engaged in ten seconds of small talk.

And then all hell broke loose.

"Umm, so before we get started, we're going to talk about the campaign contributions in the past and how you changed," Dennis said, his head buried in his notes. He launched into my husband's past donation to Obama. A donation Jeff now wishes he could get a refund for since Obama was so dismal.

Dennis grilled me for several minutes. I thought, *Wow, is this all he's going to ask me about? Is my opponent paying him to run this story? This is the first interview with me, surely he wants to ask about the issues,* but no he didn't. He continued on.

Dennis: "I've got you contributing $350 to Barack Obama."

Leading up to the interview, I had imagined many different scenarios in my mind, but an ambush on a tiny political contribution a decade and a half earlier had been pretty far down that list. Dennis had come in hot trying to catch me off guard, immediately showing me exactly what the temperature of the interview was going to be.

I knew going into the campaign that our former contributions were going to be a political liability. I wasn't ashamed of them. But I knew the establishment class would try to use them as a cudgel to question my conservatism. My mistake was assuming the liberal media wouldn't do the same.

I thought back to Reagan's platform of American Exceptionalism, economic prosperity, a smaller government with lower taxes, and the Gipper's ability to communicate that common sense-agenda directly to the American people, I was captured by it. I registered as a Republican as soon as I was old enough to do so. Because that was the political party that appealed the most to my values.

But as I matured I saw, with growing alarm, how the Republican Party started to break from that agenda, and move toward a policy that favored the military industrial complex over the common American man and woman.

By 2004, America was mired in an international conflict in the Middle East that seemed to continually escalate and that I saw no escape from. I was a young mother who looked at her children's future and saw only war. You're damn right I was looking for an alternative from the policies of George W. Bush.

Most Americans wanted to elect a president to get us out of war and work toward a domestic agenda. Obama had promised to bring peace, McCain was an unapologetic war hawk. Who would end the endless wars? It was a gamble. Too often in politics, it turns out that the lesser of two evils is still just evil.

The America First policies of Donald Trump brought me, and so many others, back to the Republican Party. Because it's not about right and left anymore. It's about common-sense solutions versus woke solutions. Freedom versus Communism. And more often than not, it's about Good versus Evil.

Well, Dennis Welch clearly disagreed with that sentiment.

"What are you getting at? Are you getting at that you can't be a conservative if you have donated money ever?" I asked. "What's your point, Dennis? What's your point?"

"My only point right now is to try to get the facts straight," he replied.

Bullshit. Dennis's game was so obvious it was infuriating. He wasn't a reporter; he was a criminal prosecutor trying to lead me toward a political death penalty.

It was not lost on me that the guy trying to impose his definition of Conservatism was a guy who probably considers everyone to the right of Liz Cheney a political extremist.

This was nonsense. I was fuming. This was going to be a total hit piece. Rather than take the bait and lose my cool, I calmly, professionally, took the gloves off and said,

"What I see is happening here is I'm running for governor. And rather than doing a story of, 'Hey, a person who has worked in our industry, had an illustrious career, and is running for governor because she cares about this state . . .' you're going to do a hit piece or try to be derogatory, which is so typical of where the media goes. If there's a story with a conservative in it, it always has a negative slant and people are onto it, Dennis. They're onto it. And you know you guys do that."

Dennis looked thunderstruck. He took a moment to collect himself:

"Okay . . . Well . . . I just want to know how you go from donating to Democrats, to running for the governor, running as a Republican candidate for governor."

Did he not understand that millions of Americans were fleeing the Democrat Party, realizing their dead-end policies were destructive? *Was he really that dense?* I was ready to welcome former Democrats with open-arms to the GOP. We have a chance to grow our base. If this was a game of football, Dennis had effectively put himself on a kicking tee, and dared me to try to send him through the uprights.

I obliged.

"You could never be a Democrat in your life and then become a Republican? If people haven't opened their eyes in the last year, I don't know how somebody wouldn't open their eyes, especially in the last year, and become a conservative after what we'd been through," I said, peering at Dennis who was squirming,

"Have you not seen what the Democrats are doing? They're for defunding the police. They're for this ridiculous curriculum that is destroying the minds of our children. They're for shutting down businesses, locking us up in our homes, making us wear masks, forcing vaccines on us. They're for abortion all the way up and past birth. Seriously, if somebody is still a Democrat . . . The Democrat Party has changed, and the media has lost their minds. I know you can't see it because you're stuck in it right now and a lot of insecure people don't want to stand up and say what we're doing is biased, but just look back at all the reporting; how often do you cover a Conservative and how often do you cover them *fairly*, open-minded without going 'well we had to have a few negative snarky remarks about the Republicans'? OK it's a time for self-reflection for everybody in the media."

Dennis, did not expect a fight, but he got one. I continued on:

"I grew up conservative. I had a short area where I was a mother. I had a one-year-old baby. I had a baby on the way. I wasn't for endless wars. We were a few years into Afghanistan, and it was looking like we weren't going to get out. You know what? I was right. We were there for twenty years. Donald Trump is the one who tried to get us out of there," I said. "I am probably the most conservative person in this race right now."

The rest of the interview was routine after that. We danced around each other like boxers in the ring. He had me on the defense but he never laid a glove on me.

I was making great points, but I knew he would use nothing that made me look good. This was your run-of-the mill hit piece. He was going to struggle putting this together.

What had started as an attempt for me to lay out my agenda for the future of Arizona had turned into a demonstration of all of the reasons I had left the news industry in the first place.

At the ten-minute mark I called the match.

"Dennis, I hate to say this, but I've seen the direction the media's gone in this town—"

"What kind of questions did you expect?" Dennis interjected.

"*Why are you running?* Maybe something like that. But you know what? I gave you five minutes and we're ten minutes in. I want to thank you for your time and I really hope you'll do some soul-searching because I think the media has completely lost their way, and I don't even know if you guys have viewers anymore because they're on to it and they're turning it off. It's pretty sad."

If Dennis was going to have a "come to Jesus" moment. It wasn't going to be in front of me.

"Thank you very much, Kari," he said brusquely. "I hope you have a good day and good luck."

I logged out of the interview and furiously dialed Ross on my phone.

"Why the hell did I do that? It was an ambush. A complete throat slitting."

"It couldn't have been THAT bad," Ross replied.

Jeff, who had been sitting next to me off-camera, put on his headphones and started to pull up the interview to watch it back.

I spent the next few minutes thinking about what went wrong—what I could have done better. In my mind, I thought I had completely lost my cool.

Jeff pulled off his headphones and looked at me with a smile, "Kari, I don't know what the problem is here. This is amazing . . . watch."

So I watched. And this time I viewed it all from the third-person perspective. And it was truly something. Ten minutes of Dennis Welch's pure discomfort. I may have been enraged on the *inside*, but on the *outside* my demeanor and composure showed a resolute, calm, strong woman who was not going to be pushed around by a liberal propagandist.

My husband was right. It WAS good. I found my superpower— the ability to be confident and strong even in a storm. And get the message of our movement out to the people. I came off the victor in this, and Dennis . . . well, Dennis looked like a total loser.

"We have to put this out," Jeff said.

He was right. And we had to put it out *immediately*. I knew Dennis was going to go into spin-mode and craft a hit-piece for the 5 p.m. news. I had to get this out and crash his narrative. So we uploaded the footage to my Rumble account within an hour of the interview and titled it: "Ten Minutes of Pure Discomfort as Candidate for AZ Governor, Kari Lake, Torches Local Reporter."

It went viral.

The clip spread like wildfire; it was EVERYWHERE. I watched in awe as the views piled up—thousands of supportive comments in response to the video. They were hilarious: "You took away his manhood and handed them back on a platter. Way to go! 'Alex, I'll take who lost his balls for $500.'"

Every conservative elected official started texting. "Thanks for putting that jackass in his place" and "You just exposed the Fake Arizona News in one brilliant clip. God bless you, Kari!" read another text. Even those who were not endorsing me, were rooting for me. Conservative media loved it. Finally . . . a Fighter! Finally someone who *understood* the media and could call these bastards out. I became a hero for Americans sick of the B.S. the media was force-feeding them. And I was saying what they were thinking.

Dennis's TV station was being slaughtered on social media and they hadn't even aired his story yet! Everyone could see this guy's bias in his line of questioning and they were pissed. The station's phone lines lit up. Dennis had to scramble to make the piece *less-biased* or he'd be exactly what everyone thought: a leftist hack who hates Conservatives.

Our strategy worked. We forced the biased media to change course. While he never mentioned that I had made donations to Conservatives like: Burgess Owens, Paul Gosar, Andy Biggs, Ted Cruz, Kathy Barnette, Debbie Lesko, Robby Starbuck. I never expected him to be *that* fair. He concentrated only on what would make me look the worst. But I did put a dent in his biased reporting and put him in his place. He behaved a *bit* more fairly each time we encountered him on the campaign trail after that unfortunate interview. He'd already been burned once. And he wasn't about to shove his microphone, so recklessly, back into the fire again.

This wasn't just some contentious conversation between an interviewer and an interviewee, it was a call to action for conservative candidates to fight back against the Fake News. It showed me that the legacy media is indeed, as President Donald Trump said, not only the enemy of the people, but the enemy of every single conservative candidate. And they need to be treated as such.

This was a realization that would permanently alter the course of my campaign.

It was really the start of something special. Never again would I dodge the press. I'd go directly into the belly of the beast. And if necessary, I would tear that beast apart.

CHAPTER 9

Trump in Heels

ARIZONA MEDIA MAY be filled with the most-biased propagandists in the entire nation. But one of them may have paid me the nicest compliment I've ever received from the Fake News.

It was in the middle of my primary for governor, June 29, 2022, to be exact, when the former Canadian citizen, turned-ActBlue Donor, turned-Fake News propagandist, appeared on a "State of the Race" panel for the 6 o'clock news broadcast. Brahm Resnik opined, "If I'm going to sum this up for Republican voters, what you saw in Kari Lake is another four years of Donald Trump. What you see in Karrin Taylor Robson is another four years of Doug Ducey."[1]

I could have thrown him a parade. This was EXACTLY the message I wanted Arizona voters to hear. It has been since the beginning.

Doug Ducey hurt so many people during Covid. He locked down the state *twice* and allowed the relaxation of the election laws that allowed Maricopa County to be stolen in November 2020 from President Trump, leading to the Worst President in the History of America—Joe Biden—being installed into the White House. The

Republican voters of Arizona had never forgiven him for it. Polling showed that he was the least popular Republican governor in the country, only two governors were below him and they were two radical Marxist Democrats—one who was driving Oregon into the gutter, the other destroying freedom while growing the homeless population in Hawaii.

I was going to be a *very* different kind of governor than Doug Ducey. Arizonans knew I would be strong on the border and finally protect Arizona and return the government to the people. We need strong leaders at this moment in history—and knowing Doug Ducey and watching him operate, the word *strong* didn't come to mind for many Arizonans. I wasn't lying when I went on stage at a massive Turning Point USA event and stated: I am an unapologetic Trump Republican. Ducey hated Trump, so that didn't sit well with him.

Donald J. Trump's unequivocal defense of American Exceptionalism, his willingness to call out the rigged system, his hardline stance on immigration and non-interventionism, all of these policies were a breath of fresh air after the milquetoast neoconservatism offered by the Bushes, Bob Dole, John McCain, and Mitt Romney.

Finally, Republican voters were offered, as Barry Goldwater once said, "A Choice. Not an Echo."

And it was Trump's words that were echoing in my head when I arrived at work the next morning. Unsurprisingly, my coworkers in the newsroom did not share my affection for the Orange Man's speech. In fact, some of the lunatics around me were completely losing their minds. One of my coworkers said of Trump's speech, "That was the most racist thing I've ever heard."

This seemed to be the consensus amongst many in the mainstream media. I think I may be understating it when I say the media had lost their hold on reality. Donald Trump truly cracked the shells off the nuts in newsrooms across the country. He was actually speaking the language of a lot of American people. And the media acted like he had just delivered the Gettysburg Address of fascism.

That's the echo chamber the media lives in. They didn't get it. They weren't Trump's audience, the people were.

I followed the growing Trump phenomenon with great interest. How could you not? We had never seen anything like it. This was a man that walked onto a field of eighteen experienced Republican candidates and systematically knocked each and every one of them out like a heavyweight champion doing drills on a speed bag.

The Republican debates became appointment television. Americans were drawn back into politics, and watching Trump relentlessly bully the presumptive frontrunner, Florida Governor Jeb Bush, had become appointment television.

"Low Energy Jeb," Trump branded him. And the uninspiring Jeb Bush had no answer for the political haymakers thrown by Donald J. Trump.

My dad was a history teacher and a football coach. And the debates brought to mind stories he had told me about the Revolutionary War, how the prim and proper British Red Coats marched in formation, as noblemen were trained to do, and how they were completely unprepared to deal with the guerilla warfare and hit-and-run tactics of the young Colonial Revolutionaries.

Jeb Bush believed in the gentlemanly rules of engagement and Donald Trump broke every rule there was. It wasn't just the Art of the Deal that Donald Trump had mastered, but the art of war. At one point during the second Republican debate, Trump turned to Jeb and said, "Your brother . . . gave us Barack Obama. Such a disaster those last three months, that Abraham Lincoln couldn't have been elected."[2] How refreshing it was to see a Republican candidate acknowledge that it was Republican weakness that got the country into the mess we're in.

Donald Trump ran as a political outsider and made himself into an unstoppable force. And believe me, I was taking notes.

I fully embraced Trumpism. It wasn't calculated, it wasn't an act; it was just an authentic depiction of where I am politically, and where I believe the soul of the nation is too.

Donald Trump vowed to make America great again, and despite overwhelming opposition from the media, the Democrats, and members of his own party, by the end of his first four years in office Donald Trump was well on his way to making good on that promise.

Ultimately, Donald Trump would gain 71 million votes—8 million more than he had received four years previously, and a *record* amount of votes for an incumbent presidential candidate in *any* election! But miraculously, Sleepy Joe Biden proved to be the *most historic political figure in our nation's history???*, drawing an unprecedented— and frankly, unbelievable (and impossible)—81 million votes, most of which have never been accounted for.

The fight for election integrity that followed would start among grassroots voters across the nation, culminating in a huge protest rally at our nation's Capitol on January 6, 2022.

Droves of patriotic Americans from across the country traveled to Washington, D.C., to petition their representatives to examine the shady election with necessary scrutiny before certifying a winner. And while the true events of what followed are still unclear as of this writing, it seems evident that the federal intelligence community played a major role in turning a peaceful demonstration into a modern-day Reichstag fire that allowed them to ignore the contesting of the certification of the presidential electors inside the walls of Congress, label the event an insurrection, imprison Trump supporters as domestic terrorists, and install Joe Biden into the White House.

Arizona played a major role in both the contested certification and the riot that followed. In the halls of the United States Senate, Ted Cruz was to have stood up and delivered his case for the decertification of the Grand Canyon State's electors. And outside the walls of Congress, Arizona native Ray Epps (mysteriously never arrested or charged with any crime) urged the charged-up crowd to enter the barely defended Capitol (at the behest of Speaker Nancy Pelosi) in what now appears to be an organized entrapment operation planned by elements of the federal government.

In the weeks and months that followed, the usual Republican quislings abandoned Donald Trump in droves and allowed the media to create a narrative damning both the president and his (and their) own supporters. However, I never wavered in support of President Trump.

When I announced my candidacy for governor of Arizona, I did so as a proud MAGA Republican. I observed that over the last few decades the Republican establishment willingly conceded issue after issue and the moral high ground to the Radical Left. And I was unwilling to give up any more cultural hills.

Like Donald Trump, I entered a crowded field full of establishment candidates and political insiders, and turned my relative lack of political experience and position as an outsider into a strength. I would often tell people that the first line on my résumé read: *not a politician*. After all, it was the so-called experienced politicians who have gotten us into the mess we are in. It's going to take patriotic, hard-working, common-sense *citizen*-politicians (like Reagan, Trump, and Lake) to get us out.

Like Reagan and Trump, I considered myself a skilled communicator and felt that both my message and my unique connection to the people of Arizona would provide me with an advantage over the rest of the field.

We had our message. In the early days of the campaign, with very few donors and no big endorsements, I decided I would crisscross Arizona bringing in the endorsements that really matter—those of everyday Arizonans. I hit small towns, Republican women's groups, churches, bars, private homes, parks. My small rag-tag team helped me get that message out to the people of Arizona. My team and I put together a relentless schedule full of multiple events a day, juxtaposed with appearances on both mainstream and independent media. We saturated the market. Within weeks, we knew this was working. We were drawing incredible crowds, but what impressed us the most, was the people who attended it. People of every age, every color, every demographic, and every political party were drawn to the Arizona First message. I had been in the homes of the great people of state 48 for nearly thirty years—Democrat homes, Republican homes, and Independent homes. My vision for Arizona was resonating with them now as I was standing before them, not as the news woman, but as the citizen candidate for governor.

Trump's movement was called MAGA. My movement was called Karizona.

I remember hearing a story about what made cultural heroes like Batman and Indiana Jones so indelible in the culture's mind. What really mattered to people was the silhouette. You could take away everything—the whip, the utility belt—but a silhouette on a black screen left an indelible footprint in people's minds. Trump had his red hats. I needed to find something that I could call my own. I was experimenting with logos, branding ideas, T-shirt looks in the weeks before I announced my run. I knew we had to get the people to help us get the word out—what better way than by having them wear our merch, or slap on a bumper sticker.

Trump was an expert in branding. He knew the power of the brand. But many people were shamed out of wearing red MAGA hats. I wanted to make red hats great again with a *Kari Lake for Governor* hat, and T-shirts that said the same. We rolled all that out immediately and raised a fortune selling it. My favorite T-shirt design came when I tapped into my inner mama bear rage I felt whenever I saw children being forced to wear masks, or really *anyone* being forced to wear masks. The T-shirt said *Kari Lake for Governor* with the image of a burning mask. That was a huge seller.

I remembered again a history lesson from my father about the power of Rosie the Riveter and how that appealed to American women who had been called upon to fill the role of the men who had been sent away to fight the war. That woman wearing the bandana flexing her strength, that one image of wartime femininity, was instantly recognizable the world over, so my team repurposed it for my race.

We leaned into iconography. I wielded a sledgehammer, I burned the mask, I even stepped on one while grinding my foot into it. After that, I couldn't attend a rally where I didn't autograph an image, whether it be a postcard or a poster with me in the pose.

We paid particular attention to our logo knowing we wanted to invoke images of a better time in Arizona's past. We modeled it after the old Arizona license plate, rust-colored with *Kari Lake for Governor* embossed across it. The license plate that Arizonans associate with a time when Arizona felt more like the Wild West state it was and less like a big suburb of California that it seemed to be morphing into.

Through rallies, viral videos, and other public appearances we were generating incredible enthusiasm among the people of Arizona. It was working. Word had gotten out that Kari Lake was now the Trumpian candidate for Arizona governor. Now, the important thing was finding a way to communicate that message to Donald Trump himself.

The perfect opportunity presented itself on July 24, 2021, when the conservative group, Turning Point Action, held a rally for election integrity in downtown Phoenix. This would have every relevant Republican candidate for office (except "Karen," [Karrin Taylor Robson] who allegedly skipped the rally to spend the weekend on her billionaire husband's yacht) in Arizona speaking, and would also feature President Trump making his first visit to Arizona since the stolen 2020 election.

This was my opportunity to not only distinguish myself from the other candidates, but also make an impression on Donald Trump. We knew my speech would have to be a good one, and it's safe to say that I went Ultra MAGA.

Before the speakers stepped on stage, we were asked what we wanted to be introduced as. I watched as my opponents chose humble responses, naming their current jobs and occupations. So when Pinal County Sheriff Mark Lamb came and asked me the same question, I decided to leave all modesty behind.

So this is how the sheriff introduced me in front of a packed crowd at the Arizona Federal Theatre:

"The next person I want to introduce, a candidate, we all saw left a very lucrative job in the media. And I asked everybody the same question, and she's the only one who gave me the answer that she wants to be introduced as the next governor of Arizona . . . Kari Lake!"

The roar of the crowd gave me goosebumps. I took my place behind the podium as they chanted my name. "Kari, Kari, Kari!"

Here's how I began my speech:

"Thank you. Oh, my gosh. All right! MAGA world is still alive and well. I see it right here. My name is Kari Lake and I am running for governor of Arizona. I am a proud Conservative and an unapologetic Trump Republican, and

I'm running to make Arizona great again. I've got to tell you I love the MAGA energy in this room and you know what's so funny about it? You know there are a bunch of dirty politicians sitting at home and they're scared to death by what they see in this room. You know the ones. The backstabbers, the ones who turned their back on President Trump on November 4. And they told us to forget about the November 3 election, that nothing went wrong and that we should get on with our lives. We're not going to do that. You know they thought that if they just made us go away, it would be the end of the MAGA movement. Well, I've got news for them. This movement is not dying! It's not dying at all."[3]

Among the roar of the crowd, I spent the next three minutes of the speech delivering my America First policy message. We would close the border/finish the wall, secure our elections, and push back against the Draconian mandates put in place by the federal government that had made our lives a living hell. We would restore sovereignty back to the people of Arizona and together we would put Arizona first. I walked off the stage to raucous applause. I couldn't stop smiling.

When it came time for President Trump to give his remarks, I was situated in the audience with the rest of the crowd. I was no longer a political candidate. I was simply a fan.

Halfway through his remarks, Donald Trump polled the audience about what candidates had left the most favorable impression. Establishment candidates like Kimberly Yee and Matt Salmon received only tepid applause. But when Trump mentioned my name, the response nearly blew the roof off the Federal Theatre.

"Kari Lake . . ." President Trump said, and the crowd roared in approval. I rose to my feet and waved at them in response. "Whoa.

Wow," the 45th President remarked. "This could be a big night for you. Thank you very much, Kari. Good job."

Charlie Kirk, the founder of Turning Point would later tell me that as soon as Trump left the stage, he turned to Kirk and asked about me, "I want to meet with her," he said. "What is her story?"

Despite the rapturous response to my speech at the Turning Point event, I continued to hear through the political grapevine that Trump was still leaning toward endorsing my opponent, Matt Salmon.

This made some sense. Upon his entry to the race, Matt was viewed as the front-runner. He was a familiar name in Arizona Conservative circles, having just retired from a stint in the United States House of Representatives, two of those years having overlapped with the Trump administration. Trump was familiar with Salmon. Matt liked to tell people he had golfed with President Trump. And told everyone he was going to get the Trump endorsement.

I knew I needed to get in front of the president and make the case for myself. So I reached out to people in the Trump orbit and managed to arrange a ten-minute phone call with one of his staff. The call lasted over an hour and landed me a meeting with the president in Trump Tower one month after that TPUSA rally.

So my husband, Jeff, and I and a few members of our team got on a plane and headed to the Big Apple. The meeting with the 45th President of the United States was scheduled on my 52nd birthday. The Trump executive office is beautiful. Molly Michael, Trump's executive assistant, greeted us as we waited for our scheduled thirty-minute meeting with the president. What a shock when Eric Trump walked by and to my surprise, he recognized me. He introduced himself and was incredibly kind. We chatted for a while about the race. By now, I've met almost the entire Trump family and I can tell you they are the most polite, kind, and down-to-earth people. To know them is to love them. The constant attacks they are under from the press is despicable.

When Molly told us the president was ready to see us, I said a quick prayer. *God, You know I'd love for this meeting to go well. Anything You can do to assist would be appreciated.* The president only wanted to meet with Jeff and me, so my team waited outside. As we walked toward the door to Trump's office, I clutched a pamphlet I had put together full of coverage from my campaign to show him I wasn't crazy when I had said I think we really had a movement going on back home.

Before I saw the president, my eyes were drawn to the office walls which were adorned with a variety of Trump-bearing magazine covers. There was a gold shovel leaning against a table. I imagined how many times Trump must have done that as he broke ground on one skyscraper or a resort. And there in the middle of the room, behind a massive walnut desk, sat the great President Donald Trump, larger than life itself. Atop the desk right in front of him, was a pile of papers seemingly stacked about ten feet tall. The stories of Donald Trump's aversion to email are legendary. Every day, his team would print out emails and news information they knew he would want to see and deliver it to his desk. And there it stood before me.

The president beckoned us over, and Jeff and I took seats in two red velvet clam-shaped chairs across from the desk. Almost immediately, President Trump launched into a recap of the Turning Point event and the reception I had received there. Clearly, that had made a huge impression on him.

"That wasn't a poll that you hire some pollster to do," the president said. "That was a real poll. That's the people telling you who they like."

I began to tell him about the movement that was forming around me in Arizona. Mama Bears, Papa Bears and even kids were rallying around me because they saw I was the only candidate promising them the same type of policies they had so loved under the president for the previous four years. I told him about how it was so important to get America First leadership in Arizona because it was a border state, and that I would be in the perfect position to fight back against Joe Biden's open borders, globalist agenda, and help finish the wall that Trump had taken to the point of near-completion.

I told the president about why I had left the news, about the time that I had interviewed him while he was in the White House, how I felt it had gone so well and depicted him in a positive light, only for some leftist middle manager to refuse to even put the full interview online for people to see it because it made Trump look good.

I told him about how my colleagues in the media had used Covid to drive him from the Oval Office and how, despite it all, I was still always going to support him and never had uttered a bad word about him.

One thing about Donald Trump is that he's a listener. He wants to have a conversation with you. The questions he proceeded to ask me showed he wasn't looking for flattery. He was looking for the God's honest truth.

The president then began an interrogation, volleying a series of questions about a variety of subjects encompassing my past, present, and future. I held serve. I was able to answer all of his questions except one that took me completely off-guard.

President Trump turned to Jeff and me and asked, "So how long have you two been married?"

For some reason, in the moment, that very obvious bit of information had completely left both of our brains. We turned to each other and did our mental math while I observed out of the corner of my eye, Trump, took that opportunity while neither of us were looking, to reach down and take a drink from a bottle of water. It was an interesting bit of behavior, like he thought we'd think him mortal, if we learned that he needed water to survive like everyone else. It reminded me of how Donald Trump had made a mockery of Marco Rubio's repeated water drinking during a 2016 Republican primary debate. I wondered if the thought crossed his mind as well.

At last Jeff and I had calculated how long we had been married—twenty-three years—and gave our answer to the now fully hydrated 45th President. We all chuckled how he had stumped us with that question. I showed the president a photo of our kids, Ruby and Leo. We talked about the crazy world they are growing up in, the race as it was stacking up in Arizona, how rigged the 2020 election in Arizona was. Little did we know in 2022 it would continue.

Toward the end of the meeting, Eric Trump joined us and we all talked about business, politics, kids. What was supposed to be a half-hour meeting had turned into more than an hour-long conversation. At the end of the meeting, President Trump rose, shook our hands, and said he would be supporting me. Eric took some photos of the president, Jeff, and me by the floor-to-ceiling window with a billion-dollar view behind us. When Eric handed the phone back, I snapped a selfie with Trump. And asked if I could share the photos and the news that we met. "Go ahead," he said.

We walked out of the office. My team was dying to hear about our one-hour-and-fifteen-minute meeting! I had no idea we were in there that long. I told them Trump was going to endorse me and we all screamed with excitement. This was a game-changer. It was my birthday, and that was the best present anyone had ever given me!

Then came the longest one month and five days of my life. *Waiting* for the official endorsement. During that time, my opponents went into overdrive trying to send their minions into Trump World to derail my endorsement. It didn't work. On September 28, 2021, President Trump made it official and sent out this endorsement. It read as follows:

Endorsement of Kari Lake

Kari Lake is running for Governor in the Great State of Arizona. She is a fantastic person who spent many years working as a highly respected television anchor and journalist. Because of this, few can take on the Fake News Media like Kari. She is strong on Crime, will protect our Border, Second Amendment, Military, and Vets, and will fight to restore Election Integrity (both past and future!). She is against Covid lockdowns, Cancel Culture, and will end the "woke" curriculum in our schools. She will do a far better job than RINO Governor Doug Ducey—won't even be a contest! Kari will make her wonderful family, and the MAGA movement, very proud. Kari Lake has my Complete and Total Endorsement. She will be a great Governor for the incredible people of Arizona![4]

I still have that pinned to the refrigerator at my home.

President Trump does not give his endorsement lightly. After his endorsement I stayed in contact with him, updating him on the state of the campaign, new polling numbers, articles, and events. He is an incredible man. A man who has given up more for this country than anyone. He didn't have to get into the ugly world of politics, but I am so glad he did. The world needed a brash, tough New Yorker to come in and wake us up and turn things around. That's why I endorsed him the second he announced his run for 2024. We need him back in the White House ASAP.

I never imagined that I would have access to President Donald Trump or be privileged to receive advice from him. He was incredibly generous with his time, coming out to Arizona on three occasions to deliver remarks on behalf of me and the entire Arizona First slate.

Talking to him, I knew that he understood the importance of what we were building in Arizona. Massive crowds, historic enthusiasm, the proof of concept that America First policies were an appealing and popular prospect on the state level.

Over the rest of the campaign, Donald Trump and I became friends and confidants. Our calls became more frequent, his advice more focused. I could tell he had taken a personal interest in my campaign.

The media began to call me "Trump in Heels." They meant it as an insult. I took it as a great compliment.

He was the archetype I'd use in every debate against my Republican opponents. Stay on offense, attack, attack, and don't be afraid to show that you're having a blast while doing it.

I took front-runner status from Matt Salmon and never looked back. Soon, the mainstream media would also focus all their attention on me. And they were *hellbent* on my destruction.

I became the main target of the news—100% of their coverage on me was negative. The media wanted to hurt Trump and they saw me as an extension of him. Kari Lake became their number one scalp.

I would lean into it. Like Trump, I would go on offense and spar with the media in combative interviews. If the media were going to be dishonest and shameless, I was going to call that behavior out right to their faces.

"The Most Dangerous Politician in America," one article said of me. Me? A middle-aged mother of two teenagers?

They called me the MAGA Queen. The Future of the America First movement.

And my favorite, an Election Denier. (I still don't know what that even means as I'm not denying an election happened, just whether it took place fairly or was run competently.)

Honestly, I didn't care what the hell they called me, as long as at the end of my campaign they had to call me Governor Lake.

But of course, the crooked political machine would never go along with that.

The Swamp is deep. The government no longer exists for the benefit of the people but rather for the benefit of themselves and their donors. The Uniparty resents America First populism because it's inclusive and it threatens their grip on power. And just as the Washington Swamp battled Trump for his entire four years in office, so would the quicksand of the Arizona Uniparty stand in the way of every single thing the Arizona First candidates tried to do leading up to the 2022 election. But these ideas are too powerful and popular. In a fair election, the Establishment simply cannot compete.

The Republican Party was on life support when Donald Trump came down that escalator in Trump Tower, but his unique style and his America First message resuscitated the dying party. The thing about Donald Trump is that he is all about "We the People"—he brought the people back into the fight.

The people want America First policies. The Establishment wants the status quo which puts America last. Something would have to give and I was more than ready to give the state the nudge it needed.

America First policies work, and Trump in Heels was going to bring them to the State of Arizona.

CHAPTER 10

Draining the Desert Swamp

THE MOST DIRECT way to break through an obstacle is with a sledge-hammer. That was one of the most valuable lessons I learned during my run for governor.

It's funny, for a desert climate, Arizona is remarkably swampy. You thought Washington D.C. was bad? Try tackling the Arizona Uniparty, also known as the McCain Machine.

Jumping into the gubernatorial race, I knew I had a unique advantage. Thanks to my nearly three decades as a broadcast journalist and new anchor in Arizona, name recognition wasn't a problem. Everywhere I went, people knew me and liked me. But even with such a gift, I knew it wouldn't be easy. I was going up against a massive, entrenched political machine—I call it the AZ Swamp—and it had a stranglehold on Arizona for *decades*. Previously led by John McCain, this apparatus has put its boot to the necks of grassroots Arizonans for decades. The AZ Swamp controlled the flow of money, the policy direction, and the selection of candidates in races throughout the state. No one could get elected without going through that establishment Machine.

I knew the machine would be an obstacle. But I had my trusty sledgehammer—made famous by my iconic ad where I take a sledgehammer to the Fake News. The ad was the brain trust of Colton Duncan, written by David Leatherwood and produced by Jason Cole of Arsenal Media.[1]

The ad is pretty badass, I must admit. I enter with a sledgehammer over my shoulder, wearing all black—the look on my face shows I'm not willing to take anymore crap, and the tone of my voice says the same thing, "I'm ready to take a sledgehammer to the mainstream media's lies and propaganda." I continue on about the lies, the *dead-end* policies that are destroying Arizona. The TV sets stacked beside me showed the faces of Fake News Hall-of-Famers like Don Lemon, Jim Acosta, Rachel Maddow, Potato Head—I mean Brian Stetzer—Chris Cuomo. I proceed to destroy the TVs with the sledgehammer. (Note: It is *not* easy to crack those old TV screens. I was sore for two days after this shoot.) It was like going into one of those rage rooms. I will be happy when each and every one of them has been run out of the news business. So far so good. A few have been fired.

The end product was a viral political ad that to this day people still mention. They loved that I called for building a wall on the border to stop illegal immigration and keep the "California crap" out of Arizona. The sledgehammer became a symbol. I brought my sledgehammer out the night I turned the corner and won the Arizona Republican primary, telling my supporters I would be taking the sledgehammer to the electronic voting machines. Too bad I couldn't have done that before the general election.

John McCain's death in 2018 created a power vacuum in Arizona. And everybody wanted a piece of that pie. In the years preceding his death, the senator had found himself in a public feud with Donald Trump. The Fake News, with a raging case of TDS, promptly took McCain's side. Even with the "Maverick's" passing, his mafia was unwilling to let bygones be bygones. They were adamantly anti-America First and unwilling to cater to the increasingly populist leanings of the Arizona electorate.

Arizona politics are disgustingly incestuous. To get in you had to know somebody. To stay in, you had to bend the knee.

But it wasn't always like that.

The godfather of Arizona politics, and I'd argue modern conservatism, was Barry Goldwater—Arizona's favorite son.

Goldwater left two indelible marks on modern conservatism. The first was his 1960 book, *The Conscience of a Conservative*—the guide for generations of freedom-loving Patriots. The second was his doomed 1964 presidential run that shifted the Overton window dramatically right, and formed the political building blocks that became the Reagan Revolution and ultimately the MAGA Movement. Goldwater may have lost the battle for the White House, but he ultimately won the war.

There's a great George Will quote (those are fewer and farther between as the years go by), that goes like this. "We . . . who voted for him in 1964 believe he won, it just took 16 years to count the votes."[2] Ronald Reagan took up the torch of Goldwater and brought it to even greater heights.

But what of Arizona? Well, that legacy turned out to be much more complicated. In 1987, Barry Goldwater retired after a storied 35-year career in the United States Senate. As his political career wound down, Goldwater went through a fascinating political transformation. The man who had charted the path of modern conservatism had become increasingly libertarian and was ideologically hard to pin down. I had the privilege to interview him and I remember covering his death on May 29, 1998, doing live reports for national cable shows all day from outside Senator Goldwater's Paradise Valley home.

With Barry Goldwater Jr. already deep into a political career in California, Goldwater's retirement left the Cactus State with no logical heir. And he left some mighty big cowboy boots to fill.

The de facto heir ended up being John McCain.

McCain was a man of unparalleled ambition. He had grown up as the screw-up son of a proud military man, and only seemed to find his direction in life following his capture and torture in Vietnam. His military service to our country is appreciated. He returned from that experience with his eyes on the presidency. So he began to climb his way up the political and social ladder. McCain abandoned his wife even as she recovered from a car accident, and started an extramarital affair that would lead to his marriage to the well-connected Cindy Hensley, heiress to a beer distributing fortune. He found his entry point into politics through his position as the Navy's liaison to the United State Senators. That combined with Cindy's fortune meant John was set.

In 1983, John McCain was elected as a member of the U.S. House of Representatives for Arizona's first district. Four years later, he would be elected to the outgoing Barry Goldwater's Senate seat. A seat McCain would hold until his death in 2018.

From the beginning, McCain consciously cozied up to Goldwater; he knew where his bread was buttered, and Goldwater was receptive. Their relationship remained cordial until 1989 when McCain found himself embroiled in the Keating Five scandal. In this scandal, McCain and four of his Senate colleagues were accused of improper conduct via a quid pro quo.

The arrangement was as follows: the senators would receive 1.5 millions dollars in campaign donations from Charles Keating, the owner of the California's Lincoln Savings and Loan Association, and in return, it was alleged that the senators would then apply pressure to the Federal Home Loan Bank Board to overlook Keating's suspicious financial activities. Keating would end up facing prison time for this scandal, with each senator's reputation taking a massive blow.

McCain would ultimately be cleared of improper conduct, said only to have exercised "poor judgment," but his reputation was permanently tarnished. And so too was his relationship with Barry Goldwater.

Of Goldwater, McCain once lamented, "I admired him to the point of reverence, and I wanted him to like me. . . . He was usually cordial, just never as affectionate as I would have liked."[3]

McCain continued to tout himself as a Goldwater-style Conservative. But the two men couldn't have been more different. John, at his heart, was a Big-Government Conservative. This was in direct contrast to the beliefs held by the individual liberty-championing Goldwater.

There's no better example of the late senator's blatant Goldwater pandering than in his 2008 presidential run. McCain arranged for the last stop of his nation-wide barnstorming tour to occur outside the historic Yavapai County Courthouse in one of the most patriotic towns in America, Prescott, Arizona (pronounced Press-kit)—a location where Goldwater had started all of his bids for office. (My second-to-last rally in the 2022 gubernatorial campaign took place in the same location on November 7—a cold night, where a thousand Arizonans gathered to fill the town square, so excited to have a governor fight for them and return our state government back to the people.)

Like Goldwater, McCain failed to win the presidency. But unlike Goldwater, McCain made sure to consolidate enough power in Arizona that all notable decisions in the state of Arizona had to be run directly through him.

John had his fingers in every piece of the Arizona pie. He and his friends in the consultant class controlled the flow of the money in the state, and the "Maverick's" conscious positioning as the "not-too Conservative Conservative" helped him cultivate relationships with the liberal media that allowed him to call on them to smear any political upstart who stepped out of line. The grassroots loathed him. This is memory-holed now, but before his passing, John McCain was the least popular senator in America amongst his constituents. The Arizona Republican Party punished him for his betrayal of conservative principles and turning his back on Arizona Republicans by censuring him. Years later his wife, Cindy, would be censured for her full-throated endorsement of the Worst President in the History of America, Joe Biden.

I had always felt sorry for Cindy. That kind of disrespect she received from her husband hurts your soul. Maybe she was partially trying to cover that pain when she admitted being addicted to painkillers and stealing drugs from a now-defunct McCain charity American Voluntary Medical Team. The story of Cindy's addiction and the DEA investigation broke a few weeks after I first arrived as a young broadcast journalist in Arizona in August of 1994.[4] Twelve years later I got to know her, when I started covering the McCains in preparation of John's imminent presidential run.

My assignment was to work on covering Cindy so our news organization had some "ins" ahead of the 2008 election. In January of 2006 along with photographer Jon Noetzel, I headed off with McCain half-a-world away to Cambodia to cover her work with The HALO Trust, an NGO that assists in the removal of landmines from formerly war-torn countries.

On one of the flights to Siem Reap, Cambodia, we ran into Cindy, her press person, and a man who I was told was a "just a friend" who traveled with Cindy.

We spent a week documenting the incredible work of brave men who remove landmines placed thirty years prior during the Vietnam War.

Cindy's other interests involved stopping sex-trafficking only to admit that for years she knew what heinous things Jeffrey Epstein was up to, and with all the power she and John wielded, did nothing to stop it.[5] To this day she is working for Biden as an ambassador,[6] hobnobbing with George Soros and his son,[7] doing everything in her power to stop America First candidates and their efforts to Make America Great Again. These are the principled Conservatives we hear so much about?

There's a story that many of the veterans in Arizona media remember of the time John lashed out at Cindy, before an interview with a reporter, the story goes: Cindy was helping comb down his hair before the interview. John's injuries from Vietnam prevented him from being able to lift his arms up to do that himself. She made a light-hearted comment about his hair thinning and he *snapped*! Enraged, he berated his wife, calling her the c-word right to her face and in front of the reporter.[8]

Not a nice man.

But then came Donald Trump. A man with enough of his own power and influence that he had no fear of the Godfather of the Arizona mafia. People forget that it takes two to tango. And Donald Trump is a counter-puncher. Trump's infamous "War Hero" salvo at the 2015 Family Leadership Summit in Ames, Iowa, didn't come out of nowhere. It was a direct response to McCain attacking the base of the Republican Party.

Only a week earlier, the senator had accused Trump of riling up the "crazies" in the party with his strong language about illegal immigrants invading the country from Mexico.[9] Can you imagine, thinking that Americans who care about national security, state sovereignty, law and order and restoring America's greatness are *crazies*?? That's how much disdain McCain carried for hard-working, patriotic Americans. But I guess a man who calls his wife a *c-word*, has no problem calling his fellow countrymen *crazies*.

McCain held grassroots voters in contempt and providing illegal immigrants with amnesty was one of his pet causes. In this case, "crazies" was his term for anyone who was more conservative than him. Which, to his chagrin, was about 95 percent of the Republican Party. For all of his self-mythologizing about his principled conservatism, the legislator who the senator's voting record most closely resembled was that of Senator Joe Manchin. That's right. John McCain, the senator for a state where modern-day conservatism was born, a state that once had a conservative supermajority in its state legislature, had amassed the decades-long voting record of a moderate Democrat. So, yeah, the people were fed up.

When Donald Trump turned to Frank Luntz and unleashed his verbal barrage, he set off a series of events in Arizona that would change the state's political alignment forever.[10]

DONALD TRUMP: "Let's take John McCain. I'm in Phoenix. We have a meeting that is going to have 500 people at the Biltmore Hotel. We get a call from the hotel, it's turmoil. Thousands and thousands of people showing up three, four days before, they're pitching tents on the hotel grass. The hotel says, 'We can't handle this. It's going to destroy the hotel.' We moved it to the convention center. . . . 15,000 people showed up to hear me speak, bigger than anybody, and everybody knows it. A beautiful day with incredible people that were wonderful great Americans, I will tell you. John

McCain goes, 'Oh boy, Trump makes my life difficult. He had 15,000 crazies show up.' Crazies, he called them all crazy. I said, 'They weren't crazy. They were great Americans.' . . . So he insulted me and he insulted everybody in that room. And I said, "Somebody should run against John McCain, who has been, in my opinion, not so hot." And I supported him, I supported him for president. I raised a million dollars for him. It's a lot of money. I supported him. He lost, he let us down. He lost. So I'd never liked him as much after that because I don't like losers. But Frank, Frank, let me get to it. He hit me—"

FRANK LUNTZ: "He's a war hero."

TRUMP: "He's not a war hero . . ."

LUNTZ: ". . . Five and a half years in a prison camp."

TRUMP: "He's a war hero because he was captured. I like people that weren't captured, okay? I hate to tell you."

LUNTZ: "Do you agree with that?"

TRUMP: "He's a war hero because he was captured, okay? And I believe perhaps he's a war hero, but right now he said some very bad things about a lot of people. . . . He graduated last in his class at Annapolis and he was upset. I said, 'Why? For telling the truth?' See, you're not supposed to say that somebody graduated last or second to last in their class. Because you're supposed to be like, Frank says, very nice. Folks, I want to make America great again. We want to get down to brass tacks. We don't want to listen to his stuff with being politically correct and everything else. We have a lot of work to do."

Predictably, the corporate media lost their mind.

"Trump attacks McCain: 'I like people who weren't captured'" screamed *Politico*.

"Trump Slams McCain for Being Captured in Vietnam" said the *Washington Post*.

"Trump: McCain only a war hero because he was captured" added CBS.

All of these hysterics missed the forest for the trees. Was what Donald Trump said tactless and boorish? Absolutely. But in the context it was given—as an impassioned *defense* of the Republican voters that McCain had ridiculed and failed time and time again—it made complete sense. But the media didn't want to take it in its context and make sense of anything. They wanted Trump's head.

And wasn't it interesting how quickly the media made the late senator a martyr? Only seven years before, the partisan press had relentlessly pummeled him during his run for the presidency. But now the media had a useful idiot. With neoconservatism on the decline and Trump's America First wing on the rise, the media would make good use of John McCain as their "Only Good Republican." And John, who spent his life craving positive headlines gladly obliged. Over the next three years, and up until his death, he happily played the foil against Donald Trump. Even when it meant hurting the good people of Arizona, which was often.

The senator did some truly nasty things over the course of this feud.

He helped create the Russia Hoax by spreading the Steele dossier around Washington. This led to the first impeachment of President Donald Trump.[11]

When President Trump fought to build the wall, McCain actively worked to thwart the construction of the wall at *every single turn*.[12] McCain hated Trump more than he loved his country. His hatred hurt Arizona.

Photo Courtesy of Bobby Bushcraft

Never in my wildest dreams could I have imagined that I would be in the center of one of the greatest political movements in history. I will forever cherish the memories and the friendships that I have made on this journey. Our brightest days are ahead of us—I am certain of that!

Photo Courtesy of Bobby Bushcraft

Each and every homemade sign we saw on the campaign trail made my heart swell with so much love. This is one of my favorites.

Photo Courtesy of Kari Lake

Never too old to celebrate my birthday with the best. I was thrilled to spend my 52nd birthday with President Trump at Trump Tower.

Photo Courtesy of Jeff Halperin

My right-hand man, Colton Duncan. He's truly one of the sharpest political minds and I thank God every day for putting him in my life.

This is the moment I found out that we won our primary election! We won all 15 counties and beat the establishment candidate by five points, despite the $30 million spent against us. What a night!

What made primary election night truly special was spending it with Jeff, Ruby, Leo, and my team. It was a late night. What began as a ten-point deficit ended with a five-point lead when they finally tabulated all the votes.

Photo Courtesy of Bobby Bushcraft

After we took the lead on primary night, I decided to give my good friend Brian Glenn, of Right Side Broadcasting, the only interview of the night. The Fake News was seething and begging me to concede. They hate America.

Photo Courtesy of Kari Lake

We knew we won, but Arizona election laws are so ridiculous that we had to wait a few days for the AP to call the race. Jeff and I finally heard the devastating news as the plane was taking off to CPAC.

Standing on the grounds that once held terror and destruction. I visited Cambodia with Cindy McCain and her "friend" Dino.

An experience like no other, interviewing the greatest President of all time, Donald J. Trump.

When I interviewed President Obama at the White House, he told me that Donald Trump would never be president. Boy, was he wrong . . .

Photo Courtesy of Jeff Halperin

This is my family: eight girls and one boy. Blessed to have grown up with them in America's heartland.

Photo Courtesy of Bobby Bushcraft

My husband Jeff and I are so grateful for our beautiful children. Forever surrounded by love and laughter with my favorite people in the world — my family.

Photo Courtesy of Jeff Halperin

Everything I did as a candidate for governor, I did for my children and the children of this great state. We must protect our most precious resource: Our children are our future. I want to see policies that protect them and prepare them for the future.

Photo Courtesy of Jeff Halperin

Photo Courtesy of Bobby Bushcraft

Photo Courtesy of Bobby Bushcraft

I wish I could have just campaigned in rural Arizona. The greatest kiddos are the ones lucky enough to grow up on a farm.

Photo Courtesy of Jeff Halperin

Photo Courtesy of Jeff Halperin

Photo Courtesy of Jeff Halperin

Photo Courtesy of Colton Duncan

Photo Courtesy of Jeff Halperin

Photo Courtesy of Colton Duncan

This was our first "Moms for Kari" Coalition meeting. We have an ARMY of Mama Bears who fuel our movement.

Photo Courtesy of Jeff Halperin

In liberal Tucson, radio host Garrett Lewis hosts a monthly "Beer Club for Men" political event. Women are allowed, but only if they don't nag.

Photo Courtesy of Jeff Halperin

The sledgehammer became a symbol of our movement. In a viral advertisement, I used one to shatter the Fake News Media.

Photo Courtesy of Bobby Bushcraft

I had to break out the trusty sledgehammer again on primary night. No Fake News journalists were harmed.

Despite it being 2 a.m., I agreed to an interview after taking the lead in the GOP primary. At nearly 53, this is WAY past my bedtime.

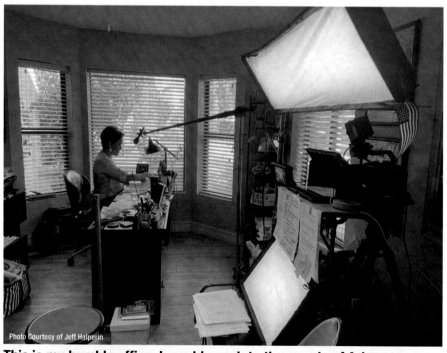

This is my humble office. I would speak to the people of Arizona on a daily basis from here.

This is the iced-over plane in which Lisa, Colton, and I nearly died. God helped land this plane.

After our emergency landing in Wilcox, Arizona, this was the tiny airport terminal that we took shelter in.

It was incredible when President Trump gave me a shout-out from the stage during his CPAC speech.

Photo Courtesy of Jeff Halperin

Colton and I find an quiet space for speech prep before heading onto the main stage. This is August 2022. I spoke immediately before President Trump (again) just after my Primary Election win. I consider this my victory speech.

Photo Courtesy of Jeff Halperin

Our government cares so little about us that their solution to the chaos at the border is a warning sign.

Their inaction has real-life, human consequences. Look no further than my friends Clark and Karen Griffin, who lost their son Tyler to fentanyl poisoning. Millions of Americans are suffering the same way Clark and Karen are and our "leaders" could not care less.

Photo Courtesy of Jeff Halperin

"Let us hope our weapons are never needed, but do not forget what the common people of this nation knew when they demanded the Bill of Rights: An armed citizenry is the first defense, the best defense, and the final defense against tyranny." —Edward Abbey

Photo Courtesy of Colton Duncan

Photo Courtesy of Jeff Halperin

Here's a photo of a forum with my primary opponents, Steve Gaynor and Matt Salmon. Matt was often sleepy on the campaign trail. They say a picture's worth a thousand words.

Photo Courtesy of Jeff Halperin

Photo Courtesy of Bobby Bushcraft

Photo Courtesy of Colton Duncan

We got pretty creative in outing our cowardly opponents who were scared to death to debate me.

Photo Courtesy of Bobby Bushcraft

Our press conferences certainly became must-see TV! These two were some of the highest-viewed live events on Rumble.

Photo Courtesy of Jeff Halperin

I was never afraid to challenge the media.

Photo Courtesy of Jeff Halperin

Photo Courtesy of Jeff Halperin

Photo Courtesy of Jeff Halperin

I joined Tim Pool's podcast twice and had a blast both times. Every candidate should have to join him for a three-hour, no-holds-barred podcast.

Photo Courtesy of Jeff Halperin

Photo Courtesy of Jeff Halperin

Photo Courtesy of Jeff Halperin

The team that makes our movement possible. I love these people so much.

Photo Courtesy of Neil A. Miller

This isn't about me. It never was. It's always been about we, the people.

Photo Courtesy of Jeff Halperin

This was after a forum with Katie Hobbs. She literally RAN out of the event as soon as she was done speaking. Katie is afraid of her own shadow.

We have the best supporters who know how to have fun.

Photo Courtesy of Jeff Halperin

Photo Courtesy of Jeff Halperin

Photo Courtesy of Jeff Halperin

Photo Courtesy of Jeff Halperin

Photo Courtesy of Jeff Halperin

Photo Courtesy of Jeff Halperin

Photo Courtesy of Jeff Halperin

Photo Courtesy of Jeff Halperin

Photo Courtesy of Jeff Halperin

We couldn't print campaign signs fast enough. People LOVED them! Arizonans were able to take a piece of our special movement home with them.

My "Black Voices for Kari" coalition was incredible. We had the largest, most robust coalition operation in Arizona history—everyday Patriots joined the fight to save their state.

Photo Courtesy of Bobby Bushcraft

Photo Courtesy of Jeff Halperin

Photo Courtesy of Jeff Halperin

We had so many amazing people come to Arizona to campaign for us. They wanted to be a part of our Movement.

Photo Courtesy of Bobby Bushcraft

The "Karizona" Movement was real. It was always great to have President Trump join us!

NFL legend Jack Brewer, and my brother in Christ, came in to stump for me. He is such an inspiration.

Evangelicals for Kari Lake laid their hands upon me in prayer. I could not have gotten through this without my army of prayer warriors.

Prolific actor and director, Mel Gibson. He is one of the few good ones in Hollywood.

Robert Kiyosaki wrote *Rich Dad, Poor Dad.* He is a veteran, Patriot, huge supporter, and friend.

Our rally turned into a John Rich concert. John may be one of the greatest friends I've met on the campaign. He LOVES America. Thanks to Senator Marsha Blackburn for joining us for this incredible event!

Colton Duncan and John Rich both grew up in trailer parks in West Texas. I grew up in rural Iowa. We all came from humble beginnings, and are working to preserve the American Dream for future generations.

(L-R) Actor Rob Schneider, Irina Wozniak, and Slawomir Wozniak

(L-R) Two of America's greatest Patriots, Steve Bannon and Charlie Kirk

Photo Courtesy of Jeff Halperin

With Governor Glenn Youngkin of Virginia

Photo Courtesy of Bobby Bushcraft

With Governor Kristi Noem of South Dakota

Photo Courtesy of Bobby Bushcraft

With former Congresswoman Tulsi Gabbard

Photo Courtesy of Kari Lake

(L-R) American Patriots Mike Lindell, Brian Glenn, and Wendy Rogers

Photo Courtesy of Jeff Halperin

Legendary country music star John Rich

This was the third rally President Trump did for us. He hasn't lost a single ounce of energy.

This rally made the Uniparty and Marxist's heads explode. We don't care. We are going to save America!

Photo Courtesy of Bobby Bushcraft

525th day of campaigning. We wrapped up with these two incredible rallies.

Photo Courtesy of Bobby Bushcraft

Voting on Election Day with my family. We were forced to drive to the liberal part of town to vote because the Republican areas' voting machines weren't working—wrong ballots printed, tabulators rejecting ballots. They sabotaged Election Day knowing that our supporters were showing up in person. We had no problem voting in the Democrat district. My entire family was able to vote in 10 minutes, while Republicans across Arizona faced 5-hour lines.

Photo Courtesy of Bobby Bushcraft

Our movement expands beyond Arizona. I went to my childhood state of Iowa and held two events. To my surprise, thousands of Iowans joined us. When they stole the election, they thought they wounded us. They only made us stronger.

Photo Courtesy of Bobby Bushcraft

Photo Courtesy of Kari Lake

My hero and attorney Kurt Olsen, a former Navy Seal, is dedicating his life to saving our Republic.

Photo Courtesy of Neil A. Miller

This was the Save Arizona rally we held after the stolen election. The venue was at four times the capacity permitted. If you look at the screen you can see Stephen Richer and Bill Gates (dumb & dumber) who have dedicated their lives to destroying our Republic.

Photo Courtesy of Caroline Wren

I told CPAC that powerful people in Washington tried to bribe me to get out of politics. They told me to name my price to suspend our political movement for two years. I said, "NO! We, the People can NOT be bought!"

Photo Courtesy of Colton Duncan

Paul Gosar invited me to the National Prayer Breakfast. Washington, D.C. needs our prayers! Congressman Gosar is "The GOAT." We need strong, America First Patriots like Gosar at every level of government.

After his terminal diagnosis of brain cancer, McCain refused to resign from the Senate because he valued being a thorn in Donald Trump's side more than preserving the Senate seat for the Arizona Republican Party.[13]

And after promising to repeal and replace Obamacare for nearly a decade, when that opportunity fell squarely on McCain's shoulders, in a complete *screw you* to the base of the Republican Party, John gave a thumbs-down on the Senate floor killing the repeal of the Affordable Care Act's individual mandate.[14] This is why he is loathed in Arizona. The narrative that he is adored is a creation of the corrupt AZ Swamp and their minions and propagandists in AZ media.

When John McCain died on August 25, 2018, all of his past baggage disappeared. The partisan press, Democrat party, and Never-Trumpers practically nominated him for sainthood. To remind people of the man's very notable flaws was an act of heresy.

At 7:32 p.m. on that day, as a journalist who had covered the McCain family for decades, I tweeted: "The 'Maverick' has died. Four days shy of his 82nd birthday Senator John McCain passed away at his Cornville, Arizona home after a courageous battle with cancer. A war hero, icon and a force to be reckoned with. Sending my deepest condolences to his family at this painful time."[15] Having lost my own father to cancer back in 2009, I know the pain of that loss, and I truly prayed for McCain's loved ones. I attended one of his numerous funerals.

John's death created a vacuum in Arizona politics. The Republican Party of yesteryear is now the America First Republican Party. Putting the needs of America and her citizens first and bringing forth common-sense solutions to the problems plaguing us. Turns out, there's still a little muckish, rotten water left to be drained out of the AZ Swamp.

CHAPTER 11

The Great Debates and the Debate Denier

FOR AS LONG as I remember, most elections were decided by candidate debates and the candidates for election were defined by their debate performance. At least that used to be the case. But, in Arizona, that may have changed forever.

On June 28, 2022, Matt Salmon dropped out of the Arizona governor's race and endorsed Karen "the RINO" Robson (a.k.a. the Billionaire's Wife).

This was a BIG deal. While I had been leading in the polls since the moment I declared, I had also benefited from the two RINO candidates (Salmon and Robson) siphoning off votes from each other. The fear from the people around me was that the consolidation of the establishment vote would be enough to put my lead in peril.

Matt had impeccable timing. It just so happened that the day following his departure from the race was the first (and only) televised debate among the Arizona candidates for governor.

The debate would be broadcast on Arizona PBS and I knew there would be a LOT riding on how it transpired. I won't lie to you. I was incredibly nervous. I was no stranger to television, and I had done candidate forums before, but I had no actual debate background. But my father taught me that "when you're facing an uncertain future, you can find certainty in the past." So I began to study debates through American history to see what lessons I could learn about what to do and, more importantly, what NOT to do.

Ronald Reagan's first term in the White House was an incredible success. He had successfully put the nation on a road toward economic recovery, following the disastrous 1981–82 recession precipitated by the Carter/Mondale administration, had kept the country out of a hot war with Soviet Russia while navigating treacherous diplomatic waters, and had shepherded the population through a significant rise in national pride, making good on his promise of a prouder, stronger and better America.

Needless to say, in 1984 Walter Mondale had an uphill battle in his attempt to unseat President Reagan. Mondale, a liberal Democrat from Minnesota, set about trying to throw shade on the "Morning in America" promised by the incumbent President.

Mondale focused his criticism on Reaganomics, the supply-side fiscal policy that had freed the country from Carter's stagflation, but done little to fix America's increasing budget deficits. Mondale also raised the alarm about Reagan's aggressive handling of Soviet leader Mikhail Gorbachev during the wind-down of the Cold War, claiming that he had the country on the verge of nuclear peril, and that America needed a steadier hand on the wheel in their dealings with Soviet Russia. Mondale would also champion the ratification of the Equal Rights Amendment returning to that classic Democrat trope that all Republicans are racists and misogynists.

But the narrative that Mondale primarily focused on was telling the American public that the aging 40th President of the United States was losing his mind, becoming senile.

Before Joe Biden was installed into the Oval Office, Ronald Reagan, at age sixty-nine, was the oldest man to ever begin a term in the White House. Four years later, Reagan was seventy-three years old, and any misspeak or stumble was picked up by the media or the Democrat opposition as a clear indicator of the onset of dementia.

The high-watermark of Mondale for President came in the first presidential debate when Reagan seemed to lose his train of thought, mistake the word "uniform" for "wardrobe," and claim that he had attended church that morning in Washington, D.C., rather than in Louisville, Kentucky, where the debate was being held.[1]

Mondale spent the next two weeks pounding the incumbent president on those mental lapses, claiming that Reagan was no longer capable of handling the rigors of the presidency.

This was the narrative leading up to October 21, 1984, when Reagan squared off in Kansas City, Missouri, against former Vice President Walter Mondale for the second presidential debate.

For the debate, Reagan and Mondale stood across from each other taking questions from a panel of four journalists. One of the men was *Baltimore Sun* Diplomatic Correspondent, Henry Trewhitt. By Trewhitt's own admission, he had worked with a colleague for hours to devise the perfect gotcha question surrounding Reagan's age.

Reagan "stumbled over words, mangled his own familiar stories, repeated mind-numbing statistics, rambled through his closing statement, and seemed to lose track of the rules at one point" in the first debate.[2] The question Trewhitt asked President Reagan went as follows:

"Mr. President, I want to raise an issue that I think has been lurking out there for 2 or 3 weeks and cast it specifically in national security terms. You already are the oldest president in history, and some of your staff say you were tired after your most recent encounter with Mr. Mondale. I recall, yes, that President Kennedy, who had to go for days on end with very little sleep during the Cuban missile crisis. Is there any doubt in your mind that you would be able to function in such circumstances?"[3]

By all rights, Reagan could have flown off the handle, but what made Reagan so wonderful was his steady calmness. While his age was always apparent, it gave him a grandfatherly quality, and those twinkling blue eyes showed wisdom, not confusion.

So Reagan took a question meant to be a political kill shot and flipped it to utterly nullify his opposition's (and the media's) primary point of attack.

"Not at all. And, Mr. Trewhitt, I want you to know that I will not make age an issue of this campaign. I am not going to exploit, for political purposes, my opponent's youth and inexperience."[4]

The response was so perfect that even the fifty-six-year-old Mondale chuckled!

Rather than give the media a story about an old man who lost his cool, Reagan's wit and sense of humor prevailed and he went on to win re-election in a landslide, scoring 525 electoral votes and 59% of the popular vote.[5]

This was lesson Number 1 that I took for my debate prep. Never take the personal attacks personally. By taking such attacks in stride and with composure and good humor, you will always look to be the better person and come out on top.

During the years and administrations following the 1984 debate, the anti-Republican bias in the media got even worse. By the time the 2012 presidential debates rolled around, the moderators had moved from asking gotcha questions to the Republican candidates to actively fact-checking them mid-debate.

This was infamously seen on October 12, 2012, during the second presidential debate between Mitt Romney and incumbent president and media darling, Barack Obama.

Romney should have had Obama dead to rights. The first four years of the Obama experience were an outright disaster. Seeing a man who had gained office promising to unite the country spent the majority of his time dividing it along racial and ideological lines while jamming unpopular nigh-Socialist policies like Obamacare down the country's throat.

The Republican Party had the perfect opportunity to offer the American public a viable alternative to Obama's Marxist flirtations with candidates like Ron Paul or Rick Santorum, who had innovative conservative solutions to the problems America was facing.

Instead, they nominated the former Governor of Massachusetts, Willard Mitt Romney, a man of flexible principles and minimal conservative credentials.

Romney, paired with spineless policy wonk, Paul Ryan, formed one of the dorkiest and least-appealing Republican tickets in recent memory. Despite this, due to the divisive nature of Obama's leadership, the pair had a realistic shot of winning the election. This was seemingly even more realistic after Romney had clearly dominated the first presidential debate, making a mockery of the incumbent president.

The media was scandalized at first debate moderator Jim Lehrer of PBS's willingness to let both candidates actually answer questions, leading to Romney's decisive victory, so they made sure that it would never happen again.[6]

To the rescue came Candy Crowley of CNN, and she made sure that Romney would be punished for making the media's golden boy look bad.

About a month prior to the debate, Barack Obama and Hillary Clinton had watched on video as Islamic militant group Ansar

Al-Sharia had invaded the United States Embassy compound in Benghazi, Libya and brutally murdered United State Ambassador to Libya J. Christopher Stevens, U.S. Foreign Service Information Management Officer Sean Smith, and CIA contractors Tyrone S. Woods and Glen Doherty.

Obama and Clinton twiddled their thumbs and did nothing for thirteen hours and afterward claimed the attack was not a planned terrorist attack, but rather a spontaneous event caused by the release of a personal videotape that the terrorists had found to be offensive.

It was a ludicrous excuse for the attack, one that promised to be a knockout blow if successfully utilized by Mitt Romney against Barack Obama. Except Candy Crowley knew that too. And she was NOT going to let that happen. Once the subject was brought up, here's how the exchange went down:

CROWLEY: "Governor, if you want to reply just quickly to this, please."

ROMNEY: "Yeah, I—I certainly do. I certainly do. I—I think it's interesting the President just said something which is that on the day after the attack, he went into the Rose Garden and said that this was an act of terror. You said in the Rose Garden the day after the attack it was an act of terror? It was not a spontaneous demonstration?"

OBAMA: "Please proceed."

ROMNEY: "Is that what you're saying?"

OBAMA: "Please proceed, Governor."

ROMNEY: "I—I—I want to make sure we get that for the record, because it took the President 14 days before he called the attack in Benghazi an act of terror."

OBAMA: "Get the transcript."

Let's stop. Here's where Candy Crowley was supposed to wave Obama's request away, and let the fact-checkers do their jobs post-debate. What she was NOT supposed to do was this (obviously prepared ahead of time):

CROWLEY: "It—he did in fact, sir. So let me—let me call it an act of terrorism."

OBAMA: "Can you say that a little louder, Candy?" *(laughter, applause)*

CROWLEY: "He did call it an act of terror. It did as well take—it did as well take two weeks or so for the whole idea of there being a riot out there about this tape to come out. You are correct about that."

ROMNEY: "This—the administration—the administration— *(applause)*—indicated that this was a—a reaction to a—to a video and was a spontaneous reaction."

CROWLEY: "They did."

Ms. Crowley was now an active participant in a 2-against-1 debate!

ROMNEY: "It took them a long time to say this was a terrorist act by a terrorist group and—and to suggest—am I incorrect in that regard? On Sunday the—your—your secretary or—"

OBAMA: "Candy—"

ROMNEY: "Excuse me. The Ambassador to the United Nations went on the Sunday television shows and—and spoke about how this was a spontaneous reaction."

OBAMA: "Candy, I'm—I'm happy to—"

CROWLEY: [Rising to Obama's defense] "Mr. President, let me—I—"

OBAMA: "I'm happy to have a longer conversation about foreign policy."

CROWLEY: "I know you—absolutely. But I want—I want to move you on."

OBAMA: "OK, I'm happy to do that too."[7]

It was the perfect set-up. Candy Crowley derailed Romney's line of attack against Obama, by providing a blatantly false fact-check, allowing Obama to turn on the charm, preemptively changing the subject and turning Mitt into a blubbering mess.

The hits would keep on coming. In total, Candy interrupted Mitt Romney twenty-eight times during the debate, only interrupting Obama on nine occasions.

Mitt Romney never recovered. His third debate performance was lackluster, and the media's kid gloves treatment of Obama (and later Hillary Clinton) allowed Obama to escape accountability for the Benghazi event to this day. And this was a fatal blow to any remaining Republican trust in the media. This was far-and-away the most concrete example to date of the media and the Left ganging-up against the Conservative movement.

And it was a learning lesson Number 2 for me to know that the moderator was NOT on my side nor necessarily impartial. When I went to debate, I needed to expect attacks from every angle. Even from the person asking the questions.

By the time the next presidential election cycle came around in 2016, the lesson from the Candy Crowley debacle had sunk in.

And to their credit, the Republican candidates showed a lot more aggression in punching back against the moderators' attempts to put their thumbs on the scale.

No one was better at policing the moderators than Donald Trump, who seemed to spend as much time explaining to the moderator why their question was stupid or biased than actually answering the question.

Like me, Donald Trump had no debate experience. His solution was to avoid being put on defense and stay on offense. He would go into a debate like the Tasmanian Devil spinning wildly and leaving destruction in his wake. But there was a method behind the madness.

A wise man once told me there's a fine line to walk between being a jerk and an asshole. Trump was the expert at walking that tightrope. He would bully his opponents on stage, but he was so damn funny while doing it that you couldn't help but be charmed. He was a jerk. But never an asshole.

The media never gave Donald Trump enough credit for his performance in those debates. They believed he benefited from a crowded field and would suffer during the one-on-one format against the politically experienced Hillary Clinton.

Here's what they didn't factor in. Hillary Clinton was not only corrupt but incredibly unlikable while being so.

Hillary spent the election cycle hammering Donald Trump on his character and temperament. In return, Donald Trump hit her on her corruption. Inevitably these two subjects would meet on a debate stage and some truly spectacular results would follow.

And they did.

On October 9, 2016, Donald J Trump and Hillary Clinton squared off at Washington University in St. Louis, Missouri. The debate was moderated by liberal stooges Anderson Cooper of CNN and Martha Raddatz from ABC News. Midway through the debate, the topic turned to a private email server that Hillary Clinton had used to correspond during her time as Secretary of State. This was not only patently illegal, but a national security risk. It was something that Trump and his "lock her up" supporters were never shy to bring up on the campaign trail. This is the exchange that followed:

RADDATZ: "I'm going to let you talk about emails."

CLINTON: ". . . because everything he just said is absolutely false, but I'm not surprised."

TRUMP: "Oh, really?"

CLINTON: "In the first debate . . ." (laughter)

RADDATZ: "And really, the audience needs to calm down here."

CLINTON: ". . . I told people that it would be impossible to be fact-checking Donald all the time. I'd never get to talk about anything I want to do and how we're going to really make lives better for people.

So, once again, go to HillaryClinton.com. We have literally Trump—you can fact-check him in real time. Last time at the first debate, we had millions of people fact-checking, so I expect we'll have millions more fact-checking, because, you know, it is—it's just awfully good that someone with the temperament of Donald Trump is not in charge of the law in our country."

TRUMP: "Because you'd be in jail."

THE CROWD EXPLODED IN APPLAUSE. The moderators panicked. Martha tried to change the subject. Anderson decided to chastise the audience for taking delight in the public humiliation of his preferred candidate.

RADDATZ: "Secretary Clinton . . ."

COOPER: "We want to remind the audience to please not talk out loud. Please do not applaud. You're just wasting time."[8]

But the damage was done. Crooked Hillary, the experienced debater, the seasoned politician, had been completely undercut by a vicious one-liner.

I knew my lack of experience would be a target my opponents would hit. But I knew, like Donald Trump, my status as an outsider also gave me a unique advantage. And, lesson Number 3, that if I could be like Trump—avoiding polite restraint and package my aggression with an equal amount of charm—I could more than hold my own in a debate.

1. Reagan taught me the art of humor to negate an attack.
2. Romney taught me the need for aggression vs. opponent AND moderator.
3. Trump taught me that a debate could be won off the strength of an unrestrained, dominant personality.

These were the lessons running through my head when I sat down for the first televised debate of my political career. I knew that the stakes were incredibly high. As the frontrunner, I had a very large target on my back, and with Salmon out of the pool, the sharks could smell blood in the water.

The circumstances surrounding the debate did nothing to allay my concerns. Arizona PBS had attempted to assign Arizona Central reporter Stacey Barchenger to co-moderate the debate alongside long-time anchor Ted Simons.

Barchenger was, and as of this writing remains, a shining example of everything wrong with the state of modern journalism—a Democrat activist who writes every article with the angle that all Republicans are evil. For months on the campaign, Stacey followed me from event to event, mischaracterizing everything I said or did, and writing hit pieces. She had only lived in Arizona for ten months, but demanded she understood the people and issues better than I had. I wanted to ban her trash paper the *Arizona Republic/AZCentral* from my events entirely, but my love of the First Amendment won out. I just stopped taking and answering her questions. She REALLY hated that.

When PBS announced hours before the debate that they would have that smear merchant co-moderate the debate, I put my foot down, and she was removed from the program. That was one problem down.

The next problem was the candidate cavalcade Arizona PBS invited to participate in the debate. With the dead fish gone, there were only two relevant candidates in the race for governor: the billionaire's spouse, and me. It was a two-person race and it should have been a two-person debate. "Karen" would not have survived that.

The issue was that AZ PBS invited the two other candidates who were on the ballot: Scott Neely and Paola Tulliani Zen.

Now, I have to be very careful how I talk about Scott, because the man tries to sue everything that moves. But Scott was an unserious person running an unserious campaign. Scott had more conspiracy theories than he had policies. He insisted on calling me a RINO plant and he once interrupted a Trump rally during the president's speech with an impassioned, "I BUILT THAT," when Trump referenced the border wall.[9]

Paola was an eccentric older lady, whose claim to fame was that she presumptively invented biscotti cookies. She was extraordinarily wealthy and used that fortune to pepper seemingly every corner of Maricopa County with her plain white campaign signs.

Tulliani-Zen was able to produce one unintentionally hilarious campaign commercial that featured her in her kitchen carving into a large chunk of meat claiming that she would chop through red tape like that tender piece of prosciutto in front of her. At one point she slapped the meat and it squealed like a pig.[10]

Needless to say, Scott and Paula were novelty acts. The corporate media used them and their eccentricities to make the rest of the Republican field look insane and gobble up time so that I wouldn't have time to expose RINO Karen and her open-borders, globalist agenda. Neither of them ever polled above 2% in a single poll. There was no technical need for them to be invited to the debate, but PBS wanted a circus so they invited the clowns.

As I entered the studio for the debate, I knew I had a high-wire act to walk. I needed to be aggressive and assertive, but I needed to come out of this thing looking like the only sane person in the room.

Scott Neely and Paola Zen kicked off the festivities which, in retrospect, set the tone for the entire evening.

When it was my turn for an opening statement, I put on my best smile, and just spoke from the heart:

"Hello, Arizona. It's so good to be back in your homes and thank you for welcoming us tonight. I had the blessing to cover this great state for twenty-seven years as a fair journalist. I walked away from my career. And the people of Arizona recruited me to be governor. And I'm running for governor now to fix some of those issues we've had. . . . Under President Trump, who I'm so honored has endorsed me, we've had the most secure border. Then on day one, Joe Biden pulled back that policy and exposed us to a criminal element, to dangerous drugs that are killing our young people, and he's taken away our ability to protect our own state. When I'm governor, we're going to come back and we're going to protect our border and secure our border and we're going to make sure our kids are learning a decent curriculum and that they are also safe at school. I ask for your vote and I look forward to the debate."[11]

My job in the debate was relatively straightforward. The media, and my opponents, had spent the last twelve months branding me as a loose cannon. My assignment was to remind the people of Arizona that I was the same Kari Lake they had spent the last twenty-seven years watching on the nightly news. I made sure to name-drop the Donald Trump endorsement as early as I could. Robson had spent almost half the cycle reminding the people of Arizona that I had voted for Barack Obama, but I had a literal Trump card in my back pocket to assuage the Republican base's fears. And I played it. OFTEN.

I also had to show them my policy bonafides and hammer home the notion that only a political outsider could be counted on to fix them.

Most of all, I wanted to show the Arizona people the Mama Bear side of Kari Lake. I wasn't just the conservative firebrand they saw viral videos of on Twitter. I was a concerned mother of two who saw the damage that the open border and the shoddy school curriculum was having on my kids and was motivated to fix these problems before they got worse. I felt good about my opening statement. I had a few stumbles, but those are to be expected when you're speaking off-the-cuff. If anything, I think they humanized me.

Which is why it was an incredible mistake for my RINO opponent to follow my statement up with an opener that she had clearly memorized and was struggling to recall. It was a platitude-riddled statement, pretty by-the-numbers until halfway through, when the RINO went for the jugular.

"I've raised my family. I've created jobs. And I get results. We need a Conservative fighter. We need a leader with a record of accomplishment, not a career talker with a teleprompter. My life is an open book. I worked for Ronald Reagan."

A career talker with a teleprompter, huh? So it was going to be THAT kind of night. She wanted to make this debate about experience and authenticity. I understood that. It was a decent message. But she was the wrong messenger.

For one, it's very hard to argue that any of the experiences Robson had did any good for the State of Arizona. For another, it's very hard to argue authenticity when you read a prepared statement and stare down at your notes to figure out what to say as she repeatedly did, while lying about her record, and keeping her ninety-two-year-old billionaire husband, who was bankrolling your campaign, as far away from you on the campaign trail as possible including cropping him out of photos and not including him in her Christmas card. The people of Arizona were getting a crash course in who KTR really was this night, and I would be the teacher.

It was also too little too late. Robson had a window early on to just be true to herself. She was to be the third term for do-nothing Doug Ducey and she should have just said it. But she was desperately afraid of alienating the America First crowd, so she put Donald Trump in her first ad. She was trying to walk between two worlds for Republican votes and she stumbled out of the gate. I don't think she ever recovered from that.

The questions were all fairly predictable: border security, education, election integrity, the state budget, and the abortion laws. I did my best to juxtapose my innovative solutions with Robson's disastrous record. I wanted to show that while she did have SOME experience.

It didn't amount to much of anything meaningful. She used her power to hurt Arizonans. She pushed forced masks, forced vax, CRT, tuition breaks for illegals and tuition increases for American students . . . the list goes on.

I often found myself distracted while I was speaking. Every time I laid a glove on Robson, she looked down. I thought, at first, that she was just avoiding eye contact. But no. She was reading from an extensive pile of notes that were laid across her lap.

I knew I had to pick and choose my spots to go on offense. I didn't want to come across as a bully.

KTR, however, felt no such compunction, as she employed her favorite insult, "Fake Lake," like a thirteen-year-old schoolyard bully in almost every other sentence. A few minutes after one round of vacuous name-calling, she told the crowd that Arizona needed a leader who was a grown-up. My eyes nearly rolled out of the back of my head.

I countered, "We do need someone who's a grown-up, and someone who calls names is not a grown-up," I said, going full Mama Bear.

Another part of my strategy was to show just how out-of-touch Robson was.

> KARRIN: "We are all sitting here with the benefit of being a Sun-Monday morning quarterback. What I'm saying is that Arizona's economy has come roaring back from the pandemic."
>
> ME: "No, no it hasn't. You know what when you're a billionaire living in a mansion everything looks bright, and shiny, and good. People have lost—"
>
> KARRIN: "You're my neighbor, Kari."
>
> ME: "People have lost—I live in a townhome."

Robson wasn't entirely off-base with the neighbor thing. We did live in the same general neighborhood in Phoenix, but she lived inside a gated mansion that you could easily mistake as a massive hotel resort and I live, happily, in a two-car-garage townhome. There was a difference.

I had clearly gotten under her skin, though. The problem was that she couldn't adapt. Her insults were packaged. I was able to score a huge hit on Robson. When I brought up the 2020 stolen election. I knew that was a political third rail for Robson. She needed to be palatable to everyone, she couldn't be caught flirting with us "election-denying" crazies.

So mid-debate I asked the panel, "If they would agree we had a corrupt stolen election, raise your hand." Three hands went up: mine, Scott, and Paola.

Robson? Nada.

Bullseye.

You could almost hear Karrin gulp.

She accused me of pulling a stunt. Hell yeah, I did. And it worked beautifully. The debate turned into a battle royale.

At one point, Scott Neely accused my campaign of being a "psy-op"—which I had no idea what he was talking about.

At another, a flustered Paola raised her hands in the air and yelled, "Mama Mia."

Toward the end of the debate a thought crossed my mind that I was being pranked. I simply had to call attention to the absurdity of the proceedings. "Is this a spoof?" I quipped. "I feel like I'm in an SNL skit here."

I was smiling, but in truth I felt embarrassed; I can be my own worst critic. And as soon as the debate wrapped, I felt it in the pit of my stomach and heard a voice in my head telling me that I had lost.

When the debate wrapped, and the light on the camera went dark, I shot Ted Simons a disapproving look, told him that was the worst debate moderating I had ever seen and headed back to the dressing room. When I opened the studio doors, I was immediately surrounded by a swarm of reporters who followed me to the green room. No one stayed to talk to "Karen."

Robson or Lake, it didn't matter. The Arizona Democratic Party and those vultures in the news were the real winners. The media had gotten exactly what they wanted from this shit show of a debate. And sure enough, the narrative in the days following was about the Republican Circus, and I was the ringmaster.[12]

I knew I was walking into a trap. I felt like I had handled it as best as I could but I still caught some shrapnel. And the lingering wounds would persist for the rest of the election cycle.

While I was duking it out with my primary opponents, Hobbs had gone Zero Dark Thirty and actively refused to engage with HER Democrat primary challenger.

This is where the Democrats have the Republicans beat. They choose a candidate and stick by them. From the moment Katie Hobbs announced she was running for governor, her state party decided she was going to be the nominee for governor. So, she didn't have to spend any money on a primary campaign, saving all her dollars for the general election, and she didn't have to break a sweat.

Meanwhile, I'm in a political thunderdome with a billionaire and two novelty acts.

It was unfair. But I was never under the misapprehension that anybody had said it wasn't supposed to be.

Besides, I told myself, when it comes to a two-person race—Lake vs. Hobbs—that would change. She would be forced to come out of hiding and Arizona would get to see its two prospective governors clashing swords on stage.

I won my primary. Hobbs won her primary.

I was out every day talking to the people of Arizona, and she was nowhere to be found.

I campaigned. Just like Joe Biden's basement campaign in 2020, Hobbs didn't.

What did she know that I didn't? Boy, was I naive! Just like Joe knew he didn't need to campaign, the fix was in, so did Hobbs.

Throughout my entire run for governor, I treated it like a job interview. I was applying for a position as governor, and the people of Arizona would be my hiring manager and boss.

I was strong and she was weak. I was charismatic (if I say so myself) and she was lackluster. A dud and drip as President Trump called her during one of our conversations. He was right.

I spent months healing the divides of the Arizona Republican Party. I was proud of the work we did building bridges. I still am. I brought Democrats and Independents over to vote for me and I brought Republicans of all stripes together.

While I was crisscrossing the state and keeping my boots on the ground, I made sure to keep one date on my calendar free of any potential conflicts. Wednesday, October 12 at Arizona PBS, I would be reunited with Ted Simons, for the traditional "Super Bowl" of Arizona political debates between me and Katie Hobbs. This debate would fall one week before early ballots were to be mailed to Arizona voters. The stakes were huge.

Sure, the Fake News hated me. But there was no doubt in their minds that it was to be a ratings bonanza. It never crossed my mind that Katie Hobbs would end up not debating. Sure, her wishy-washy refusal to commit had been odd, but I just thought it was part of her plan to cast me as a crazy person and that she didn't want to give me the time of day.

Even in late August when the Hobbs's campaign came forward to say, "We will be seeking changes to the format to ensure that

Arizona voters get a robust policy debate based on fact, instead of regurgitated lies about the 2020 election," they still capped off that garbage with, "We have every intention of participating."[13]

My campaign and I seized on their hesitation. We released a video addressed directly to Katie Hobbs, "To make things even easier for you, I'll allow you to choose the moderator. Hell, I'll even let you write the questions."

And I meant it. It's like the Dr. Seuss story, *Green Eggs and Ham*.

I would debate her on a boat.

And I would debate her with a goat . . .

And I would debate her in the rain.

And in the dark. And on a train.

And in a car. And in a tree.

It really didn't matter to me.

The jockeying between the two campaigns continued for the next month. By then, alarm bells were ringing. Katie actively refused to appear on stage with me anywhere. Even forums where we wouldn't even share the stage at the same time took place only with caveats.

During one Hispanic town hall, where Hobbs humiliated herself by being unable to list a single lesson she had learned from Arizona's Hispanic population—which make up a third of our population—Katie demanded we be separated by curtains and tried to get me kicked out of the venue. My husband and kids are Latino, and they were flabbergasted at her answer which was a minute of "uhs" and "ahs" unable to answer a softball question.

By September, even Katie Hobbs's friends in the media were beginning to sound the alarm. Her loyal Pravda in the *Arizona Central* wrote, "Katie Hobbs tells Arizona she is a coward—and it's Kari Lake's fault."[14]

Katie's cowardice became a national story, but Katie didn't budge.

In early September, Team Hobbs petitioned the Clean Elections Commission to hold separate town hall forums. I adamantly refused this format. That simply wasn't a debate. And to their credit, the Clean Elections Commission stood by me and refused to alter the format.

Hobbs's campaign manager released this petulant statement, "Unfortunately, debating a conspiracy theorist like Kari Lake—whose entire campaign platform is to cause enormous chaos and make Arizona the subject of national ridicule—would only lead to constant interruptions, pointless distractions, and childish name-calling. Arizonans deserve so much better than Kari Lake, and that's why we're confident Katie Hobbs will be elected our next governor."[15] The statement continued, "We must respectfully decline the invitation."

Yet *I* was the one lacking maturity here!?

I responded, "It's becoming clearer every day that Hobbs' strategy is to hide from Me, the Press, and the Voters throughout the entirety of this campaign and run out the clock on the people of Arizona. Fortunately, the Clean Elections Commission refused to play into her game and voted down her proposal for a town hall safe space."[16]

I extended my invitation to debate her at any time and any place if she grew a spine.

At this point in the campaign, I was starting to get VERY worried. I was surging in the polls. By all rights, Katie Hobbs should have awakened from her slumber and started to throw punches. But she didn't. She didn't change her "non-campaign" strategy at all.

Colton Duncan, my right-hand man, and I knew she had something up her sleeve. We just couldn't narrow it down to WHAT that might be.

The back-and-forth among my team continued. And we made a meal out of her cowardice. Poultry was the main course. We called Katie a chicken and went all-in on this particular comparison.[17] My team sent staffers dressed as chickens to her events. We even borrowed some actual live chickens from the father of one of our interns.

After a few weeks of deliberation, the Clean Elections Commission reached the only logical conclusion possible. If Katie Hobbs wouldn't debate, she could stay at home. And I would be given the entire hour to answer questions and speak to the people of Arizona.

I wasn't overly pleased with this. I wanted them to make Katie debate. I wanted to show the people of Arizona the stark contrast between the two candidates. But getting the opportunity to make the case for myself uninterrupted was far from the worst-case scenario.

So this was the plan until October 12, 2022, when Hobbs went on MSNBC and revealed that "PBS is also giving me the same format that Kari Lake has."[18]

What the hell? That certainly wasn't the deal.

It turned out that Arizona PBS had made a backroom deal with the Hobbs campaign for a one-on-one interview. PBS did this without communicating their planned format to the Clean Elections Commission.[19] This betrayal led the Commission to cancel MY appearance, and send me out to find a new broadcast platform.

At some point when this chaos was unfolding, I was made aware that all of this had been orchestrated by the President of Arizona State University, Michael Crow.

Michael Crow, the self-professed "most powerful man in Arizona" had taken over Arizona State in 2002 with the intention of turning it into America's first Globalist University. Crow had made inroads with Communist China, letting them establish a major presence on his Tempe, Arizona Campus.

Crow had used Covid to punish his students for daring to exercise personal medical freedom, while simultaneously petitioning anyone who would listen to grant the children of illegal immigrants free tuition. Crow's priorities were America Last and Arizona Last. Thus, they were diametrically opposed to my own.

I had made my intentions known to some of the Regents at ASU, that this would not be tolerated under a Kari Lake administration. Needless to say, Crow was not a happy camper. Some very powerful people reached out to me and told me I had to bring Crow into my inner circle—it was required of any governor. I forced a painful smile, and told them that, while I couldn't make any promises, my door would always be open.

In truth, I had every intention of pushing back against Crow's attempt to expand his University's global outreach. And Crow is a smart man. He knew that. So he began orchestrating the election of Katie Hobbs.

Arizona State University owns Arizona PBS. The channel is broadcast out of the university's Cronkite School of Journalism. Crow had reached out to the station to "let his preference be known" that Hobbs deserved her own forum.

The Commission's Executive Director Tom Collins would later agree that, "ASU was playing favorites with the candidates."[20]

I was furious. So I called for an emergency press conference outside of the ASU Cronkite building to make my feelings on the debacle known. Swarmed by an army of reporters, I took to the podium and said,

> "We cleared our schedule immediately when we were asked
> to show up and do a debate for the people of Arizona to hear
> what the two candidates running for office, this ever important
> office, want to do for this wonderful state. They changed

the date on us and we cleared our schedule again for today. Unfortunately, I'm running against a coward who's afraid to stand on a debate stage and talk about what she wants to do for Arizona. And, unfortunately, PBS and ASU have done a backroom deal with that coward to give her airtime that she does not deserve."[21]

By this point in the campaign, my voice was almost gone. I was recovering from laryngitis. But I spoke very clearly and concisely when I said that I would explore defunding Arizona PBS. They were operating with Arizona tax-payer funds after all, and putting their foot on the scale in this campaign.

In agreeing to do this shady workaround, Michael Crow, PBS, and Katie Hobbs destroyed a decades-long Arizona tradition and likely signed the death warrant for all future Arizona political debates. This deal basically tells every Democrat in the future that you don't have to debate the Republicans, because if you bow out, PBS will just give you an opportunity on your own. You never have to have a debate. And I find that to be absolutely tragic.

Hobbs got her uncontested forum. After her thirty-minute puff piece with Simons, she locked reporters in a back room at ASU, so she could flee to the service elevator to avoid questions.

That's how the rest of the campaign played out. I continued my relentless campaign schedule and Hobbs hid. I was there and she wasn't. I was strong where she was weak.

The narrative was that Hobbs was conceding the race rather than face her challenger. And by Election Day, I had a 3.5 percentage point lead in the polling average of Real Clear Politics.[22] But internal polls showed me 10 points up with my lead growing.

The exact part she played in the Election Day sabotage of November 8 is still up for debate, but there's no denying that she had a very good reason for not debating and not campaigning.

The fix was in for the Debate Denier.

This may be the first time in recorded history where a Crow saved a chicken.

CHAPTER 12

David vs. Goliath

KARRIN TAYLOR ROBSON was the ultimate insider—which was ironic because she was running as a political outsider. She came from a family with an incredible political pedigree. Her father, Carl Kunasek, had been the President of the Arizona Senate and the chair of the Arizona Corporate Commission. Her brother, Andy, had been a member of the Maricopa County Board of Supervisors. Her husband, Ed—an Arizona icon—was the Chairman and CEO of Robson Communities, and during his time in the development business he had amassed an incredible fortune. Karrin had political aspirations and connections, but she needed money to make it in politics. She married Ed, the ninety-year-old billionaire, in 2017, and when she signaled to her husband that she wanted to run for governor, he handed her a blank check. Other than bankrolling the operation, Ed stayed mostly out of sight, a decision that seemed like a grossly calculated attempt by her consultants to hide the fact that there was a nearly forty-year age gap between the couple. The public perceived her as a cold and calculating woman trying to buy the governor's seat.

She was a social acquaintance of Cindy McCain and a good friend of Doug Ducey and his wife. (I told you Arizona politics was incestuous.) She was the ideal insider politician—married into money with friends in high places. After McCain's death, KRT heavily lobbied Ducey to appoint her to the vacant U.S. Senate seat. Ultimately, Ducey chose Martha McSally, but as a consolation prize he appointed Karrin to the Arizona Board of Regents.

The Arizona Board of Regents is the supreme governing body for Arizona's public university system. It provides policy guidance to Arizona State University, Northern Arizona University, the University of Arizona, and their associated campuses. A regent has a tremendous amount of influence in shaping the course of Arizona's premier learning institutions. By appointing Robson to this position, Ducey gave her the opportunity to establish her policy bonafides and help accelerate her up the political ladder.

Unfortunately, for Ducey and Robson, her voting record was appalling. She sat idly by during the rise of CRT, abstained from a crucial vote that would have kept our young university students from having to wear useless masks in Arizona's 115° heat or from having to get experimental Covid shots in order to go to college, she supported gun-control and championed anti-second amendment legislation, and seemed hellbent on providing illegal immigrants discounted tuition that meant they would pay less than American students, meanwhile she voted to raise tuition and fees more than seventy times during in her short stint as a regent.[1]

Throughout her campaign for governor, Robson promised that she would be tough on the border. She even shot a commercial at the wide-open Arizona border touting her *six-point plan!* In her ad a stream of illegal immigrants come across the border and walk right by her.[2] *What a terrible image*, I thought. Did she pay high-priced consultants to put that piece of schlock on the airwaves?? Karrin's real border policy would look very much like her TV commercial; Karrin standing by like a potted plant, doing *nothing*, just *watching* as illegal immigrants pour into our state and country. It was an effective critique, I must say. Arizonans even found her ads to be a joke. I remember one tweet that made me chuckle. It laid the RINO's consultant-created border ad to waste.

The tweet from a man named Connor Clegg summed up what many Arizonans were feeling:

> *Out-of-touch billionaire housewife *literally* stands by and watches illegal aliens invade Arizona—that's all this ad says to me. I have a feeling @KariLake would have hogtied these criminals and tossed them back over the border herself. That's my Governor.*[3]

Karen's dismal voting record exposed who she really was. Worse still was her donation history. Karen used her husband's immense wealth to help fund Arizona's most extreme leftist Democrats like Ruben Gallego, a man who is a flat-out socialist, though his tweets and votes in Congress may make you wonder if he's a communist. Isn't it funny how it's always the self-professed principled Conservatives who are willing to sell out their values to the highest bidder?

She had connections and allies across the state. Her consultants, Camelback Strategies, a brainchild of former McCain staffers, were the political heavy-hitters in the AZ Swamp. And using Ed Robson's seemingly unlimited supply of money, Robson was able to relentlessly bombard me over TV and radio for the duration of the primary. Robson ended up spending $25 million in her pursuit of the nomination. About $20 million of that was her husband's money.[4] I had incredibly generous supporters, but I couldn't compete with that. Robson ended up outspending my campaign 20-to-1 in ads in the primary.

We knew that we couldn't buy the election. We would have to earn it. What helped us was that Robson's campaign was a boring relic and ours was wildly interesting.

Arizona has never seen anything like it before. The Karizona movement, as it came to be called, was a collection of grassroots Arizona Patriots from every background. And what Robson had in money, my supporters more than made up in enthusiasm.

Expertly steered by a bunch of fed-up Mama Bears—lifelong Arizonans who didn't know politics as much as they knew Arizona—and Colton Duncan, my young, quick-witted, messaging genius from Texas. Colton expertly knew how to create and seize upon viral moments, making him indispensable. I was probably the only candidate in the country who was also the campaign manager. Publicity, combative interviews, anything that could attract attention and eyeballs and content worth sharing would translate into earned media—that is media you get for free and is worth more than commercials that you would have to pay for. By the end of the campaign, we had more than $1 billion in earned media. A record. We learned this from Donald Trump: when you take up *all* of the oxygen in a race, all the rest of the candidates would struggle for air.

We deliberately made the Republican Primary focus on what Kari Lake and her supporters were concerned with. And while Robson was assaulting me on the airwaves, we were outworking her on both the ground and in the media. Yes, the media hated me. But they couldn't resist covering me. Even if all of it was spun into negative hit pieces, the local national and international press was obsessed.

While I had been leading wire-to-wire in every poll, Robson's money WAS having an impact. Adding to my increasingly precarious position was the consolidation of the Never Trump political establishment around her, and more importantly, *against* me.

Jan Brewer went from urging me to run, to co-chairing Robson's campaign, and doing weekly radio hits on the local AZ Swamp radio station attacking me.

Doug Ducey, the head of the Republican Governors Association, went from suggesting I run, to breaking a promise of neutrality, endorsing "Karen," and going on a warpath against me.

Dobson even managed to secure the endorsements of Chris Christie and Vice President Mike Pence.

For the bulk of the primary, KRT bought ads and lied to voters to walk the line between America First and the Establishment class. It was those back-to-back swampy endorsements that sealed her fate as the RINO in the race.

But even before that political kiss of death. I knew we had her on the ropes. Because I had a ticking time bomb of Robson opposition research just waiting for the right time for me to set it off.

You see, the Establishment plays dirty. They like to pretend they're civilized, move to shake your hand, and then stab you the moment your back is turned. Robson pulled out ALL the stops. She got her old friends the McCains to accuse me of smearing their sainted patriarch. They got one of the former human resources managers at my old news station to lie about me on TV.[5] Through donations and connections of the dirty consultant class, they managed to get big endorsements like the Border Patrol Union,[6] even getting the chair of the Union, to attack my border policy in TV ads, one that he, himself, HAD PREVIOUSLY endorsed. They found an old drag queen acquaintance to lie about me and accuse me of hypocrisy by misrepresenting my stance on Drag Queen Story Hour.[7] And in a particularly bonkers moment, they arranged to put up campaign signs all across the state featuring images of myself and Barack Obama with the caption, "Kari Lake Donated to Barack Obama." That seemed like a setback, until hundreds of Independents and Democrat voters who crossed over to support me told me they thought it was "cool" that I was endorsed by BOTH Trump and Obama.

That was all well-and-good for them. But when I fought back, they immediately retreated into their political tortoise shell accusing me of being a bully. That's how the machine works. They set the rules, but never play by the rules themselves, and then they're absolutely *outraged* when you decide not to play along too. Screw that—I didn't have a ninety-two-year-old sugar daddy to spread lies. I had the truth and a lot of fight in me.

Weeks before the primary election, I pulled out my "Trump card." A series of recordings that had been given to my campaign by Steve Gaynor, one of my other primary opponents, upon his departure from the race.

It all started with a call from my daughter, Ruby. "Mom," Ruby said. "Did you know that Karrin Taylor Robson screwed old people out of their money?"

It was an indelicate way of putting it. But it was true.

It turned out that Steve Gaynor's team had gone through Robson's FEC page and found an inordinate, record amount of refunds. Thousands of them. Team Gaynor started calling the refund requesters and here's what they found out.

Karen Taylor Robson had been engaging in misleading fundraising practices where she would send out texts tugging at the heart and soul of patriotic Conservatives.

Texts like:

Democrat Beto O'Rourke is jumping into the Texas Governor's Race is bad news for Republicans everywhere. He's raised millions, and we need to fight back. Rush $5.

And this:

Are you excited? Trump is back! His team launched his new social media and he needs your support!

And this:

GOP is going to miss its end-of-month goal without your help. If we fail, AZ is lost. Rush $5 here.

Texts asking donors to help Donald Trump get Truth Social off the ground and fight censorship, or helping Greg Abbott build a border wall in Texas? It all sounded noble, but the money wasn't going to those causes: it was going to a political unknown, a "Karen" from Arizona.

And here's the *worst part* . . . Unbeknownst to the donor, this contribution was a slow-bleed of their bank account; it was a recurring donation to someone they didn't know and didn't care about. Despicable.

I will never forget how disturbed I was at one of the calls. Gaynor's people had contacted a woman who said she put her mother in a nursing home and had also taken over her accounting. When she looked at her mother's Visa account, she saw a recurring donation to someone named Karrin Taylor Robson. Neither mother or daughter had any idea who that woman was. Her mother was on a fixed-income and part of her income was being drained for a billionaire candidate's vanity project. When told about the scheme on the phone, she described Robson perfectly:

"She's a thief!" her voice shaking.

It was horrifying. I was blessed to have the incredible support of first-time donors who would chip in $10, 20, whatever they had on hand. But Robson . . . she didn't need the money. She had an inexhaustible supply of it. But she wanted more.

We knew we had the goods. Now it was time to turn it into a bombshell.

Theodore Roosevelt had the bully pulpit. Donald Trump had Twitter. And Kari Lake? Well, I ALSO had Twitter.

Social media was our secret weapon. Thanks to my husband Jeff, a videographer, agreeing to go on the trail with me, we filmed *everything*. We had an infinite supply of content. These videos in conjunction, with fiery tweets by yours truly, and contributions from my wonderful communications staff, we had the ability to draw oxygen and start news cycles with a single tweet.

So we put together a video with me explaining what would later be known as the #RefundRobson scandal. I had piles of paper set in front of me meant to represent the donors who had been bilked out of their hard-earned money, we had video playing in the background, and we also had those phone calls. We ended the video asking people to call Karrin's campaign manager if they'd been burned and wanted to request a refund. We had his phone number on it and everything. People were NOT happy about that. We ended up having to remove that after my account got shut down on Twitter.[8]

After wrapping the shoot, we started to build suspense.

Colton got out his phone and started typing out a perfect tweet:

We just found out the most horrible thing about my opponent Karrin Taylor Robson. We're triple checking.

With giddy anticipation, he pressed *send*.

We sat on the video for twelve hours. Twelve long hours for Karen to panic. Her high-price consultants must have been wracking their brains wondering what dirt we had.

The next day was one of the oldest, most iconic Republican candidate events in all of Arizona—the Mohave County Republican Picnic at the top of Hualapai Mountains in one of most patriotic, America First counties in America. No candidate would *dare* miss this. Each candidate was instructed to walk in and put their name on the list and they would be called to step up on the small stage and speak in a "first-come-first-served" order—that way no one could be accused of playing favorites. I had a plan. I walked into the venue and simply waited to put down my name. KRT and I had been engaged in a game of chicken for the past month. Each of us tried to outwait each other in an effort to speak last. I was the frontrunner and "Karen" hated that, so she needed to have the final word. Really, Dobson had an unfair advantage here. She had a private jet that she would circle around in and wait to land until the last minute—just so she could speak AFTER me. What she didn't realize was that on *this* day I actually *wanted* her to go last. I wanted to speak immediately before her and then she would have to respond to the can of whoop-ass I was about to open up.

So I waited . . .

Five minutes . . . ten . . . fifteen minutes . . .

Touchdown.

As Robson and her entourage approached, I walked over to the table and put my name down. With a smirk, a member of her team put her name directly below mine. They had "won"—or so they thought.

As I took the stage and grabbed the microphone to speak, Colton posted the video live online.[9]

Here's what I told the audience:

"I don't know if my opponent, my RINO opponent, is going to show up." (I already knew she was there and could see her out of the corner of my eye.)

"She's here!" came a voice from the crowd.

"I think she's here," I said, acknowledging the people pointing her out. "Oh good, Karrin, where are you?" I put my hand above my brow to search for her in the picnic area. She was off to the left of me just outside of the covered ramada.

"She's over there!" came voices.

"Karrin, we want answers for all your duping thousands of people out of money. It's wrong. Here's the sad thing, guys. She doesn't need the money. The sad thing is . . ." I took a quick moment to sneak a peek at Robson. She was as white as a ghost.

". . . Let me say something. The sad thing is she's being funded by a billionaire. She doesn't *need* to dupe senior citizens out of their paycheck. But she did it to trick people into thinking that she has grassroots support. It is unethical and it is outrageous. And I think she should give every single one of them a refund!" I could feel the energy building in the crowd. I fed off of it.

"Every single one of them deserves a refund. That's deceptive. Let me tell you, real quickly, because I don't have a lot of time. But I had to lay that out because you've got to know who's on the ballot. We cannot put an unethical person, with no integrity, who's trying to *buy* this election on the ballot, we can't put her in the governor's office." Karen was now translucent.

"We're at a crossroads in Arizona, guys. We're at a crossroads where—Do we want to go back to the McCain style, McCain Mafia running the show?" Patriotic Arizonans started booing. Several shouted, "No!"

I continued, "Or do we want to go to America First?"

"America First!" screamed the crowd.

"I don't want to go back to an Arizona, where the high-priced McCain consultants are running the show. I want to go back to an Arizona where We the People are in charge of our government."

Honestly, I should have just dropped the mic. I thanked the crowd and I left the stage. You could hear a pin drop as KRT got up to speak. Everyone was looking at her wondering *what* she was going to say. And then she made a critical error.

She climbed up on that wooden stage and she gave her *memorized* spiel. Her stump speech.

Stick a fork in her. She had lost that audience forever. I still have voters from Mohave County tell me that was the most exciting moment they've witnessed in all of their years attending that political event.

Between Ms. Moneybag and her friends with PACs, they ended up spending more than $20 millions in ads against me.[10] The most *ever* spent in an Arizona gubernatorial campaign (and this was just the primary)! They had an impact, but not a sizable one. Our data showed that while older people still believe what they saw on TV, the younger people didn't buy it.

"They're lying about Kari Lake!" the kids would say.

We had some ads of our own. The one I was most proud of aired smack-dab in the middle of my old news station's broadcast.

It was thirty seconds. I looked at the camera and said, "If you're watching this ad right now, it means you are in the middle of watching a fake news program."[11] I told voters why they are fake; mentioned the important stories they wouldn't touch or talk about, then I grabbed a remote. And I turned it off. That thing ended up becoming a national story—and only cost me a measly $10,000, at most!

We knew it would be a story. A campaign ad, running during newscasts calling them out for being liars and fake. And the television stations couldn't do a damn thing to stop us. By law, political campaign ads run by a candidate are virtually impossible to censor or edit. Our $10,000 ad secured me $325 million in earned media. We used very old traditional methods of politicking combined with social media to add a new angle. And it caught everyone by surprise.

Still, Election Night was interminable. Arizona has a backward, frankly, corrupt way of counting ballots—meaning all of the early returns would be highly unfavorable to me. They had to pump in a bunch of invalid ballots that came out of nowhere with no chain of custody to pad the count for their chosen candidate, but they didn't prepare for the onslaught of fed-up voters who showed up August 2 at the polls. In Pinal County, they *ran out* of Republican primary ballots ONE HOUR into primary election day. A quarter of polling locations in that county ended up *running out* of Republican ballots by the time voting was done. Our supporters showed up in DROVES!

Much of election night was sending surrogates out to tell the vultures in the media not to call the race for my opponent till the Maricopa County numbers came in.

Robson had one last card to play. Sometime during the night someone on her team texted mine asking if I was ready to concede. We didn't answer. By midnight, we knew we had won. I went from the first count of ballots being released and being 9 points down to defeating the billionaire by 5 points. Three days later it was official.

David beat Goliath. Kari beat Karen.

I was *officially* the Arizona Republican nominee for governor.

I gave my "victory" speech with a sledgehammer in my hand around midnight or one a.m.[12] As of this writing, Karrin Taylor Robson has still never called me to concede her loss in the primary.

Sometimes a "giant" with the most money and the powerful connections falls hard to the fearless fighter with her own special ammunition—truth, grit, and the determination to defend America First.

CHAPTER 13

A Short Meeting

I NEVER RECEIVED a congratulatory call from Doug Ducey. (I did receive one from Iowa Governor Kim Reynolds, a class act, and Montana Governor Greg Gianforte, a nice man.) I thought it was weird that Ducey didn't call. I understood there was bad blood, but "politics isn't a game of beanbag," as McCain used to say. It's a blood sport. Sure, I had pointed out Ducey's absolute failure to protect Arizona and secure our wide-open southern border, and dubbed him Doormat Ducey for letting the cartels run roughshod over the sovereignty of Arizona and the citizens. And maybe I called him Do-Nothing Ducey for failing to stand up to Biden and do *something* to secure the border.

In return, Ducey said some terrible things about me. And just plain lied.

The primary was all about the politics of personal attack. I didn't want to play that game, but my opponents spent millions attacking me. I had no choice but to fight back with my fists and mouth. It was a dirty game, but I had to take part in order to win so I could get into office and help the people.

Ducey was a lame duck; I was the leader of the party now, the nominee, the presumptive governor. And it was up to me to extend the olive branch, and do the work, to bring the Arizona First and the Establishment wing of the party together. So I set out to do that.

After days of not hearing a peep from Ducey, I broke the ice and reached out with a text message that read:

Governor,

Good morning.

I've been thinking about you the past couple of days. In the heat of battle things may have been said, but I want you to know that I would like to get together with you and take advantage of your knowledge and experience and get your thoughts and suggestions on the race, etc.

I hope we can meet soon if your schedule would permit.

I want you to know that my door will always be open to you and I will always be receptive to your thoughts and suggestions.

Kari

An hour and a half passed. I knew through sources inside Ducey's inner circle that he received it. Finally a reply:

Kari,

Thank you for reaching out. Congratulations on the nomination.

We will get together. Please have your team reach out to mine to find an appropriate time.

Thx.

I took it all with gladness. I was ready to unite and FIGHT.

We scheduled a meeting. I brought Colton Duncan and Lisa Dale along with me. We showed up happy to meet and were very friendly. We were sent into a conference room where Doug Ducey stood up and made me walk to him. Power move. I obliged. No need to bruise an ego.

I brought nothing but kindness and confidence in my attitude. I thanked Ducey for taking the time to meet with us. I was ready to work with him to bring Arizonans together. Doug had two staffers with him sitting in chairs. They were pleasant. All of them seemed a bit shell-shocked that I won.

We sat down across from each other, three one each side of the conference table. We exchanged pleasantries with his aides while Doug Ducey sat there silently. Seeking to cut the tension coming from Ducey, I wracked my brain for something conciliatory to say. *Quick! What could I say to compliment him?* It wasn't easy. Doug Ducey did not protect the people of Arizona. He was incredibly weak on the border, had shut down the state TWICE during Covid, and had signed off on the stolen election in 2020. I was at a loss. Eventually, something came to mind.

"Governor, your legacy with education freedom is so important, as a mother I appreciate that you signed those protections into law. I want to make sure that we win and protect that legacy."

He stared at me and gave a long, awkward pause. "Yep," he said with a nod. And nothing more. He proceeded to stare at me for an interminable amount of time. After the long, awkward passive-aggressive pause, I chuckled and looked to his aides. What the hell was going on? Why did he agree to meet if he was going to sit there like a dope? It was actually funny. Ducey agreed to a meeting and turned it into a staring contest?

"Governor," I said with confidence and joy that only pissed him off more. His stare-down didn't scare me. "You've been through a lot of elections. Do you have any advice for me as I enter the general election?"

Again, a dead stare and a l o n g pause, then in monotone he said, "You get more votes. The person who gets more votes wins."

Okaaaay, Mr. Obvious.

This is Ducey's way of pouting. But I've raised toddlers and teen-agers, so this was easy. I have to acknowledge that he is hurt and say something. So I took that route: "I know that the primary was brutal. It was painful for all of us. In the heat of battle we take incoming," I began. "It was difficult for me being on the receiving end of tens of millions of dollars in attack ads, but we're moving forward, and I'm bound and determined to bring people together. We have great policies for Arizona. I'm really hoping you're for that as well." He nodded again.

More silence. More staring.

And we just sat there.

I checked my watch.

The meeting had only been going on for ten minutes—at most. Ten excruciating minutes.

Screw this! I thought to myself. I physically indicated that I was ready to go. *No sense staying in a room with Grumpy. I have voters to reach and a state to save. Let's get out of here and get to work,* I thought.

"Well . . . again . . . thank you, Governor, for your time." I could see a look of panic cross his aides' faces. I'm sure they were worried we'd walk out and use our massive social media presence to call out Doug Ducey for his juvenile behavior in the meeting and tell Arizona that Ducey was *not* about uniting. And *not* about supporting the Republican nominee.

I imagined the tweet already, probably from my Kari Lake War Room Account:

*In classic Ducey fashion, his meeting with @KariLake was, well
. . . short. America's 49th favorite Governor refused to speak to
Kari, instead challenges her to a staring contest. Odd.*

That would be bad for Doug. The staffers quickly started some
conversation about this-and-that. We managed to squeeze about ten
additional minutes out of the affair. They wanted to be able to say
Ducey met with me, but this meeting was a joke. I truly wanted to
bury the hatchet and move forward. Ducey had no such intentions.
At last, we said our goodbyes and headed to the car. Safely away from
the outgoing governor, I turned to Lisa and Colton broke into laughter. "What the actual hell was that??"

That was definitely the most awkward meeting of my life.

I would find out later from someone in my campaign who knew
someone in his inner circle that Ducey had just finished reading
some self-help book that taught him that the dominant person in a
negotiation should not speak for the first thirty seconds of an inter-
action. The whole thing had been some insane new-age power play.
Utterly baffling.

Doug Ducey did the bare minimum to help me during the primary. He gave one positive sound bite for me, basically saying I was
better than a Democrat, and helped oversee some truly sub-par commercials produced by the RGA, ostensibly in support of me, that
didn't mention me AT ALL.

After the sabotage of Election Day in Maricopa County, where
countless numbers of HIS constituents were disenfranchised, Ducey
wasted no time legitimizing my Democrat opponent Katie Hobbs,
publicly embracing her as his successor. And signed all the documents to formalize and certify the stolen election. I found out later
that Ducey walked around the next RGA meeting gloating over our
stolen victory.

I thought the primary was the end of it. That the Establishment holdouts would fall in line. Surely, an America First Conservative is better than a full-blown Marxist? But I underestimated the moral rot of the Arizona Uniparty. They simply decided if they couldn't win, I had to lose. Their power grasp was at risk. I thought I put a stake through the heart of the corrupt beast. But it rose, like a zombie, and dragged me and the people of Arizona straight to hell. You see, the Uniparty only allows pre-approved, controllable candidates. In their corrupt world, "We the People" don't matter and most certainly are NOT permitted to choose our elected representatives.

But I'm clawing back. And if the machine thinks I'm going to roll over and die, then they don't know Kari Lake.

CHAPTER 14

Moving America Forward

SOME OF OUR most consequential presidencies were a direct ideological reaction to the one that came before.

Carter begot Reagan.

Bush made Obama.

Obama resulted in Trump.

Biden was installed to reverse Trump and return to Obama.

Carter's weakness in dealing with foreign adversaries made Americans long for a strong leader and advocate for American principles.

Bush's strength in dealing with 9/11 during his first term was followed by years of pointless war throughout his second term which soured Americans on Republican foreign policy.

Obama's rejection of American Exceptionalism, contempt for middle America, and divisive policies and comments led Americans to seek a political outsider/straight-talker who believed in the greatness of our nation and who had achieved the American Dream.

Finally, with the unwavering support of social media, the corporate media and the amplified Covid pandemic, Trump was portrayed as an evil, nasty man incapable of returning the country to unity and health, with Biden as the man to unify and beat the virus.

Assuming our elections are properly secured, and the American public gets a fair shot at choosing their next leader, the question needs to be asked: What comes after Biden?

I think it'll be Trump. I pray it will be Trump because his America First policies are the answer to the problems that have been plaguing this country for decades. And they worked for the four years of his presidency. But regardless of the man, the America First/MAGA policies must be reinstituted.

But the MAGA movement needs to think bigger. It cannot afford to be complacent. Democrats play the long game, and our movement must do the same. So the question must not be what to do in 2024, but what we are going to do to ensure the survival of our movement and the energization and improvement of your country for our children and generations to come?

How do you have hope for a country when you feel like you're losing it? The answer is easy to me. You remember all the things that were great about it in the first place. You remember all the moments when it lost its way. All the hills previously hard-won that were sacrificed. And then you pick yourself up and you get to work on taking them back.

I believe that America First has the solutions we need to turn this country around.

It was America First solutions that, for a time, got us out of a decades-long political freefall. And it's those same policies that will help us bounce back after the Biden disaster comes to its merciful end.

The fight we have before us is a difficult one. The obstacles and opposition are more deeply entrenched than ever. But I've found that it's the hardest fights that are the ones worth having.

So what are we fighting for?

I think everyone will have a different answer to that question.

For me, it's my children. I don't want them to grow up in a Communist country, where they spend every day censoring themselves and fearing the consequences of what would happen if they step out of line. Living in a country where opportunity is reserved only for the ruling class and their allies.

I believe that my children's greatest inheritance is the freedom and liberty that we are fighting for, the underlying values that have always made our country the foremost among nations.

I try to lead by example. That's why I ran for office. If I had watched my country come apart at its seams, and not had stepped up to try to turn things around, I know that's a decision I would have regretted for the rest of my life.

So, I walked away from a hefty paycheck, and when the people reached out asking me to run for governor of Arizona, I said Yes. I spent eighteen months of my life being pilloried by the press and having all the baggage assembled from the course of my entire life aired before the people of Arizona. And mountains of lies told about me. And I don't regret a single moment of it.

Fame is fleeting. The richest man or woman alive is worth nothing if they are morally broke.

After all, what good is a paycheck if we don't have a country anymore?

Our Founding Fathers did not intend for politics to be a life-long career. They intended for citizen politicians to be the ones to hold office. President Trump understood that and so do I. Political outsiders can't be bought. They are untethered from the swampy shackles of the political machine, the self-interested mega donors, and the consultant class. The future of our movement is people who are not just unafraid to challenge the political machine, but actively looking for ways to break it apart.

We need people who are no longer content to accept the status quo. We need people who make progress, not excuses. We need people who understand that when our Founding Fathers offered us Life, Liberty, and the Pursuit of Happiness, they did so with the knowledge that those offerings were under constant threat, and they must be protected.

Recall what Ben Franklin once said, "A Republic. If you can keep it."

Most of all we need people who know this fundamental truth. It's the people who they are attacking the most that are the biggest fighters for America.

Who are "they," you ask?

I believe "they" are the greatest existential threat to the survival of the United States of America that we have ever seen.

Globalists.

Every advancement in technology makes the world a little bit smaller. And there's an ever-present syndicate of globalist elites and corrupt world leaders who spend almost every waking moment of their day trying to close that gap even tighter.

They seek the homogenization of the world under one flag. I can't think of anything more terrifying or regressive.

Our Founding Fathers did not free themselves from the shackles of King George only for the inheritors of this great nation to bow before globalist King George Soros.

Globalism is inherently Godless, secular. This is in direct conflict with the Judeo-Christian values on which this country was founded.

There is room for all peoples who worship God their particular way in this great country, just not room for a country without God.

This notion that absent God and Country, the people of the world would come together around some shared purpose is lunacy. By denying the importance of both God and Country, you are TAKING away that purpose. This isn't nirvana, this isn't liberation. This is anarchy. This is atheism. But that's their endgame here. Do not worship God. Worship your leaders.

Our expert class of globalist leaders: Bill Gates, Klaus Schwab, George Soros et al. have replaced God and instead worship the false idol of their expertise. "Don't trust your gut. Don't trust your God," they say. "Trust *us*. Trust the *science*." But they never seem to bother to explain what any of that actually means. That's because they seek to create a world absent of meaning. Not agnostic, no. They want to DENY people that study the truth.

They seek atheism. Because when you detach people from existential comforts, you leave them desperate and malleable. They will seek meaning in anything. And therein comes the false idols of science, climate change, and a belief that the answers come from collectivism, not individual discovery.

Not as Barack Obama once mistakenly told working Americans, "You didn't build that!" Not as Hillary Clinton would have you believe, "It takes a village."

I see a world where we can work side by side. But that doesn't mean in unison. We must not allow ourselves to be shackled by conformity. The world is a very big place. That's what makes it special. There is strength in diversity, but not the diversity of race, gender, sexuality, etc. that you have been lectured about. Strength comes from diversity of thought and opinion.

America was truly birthed in 1776 through a unique set of circumstances. And while some other nations have been served well by essentially copying our example (see: Israel), whenever we attempt to impose the American experience via nation-building, we are met with historic failures (see: Vietnam, Afghanistan, Iraq, and Iran).

Democracy is an incredible system. It's one well worth spreading. But time and time again, history has shown us that nation-building leads to collapse—not a sustainable system. I believe America would benefit from giving up on nation-building, severing most foreign entanglements and focusing on itself.

Let's look at English Puritan lawyer John Winthrop's sermon from which the concept of the "City on the Hill" was born. "We must consider that we shall be as a city upon a hill. The eyes of all people are upon us. So that if we shall deal falsely with our God in this work we have undertaken, and so cause him to withdraw his present help from us, we shall be made a story and a by-word through the world."[1]

At its core this is an incredibly flowery way of saying we need to lead by example—feel God's guiding hand on our shoulder. Ignoring the clear religious intonations of this speech, warmonger leaders have misrepresented this passage to mean we need to take other countries by the hand, mold them, and fight their battles for them. This has been the pretext for America to invite itself into all manner of foreign conflicts and enter an inexhaustible supply of international quagmires and pointless wars. Actions that weaken America—and destabilize the world.

This forgets the fact that Republican Democracy is uniquely American. It's not just a system of principles and structures, but it's in the basic DNA of the country. The same blood that flowed through our Founding Fathers when they built this nation is still flowing through OUR veins.

Without those experiences, what we get is a purely secular psychology. This need to fill the vacuum caused by the absence of God leaves these people to worship the war machine.

That's why we need to bring God back into the picture. When we kicked God out of our society, that's when our troubles ramped up. We have to invite Him back into the culture, our homes, and our hearts.

When we recite the Pledge of Allegiance, we do so under "God." When we flip a coin, we see "In God We Trust."

In its most biblical sense, the concept of leading by example, of showing that City on the Hill, is working alongside your fellow countryman and creating a story for the rest of the world to see. Like the shepherd to his flock, we show the way—it's up to the congregation to finish the journey for themselves.

But this requires belief. God *is* on our side. And with His help, we *will* save this Republic. When you have God on your side, and you employ America First policies, we are all going to live a better life because of it. We must never forget we are Americans. And we kneel before only one king and that is our Creator.

There's no denying that some elements of our history are flawed. The scourge of slavery being the prime example. But these flaws come not from the structure of our government or the tenets of God, but instead from the fallibility and weakness of basic human nature. And it was Americans who fought to end the slave trade in Africa and brought an end to slavery in our own country.

Enlightened Americans must always seek to address and counteract the mistakes of the past, but we must not let those errors blind us from the fact that America has been an overwhelming success for its citizens and a positive force for good throughout the rest of the world. America has always moved to remedy its faults once they have become apparent.

I am very troubled with the present, but I have great hope for the future. Current state and national leadership has us on the wrong path with no plans to course-correct.

In the simplest terms, I have hope because we're right and they're wrong. Our ideas make sense and theirs don't. This isn't about Republicans or Democrats anymore. It's not about right or left. It's about common sense versus lunacy. It's Globalism versus Americanism.

The programs and policies currently in place that have brought us to this low point arise from a legacy of unintended (or perhaps very much intended), yet totally predictable consequences. Just a few examples:

- Relaxing immigration enforcement resulted in far greater illegal immigration.
- Spending more on public schools resulted in poorer education.
- Increasing unemployment compensation resulted in fewer people employed.
- Providing more "support" for the homeless only enabled them to stay on the streets.
- Replacing punishment for crime with rehabilitation resulted in more criminal activity.

The fight we have ahead of us is daunting, but not impossible.

We need to return to the same Revolutionary spirit that made this country what it was. The poison is Orwell's *1984*; the antidote is our Founding Fathers' 1776. This is going to take courage. Remember the Founders put their lives, fortunes, and sacred honor on the line when they signed the Declaration of Independence. Fifty-six men essentially signed their death warrant when they declared freedom from the monarchy. If those Patriots way back then could give those tyrants the middle finger, why can't we?

What do we have left to fear? Cancellation? Ostracization? Repudiation? Aren't those risks worth taking to save this country?

Even job loss. All of us who have fought to preserve our freedom and liberties will take a personal hit. Face a personal sacrifice. We will all be better, stronger for it.

Since its inception, America has been the foremost force for good in the world. That's why civic pride is the first line of attack from the Radical Left.

Barack Obama spent an entire presidency apologizing for American Greatness. Who can forget when, on the eve of a NATO meeting, Obama obsequiously told a town hall in Strasbourg, France, that "There's a failure to celebrate Europe's leading role in the world. . . . There have been times where America has shown arrogance and been dismissive, even derisive."[2]

Can you think of anything more demeaning than the leader of the free world telling the world that the country he leads is unworthy of holding that distinction? Disgusting. As the liberators of Europe in World War I and World War II, we apologize to no one. We must remind the rest of the world what we have done for them. And we need to take pride in those accomplishments. We must embrace American Exceptionalism. And those who do not appreciate what America is doing or has done for them in the past, can choose to face an increasingly uncertain future without us.

What has historically bound Americans together, in spite of all our differences, has been our love for this country. We all pledge our allegiance to one flag, the Stars and Stripes. We rise to sing only one National Anthem, "The Star-Spangled Banner." But while we are one nation under God, we must never forget that we are fifty separate states, each with a myriad of different experiences, needs, preferences, and goals.

Arizona is not California.

Florida is not New York.

Montana is not Oregon.

Nor were they ever supposed to be.

Our Founding Fathers brought us the concept of Federalism for precisely this reason. *E Pluribus Unum*—"out of many one."

The Tenth Amendment of the United State Constitution states: "The powers not delegated to the United States by the Constitution, nor prohibited by it to the States, are reserved to the States respectively, or to the people."[3] Federalism, in essence, created a central government with specifically defined powers, such as national defense and international relations, while reserving most other powers to the individual states to proceed on their own paths as they saw fit.

The Radical Left who seeks to open our borders, eliminate our electoral college, rule through executive order, control our schools, and meddle in local affairs forgets that this amendment was created to ensure that the federal government only exercised its defined powers allowing the maintenance of distinct differences among the states. Our country is not one size fits all. Instead, each state was granted the opportunity within stated guardrails to mold its own future from the same set of American clay.

The federal government has overreached on many occasions. They have used the power of their purse to force the states into submission. And too often weak governors forget that the Bill of Rights has given them the means to slap that meddling government's hand away.

This interpretation of the Tenth Amendment also requires a judiciary, particularly the Supreme Court, dedicated to originalist interpretation of the Constitution and not courts packed with activist judges who seek to legislate from the bench.

Personally, I'm so sick of these weak politicians and weak governors who act like there's nothing they can do. "Oh we need the federal government to help!" No, we don't. You lead a sovereign state. Do your job, protect your citizens, their rights, their futures, and their prosperity.

In order to fight the federal government, individual governors working with their legislatures must have the political backbone to do what's right. A number of previous Arizona governors have lacked that particularly skeletal structure.

As governor of Arizona (and I *will* be the rightful and duly-elected governor—the truth will come out), I intend to set a positive example in the hopes that spinal courage proves to be contagious. But this entire system collapses when the people are denied the right to exercise free choice in voting for their elected officials.

This is why I believe that election integrity is the single greatest issue confronting our state and our nation. WE see what stolen elections can do, the consequences impact our country and the world. Case in point: Joe Biden.

The America First movement and Arizona First movement are really one in the same. We can take those lessons in courage and those policies as outlined by President Donald J. Trump and customize and apply them on the state level. These policies work. Populism sells. Because the people, deep down in their soul, know it's right—it returns the governor back to and the *power* back to the people. That's why the corrupt ruling class wants to take it off the market.

I have said America First is at war with Globalism. And I truly believe that. The Uniparty plans to transition this country from a constitutionally-balanced Federalist government to a strictly centralized National government. I believe that this is an intermediate step in handing off that centralized government to some homogenized globalist conglomerate.

We see it in NATO, the United Nations, the Paris Climate Agreement, the World Economic Forum, the World Health Organization, and other organizations and pacts seeking to strip us of our national identity and independence.

Similarly, Arizona First is at war with the corrupt Uniparty-controlled AZ Swamp.

For nearly two years, I worked with Arizona's grassroots to assemble the greatest movement the state of Arizona has ever seen. We did so by honoring God, our Constitution, and championing Arizona/America First values.

But our victory was denied from us by a corrupt Uniparty, Democrats, and America Last Republicans and AZ Swamp creatures, put in place to preserve the status quo. So, I turned to the legal system for remedy and have unfortunately found that judges are cowardly and ALSO more highly interested in preserving the status quo than enforcing the rights of the people. *Leave well enough alone. Don't rock the boat* is their mantra!

I pray this changes. We are watching judges who wear the black robes and whom we call "your Honor" ignore the law, look away from the crime, and put their Stamp of Approval on the most corrupt election of our time. That is something they will have to live with. History will not look kindly on these men and women.

I am the rightful governor of Arizona and I owe it to the people of Arizona to continue the fight, exploring all options to restore integrity to their elections. Ask any Arizonans and they will tell you they believe this election wasn't just stolen from *me*, but from *them*. The chance to *finally* have a governor who represented and worked for the people excited the electorate in a way that hasn't been seen in Arizona before. The good people of Arizona have been wronged. I pledge to stand up and fight for them.

If they destroy our elections, they take away our freedom and free will to choose. And the minute we allow that, we sacrifice those freedoms the Founders fought so long and hard for, and put our future in the hands of people who do not see us as individuals, but as pawns in a larger game.

But what if the legal system fails us? What's next for Kari Lake? Well, one thing for certain: I am NOT going away.

One way or another, I intend to make my voice heard and lead by example, as I have always done. We, the people, will *never* be silenced. We will continue to speak the truth.

I will support policies and candidates who share my vision of the future and work to thwart all attempts to undermine the success of those candidates and that movement.

The future I see is a bright one, an achievable one. Just as fast as Joe Biden and the America Last Uniparty crowd has destroyed America, good strong leaders who put the needs of our citizens first can turn this Titanic around. As long as enough of us are working toward the same goal of putting Arizona First, America First, we cannot be stopped. As more and more people feel that nudging by God to be courageous in this moment, we will see victories. We need national *and* state leadership that believes in this vision. In order for us to create this future for ourselves, our children, and for generations to come, we must set these priorities, abide by these principles, and pursue the following policies.

Election Integrity

In 2016, over 60% of Democrats believed the presidential election was stolen.[4] In 2020, over 60% of Republicans believed the presidential election was stolen.[5] In 2022, 71% of all voters agreed with Republicans that issues in Arizona affected the outcome of the midterm elections. That includes 65% of all Democrats.[6]

The media and the Left want to make election integrity a taboo subject—disparage anyone who questions our election results as "election deniers." But most Americans overwhelmingly agree that we need to secure our elections. To put it simply, we cannot continue to have disputed elections and expect this country to survive. There are relatively easy fixes. But they require both a spine and the political willpower to do them.

1. Eliminate early voting and return to a single Election Day with strict requirements for limited absentee balloting. Early voting makes a mockery of the campaign cycle. And counting votes for two weeks *after* Election Day is wrong. The Constitution mentions Election Day, not Election Month.

2. Require voter ID. One person, one vote. Call BS on those who say this disenfranchises anyone. You can't buy an alcoholic beverage or board an airplane without an ID. Does this deny anyone a drink or a flight?

3. Require pre-printed paper ballots—no printing ballots on-site at polling stations, which increases the likelihood of individuals casting multiple ballots, or as my campaign found, printer settings being deliberately altered to make certain ballots unreadable through scanners.

4. Take all equipment that uses software or has components made by our adversaries in China, or elsewhere, out of the counting process. If it has software, it can be hacked. Elections are simply too important to take that risk.

5. Insist on a verified chain of custody for all ballots at all stages of the process. Ballots with a broken chain of custody must not be counted.

6. Go back to small precinct voting. During Covid, closing down churches and schools—common voting locations— led to the opening of massive voting centers. It's easier to detect fraud in small precincts; it's easier to commit fraud in massive voting centers. All votes can be counted by hand in small precincts at the end of the night and reported back to

the county. Before you say that would take too long, remember here in Arizona where machines count our votes it takes 10–14 days to count our vote. That is outrageous.

7. Audit everything. Elections should be followed with regular, highly accurate audits of the results to ensure transparency and bolster public trust.

8. Oh, and of course, ONLY American citizens will be allowed to vote in national, state, and local elections.

Border Security

I believe that every state is a border state. The fastest way to save our country is to secure our southern border.

The drugs, the weapons, the human suffering that the federal government is intentionally allowing to stream in through our open border doesn't just affect Arizona, New Mexico, Texas, or California. No, they spread throughout the country bringing third-world problems to what's supposed to be a first-rate nation.

The federal government has made it perfectly clear they have no interest in solving the problems they have caused. In turn, the individual states must step forward and do what Washington, D.C. will not: protect their states and put a stop to the violence, death, chaos, and human misery caused by our unsecured border with Mexico.

We are being invaded, not only by future Democrat voters, but by human traffickers, drug dealers, and possible terrorists. And it's time we treat it as such.

Federalism provides us the remedy to this problem. A group of like-minded states must come together to form an interstate compact. In doing so, they can exercise their inherent Article I (of the U.S. Constitution) authority to issue Declarations of Invasion and affirm their sovereign right to protect their citizens and secure the borders of the United States.

They must authorize the creation of a dedicated border security force consistent with state law enforcement functions to engage in joint border security operations.

Give this border security force the authority to arrest, detain, and return illegal immigrants back across the border. No more sending illegal immigrants on publicity stunt relocations deeper into the country. If you get caught, you're turning around and going back from where you came.

We must also communicate the message that our borders are once again closed and that there will be NO path to citizenship for someone whose first act in our country—past, present, or future— was to break the law.

By invoking their constitutional authority, the states may invalidate federal restrictions and regulations on border enforcement as administered by agencies like Customs and Border Protection, the EPA, and the Bureau of Land Management. Instead, the states must be prepared to work together as a unit.

States must also commit to finishing Trump's Border Wall and providing the National Guard with the resources they need to do their jobs. The interstate commission will keep the federal government in the loop about all actions, but this is a courtesy, not a request for approval or affirmation.

If Joe Biden is unhappy at this turn of events, he's more than welcome to try to arrest a sitting governor: me. He will have to deal with the consequences as a result of that.

These measures must be done until the federal government resumes its obligations under Article IV, Section 4 and recommits itself to its constitutional duties to defend our nation's borders and protect the states.

If Washington refuses to fulfill its constitutional requirements, states have every right and responsibility to take matters into their own hands. When they do this, they will send the federal government an unmistakable message: Close the border and stop incentivizing people to cross it. The states are back in charge.

Protecting Mothers and Babies

I am pro-life and believe that every life is worth saving. The pro-life movement stands strongly in support of providing the resources necessary for mothers to embrace life.

My mother was a nurse. My father was a high school history teacher. When my mother became pregnant with me, they already had eight other children to reckon with. The thought of denying me the right to exist never even crossed their minds.

Thank God my mother was pro-life. I mean, if you are reading this, you really should thank your mom. Everyone here debating this issue has the luxury of being born.

God has a plan for each and every one of us. He created us. We are not meant to be destroyed in our mother's womb. The pro-choice movement is a lie. They are not about choice at all. They are about one choice. The worst one for both mother and baby. A scared, pregnant mother walks into a Planned Parenthood abortion clinic, and she's not offered a choice except a fatal one. They don't ask her why she wants to have an abortion, or if there is a way she would be interested in finding an adoptive family to love her baby, or if it's financial reasons she is there—if they could help her overcome those issues so she can be the mother God wants her to be. They just schedule the abortion, take her baby's life, and oftentimes that abortion leaves the mother infertile.

When I ran for governor, it was very important for me that I never wavered on the matter of life. I had a lot of people in my ear telling me otherwise. This was before the official overturn of *Roe v. Wade*, but we all knew that the reversal was coming. And the Radical Left was just salivating over the idea of pummeling Conservatives with accusations of forced birth and wanting to deprive choice from women. They even tried to accuse Republicans of wanting to ban medical procedures to help a woman having a miscarriage. Truly despicable.

That framing disgusts me. This is a human rights issue. What choice are we offering the unborn child? What has happened to the rights of the child?

You want to hear a compelling case against abortion? Find any mother out there and ask them if they regret having a baby. You will never find one who says yes.

On the other hand, go talk to the young women who did have an abortion, who were preyed-upon by the Radical Left. Talk to the women who were told they have no options and how that feeling of desperation *led* them to make a truly tragic choice. I've met these women. There's a countless number of them and each story is more heartbreaking than the last. The pain of that "choice" that was hoisted upon them can never go away, and sadly many can't conceive so the pain is even more unbearable. I want to help as many women as possible so they never have to face that pain. I also want to save as many babies as possible.

I believe in protecting life, liberty, and the pursuit of happiness for all Americans, even the unborn. I hope all America First leaders will not shy away from wanting to protect mothers and their babies. We must put significant resources into helping pregnant women choose life-saving options including adoption, parental support and guidance, and neonatal treatment. So that no woman feels the need to make that irreversible decision to have an abortion.

I am most proud that I showed other Republicans how to speak out on the issue of abortion without feeling ashamed that we are pro-life. We are on the right side of this human rights issue. We are not radical or extreme. The far Left's stance is extreme. This push for abortion up until the baby is in the birth canal ready to be born, and pushing for infanticide once the baby has been delivered, is truly demonic. My opponent was against offering any medical treatment to a baby who survived an abortion. Letting the baby die on a cold metal medical tray is their heartless, cruel stance. Make the pro-abortion crowd explain that. We have nothing to apologize for or run from when we are pro-life because we are for mothers and children. And that is a good place to be.

Second Amendment

The American people have the right to defend their rights, their lives, and their property both from criminals and a potential future authoritarian government. The right of the people to bear arms SHALL NOT BE INFRINGED.

End of story.

Education

The globalist agenda only wins if they are successful in undermining national pride via indoctrination of our children—making the next generation of Americans ashamed of where they came from and what their country stands for.

That's the ultimate goal of the Critical Race Theory agenda. And we have to excise that bullshit from our education system root and branch.

It's time we return to teaching American history, not anti-American history. That doesn't mean ignoring our flaws, but it does mean standing up to the revisionist attacks that focus on the negatives and ignore the positives of the past, that Progressives are using to promote their ideology.

Our teachers must focus on education, not indoctrination. That means we need to RAPIDLY improve the standards of our public schools. To do so we need to increase competition. I am a huge proponent of ESAs, or Empowerment Scholarship Accounts.

ESAs allow families with a child in kindergarten through 12th grade to take a portion of their education dollars and use it for the school or educational program that works best for them and their child.

We must ensure that parents have every available option to give their kids the best education possible—great public schools, great charter schools, great technical schools, and real support for home-school parents. It's intended to fund *students*, not systems, and replace woke curricula with education that gives our kids the real-world tools they need to thrive. And competition will make our public schools better and ultimately a more attractive choice for parents.

When I was running for governor, I championed Dual Track Education after 10th grade. This would allow students to choose between going to college or learning a trade that would help them qualify for a high-paying job immediately upon graduation. We need to recognize that college isn't for everyone. And truth be told, some of the dumbest people I know have a college degree. I believe our country would benefit tremendously from returning to teaching students the valuable lessons they need to thrive in the real world.

The world has more than enough Gender Studies Majors. Let's bring back the engineers, scientists, and those who work in the much-needed trades.

Our children *are* the future. We can no longer take them for granted. We are educating the next generation of Patriot leaders. It's time to give them the skills and values they need to help put America First and make it even greater.

These ideas of moving America forward work. So let's put them into action.

CHAPTER 15

A Dream Becomes a Nightmare

I DON'T DREAM often, but when I do it has extra meaning. One dream, in particular, was unnerving. It felt like being doused by ice-cold water. One minute I was unconscious. The next, I was jolted awake. It took me a moment to collect my bearings. Except there wasn't much to collect. All I could see was darkness, pitch-black darkness. I blinked rapidly and felt my eyelashes drag across something soft. Fabric. *A sleep mask?* I thought. *Weird. I don't wear a sleep mask.*

I tried jerking my arm up to strip off the mask, except my arm didn't oblige. All I could accomplish was flapping my arm limply like a bird with a damaged wing. *Am I drunk? Am I drugged?* I moved to try my other arm and felt the pinch of hairs being yanked from my skin. Duct tape. Which meant it definitely wasn't a sleep mask obscuring my vision. It was a blindfold.

This changes things, I thought. I felt a little flattered. I didn't think I had reached the point of public infamy to be kidnapped. I figured I'd hit that point after my inauguration when I closed the border and showed the Mexican cartels I wasn't bluffing when I promised to put them out of business. But this? Way too soon. So who was it? And where was I?

As if to answer my question, my body was thrown upward and I slammed back down hard on unforgiving aluminum. I could hear a steady humming below me. I was in a truck bed, and we were moving, but to where?

Delicately, I shook my head against my shoulder until I felt the soft sensation of the blindfold falling off. Freedom. I rolled onto my back and was greeted by an effervescent desert moon. I craned my head over the side of the truck bed and saw an imposing green structure with arms extended toward the sky. It looked like Mother Nature flipping me off. It was a Saguaro Cactus, which put me somewhere in the Sonoran Desert in Arizona, or (please no) in the vicinity of San Bernardino, County California, or Sonora, Mexico. I willed the Lord to make it be Arizona.

Morbidly, my mind wandered to the stories I used to hear of the mobsters who would drive down from Vegas, with an expendable human being and a shovel. Whether this was the mafia or cartels, I wasn't feeling particularly expendable. I'm a mom, a wife, and a candidate. So I pulled an old cheerleading maneuver called the tuck, and bent my knees and raised my ankles to my fingernails, and slowly whittled myself free. Duct tape is no match for a sharp, strong acrylic nail.

Freedom. The truck began to slow, weaving unevenly across the rugged road until finally coming to a rest. A tall, lanky man unfurled himself from the vehicle wearing an ill-fitting suit jacket. He sported a batch of ginger stubble, a color match for his thinning hair. He looked like Ron Howard amidst a mid-life crisis. If the mafia or cartels had sent this guy, they weren't sending their best. To my surprise, I heard a lock unlatching, and with a mechanical squeal the passenger side door swung free. "Damn, Stephen. Is this the first time you've driven a truck?!" snapped the passenger.

"I'm sorry, Mr. Bill. I'll do better next time," squeaked his ginger companion.

As the passenger crossed in front of the truck, I could make out his profile—short, with greasy black hair, and a face that seemed incapable of bearing any expression other than smugness. His tiny hand reached down into his waistband, revealing a shiny black object that could only be a—

"Glock," stated Mr. Bill, trying hard to be alpha, but failing.

"Wha?" Lanky Stephen asked absentmindedly.

"It's a gun. Take the damn gun," Mr. Bill snapped.

As the tall man took the firearm from his companion, the gun slipped from the Ginger Man's fingers and fell to his feet, which only infuriated Mr. Bill, who seemed to be the one in charge.

"Use both hands if you have to. Now! So are you going to do it or what?" I knew exactly what IT was. These two were like Dumb and Dumber. But even a dumb guy with a gun can be dangerous.

I threw myself off the back of the truck. My bare feet hit gravel. I tore off as I ran into the desert night—the sharpness of the gravel felt good. Made me realize this was real. My adrenaline kicked in as I remembered running track in school, but this was dangerously different.

"DON'T JUST STAND THERE. GET HER!" shouted Shorty.

The only thing that gave me confidence in my continued survival was the obvious incompetence of the two men looking for me. After a few minutes of sprinting through the rocky terrain, I hid behind a boulder to collect my bearings.

My heart was pounding, my breathing was ragged, as I rested the back of my head against the rough stone. I gave myself a moment to collect myself. And I listened.

"Do you see her, Stephen?" shouted Shorty in the distance.

"It's too dark, Mr. Bill. I can't see a thing," squealed the balding man.

Shorty swore to himself and snapped, "Give me the damn gun."

I was a good fifty yards away when Mr. Bill raised his arms in my direction. *Boom!* A shot rang out. So loud it pierced the still air of the desert.

Boom. Boom.

Mr. Bill continued aimlessly shooting the gun in my direction. My heart was beating fast and so loud I feared it would give away my location.

The scraggly ginger whined, "Did you hit her?"

"How the hell am I supposed to know! I *hope* I did. She's got to be eliminated. Hopefully she bleeds to death. If I missed, she's still toast—the desert will kill her."

The dumb duo walked back to the pickup. *How on earth did they manage to kidnap me?* I peeked to the side of the large boulder to confirm both of them were in the truck as they started the engine and drove away.

The nearly full moon shining down, I was starting to plot my return from the unforgiving desert back to safety when a startling cacophony of bells coming from a xylophone tore through the cool desert air. *Oh thank God!*

My hand, still sore from ripping off the duct tape, reached into my back pocket to answer it . . . but no phone was there!

———

"Answer your phone, hun," I heard Jeff say from beside me. I opened my eyes. My clock read 6:30 a.m. My phone sat on the nightstand ringing. *What a weird dream!* I thought.

"Kari, you have a minute?" said my lead attorney in my election lawsuit.

Me, trying not to sound like I'm still half asleep, "Sure, Kurt. What's going on?"

It was a couple of weeks past the November 8 election. The entire state of Arizona had a pallor of depression hanging over it as we came to terms that another election had been stolen from the people. This time in broad daylight, like a highway robbery. I was oscillating between anger, sadness, and despair. I was praying constantly for peace, strength, and patience. So many people around the world were rallying around me encouraging me to fight. Letters arriving in the mail, with encouraging words or Scripture. Messages and emails of support. It all kept me going and pushing forward.

Kurt had warned me this was going to be a protracted fight, but urged me to stay in it for the sake of the entire country and the future of our Republic. Nothing like added *pressure*! Ha! I knew God did not lead me on a fantastical journey and led to an incredible movement of the people, to have me bow out like a coward now. THIS is when the true fight was beginning. As Kurt started in on some of the counts he wanted to include in our case, I found my mind wandering back to that bizarre dream about those two men—who curiously reminded me of the two men running the Maricopa County elections. I was wishing I knew then what I know now about how Stephen Richer and Bill Gates would destroy any trust the voters still had in elections. Maybe I could have done more to stop them. I thought back to how that day started with an early morning phone call. The familiar tune of "Hail to the Chief," the ringtone I set for President Trump, rang out in my dark bedroom. Election Day, November 8, 2022, had finally, *finally* arrived.

That morning Jeff turned over beside me hearing the familiar ringtone as my hand swept the nightstand beside me searching for my phone. Finding it, I tapped my finger onto the screen and heard a familiar voice of my friend.

"Kah-ree," said a familiar New York accent. "Big day for you, Kah-ree. How are you feeling?"

"Mr. President." I sat up, trying not to sound too groggy. "It is. I'm very excited—relieved."

It was an incredible way to start the morning. The Big Day. Election Day—525 days of campaigning had come to an end.

I told him about the three rallies we did the night before to massive crowds. Including one on the courthouse steps where Barry Goldwater launched his run for president. A full city block of elated voters showed up last night, I said. It was magical. They were ready to vote for a governor who would work for them. I had invited, as I always did with my big event, the entire slate. Blake Masters, Abe Hamadeh, Mark Finchem, those running for legislative seats, my friend, Stephen K. Bannon was there too. It was exhilarating. Trump was happy to hear that. Talking to my friend—who also happens to be the greatest president we have even known—was an amazing honor I was so thankful for.

He was on the golf course in Palm Beach, Florida. Some of his golfing buddies had asked about me and told him how much they loved our energetic, common-sense campaign here in Arizona. And how they enjoy watching me take on the Fake News. President Trump said he was proud of me and my campaign, calling it the best in the country. We said goodbye and hung up, though still exhausted from the night before, at that moment I felt like I could take on the world. I would need that attitude to survive the day, weeks, and months that lay ahead.

Following the conclusion of the 2020 stolen general election, the media had come up with this wonderfully dystopian talking point, "No Widespread Evidence of Fraud."

We heard this quite a bit in Arizona. This was a favorite phrase thrown around by the detractors of the Maricopa County Audit.

Its usage grew to a fever pitch after the audit's completion revealed a complete breakdown in election procedures, and a discovery of enough unverifiable ballots with no chain of custody, that equaled 10 times Joe Biden's margin of "victory."

No widespread evidence! The MOST secure election ever! the media declared in unison, as if coordinated from some central messaging point. Our cowardly Attorney General Mark Brnovich refused to act on the audit's findings, and a select group of Arizona Republican legislators (Rusty Bowers, Paul Boyer and Michelle Ugenti-Rita, to name a few) set about killing every worthwhile piece of election integrity legislation leading up to the 2022 election.

To put it simply, the 2020 Election in Maricopa County was an absolute disaster, and the Arizona establishment spent the following two years ensuring nothing changed. In retrospect, it's crazy that I ever deluded myself into thinking the corrupt machine would let me win.

Here's the thing about "Widespread Election Fraud" in Arizona.

Maricopa County is the fourth-most populous county in the United State of America. It makes up about 62% of the entire state of Arizona.[1] Election fraud doesn't have to be widespread. It only has to be located in one county. And it was—largely. We don't have enough pages to elaborate on Pima County, whose seat and major population center is Tucson, the ballot harvesting capital of the world.

Maricopa County is run by a five-member Board of Supervisors. They control the elections, the budgets, and set the agenda for the mega county. During the 2020 Election, the five members of the Board were as follows: Bill Gates (not the Microsoft vax pusher), Clint Hickman (R), Steve Chucri (R), Jack Sellers (R), and Steve Gallardo (D).

It was the Board of Supervisors who stonewalled the Arizona legislature's attempt to investigate the 2020 Election. They are the biggest impediment to election integrity in the entire state of Arizona.

In the fallout of the 2020 Election, Jordan Conradson, a reporter from the *Gateway Pundit*, released a recording of Steve Chucri confessing that the election was stolen and his fellow board members were spineless cowards.[2]

Chucri would then resign and be replaced with one of Bill Gates's proteges, Thomas Galvin. To date, Chucri is the only Board of Supervisor who has ever faced a consequence from his role in the stolen election. He was a reluctant whistleblower. But that whistle fell on deaf ears.

Following the 2018 election, where Kyrsten Sinema was elected through late-arriving ballots, the Board of Supervisors hired a Koch Brothers network attorney named Stephen Richer to do an investigation and write a post-mortem of the 2018 election. This post-mortem excoriated then-Maricopa County Recorder Adrian Fontes (D) a former cartel lawyer who ran the elections. The report showed numerous flaws in the county election and recommended some sensible changes.[3]

Stephen Richer leveraged publicity for this report into a successful 2020 election victory against Fontes. Using Trumpian-language, Richer promised grassroots Arizonans that he would "Make Elections Boring Again!" However, upon winning the election, Richer reversed these positions completely. He started buddying up to Fontes, claiming that anyone who questioned the integrity of Arizona elections were QAnon-worshipping, tin-foil-hat-wearing, election deniers, and began providing cover for the Board of Supervisors.

But his 180-degree turn didn't stop there. Stephen Richer wanted to be on the frontlines in this battle against (America First) candidates whose existence "threatened our democracy." So Richer, with assistance from Bill Gates, started a super PAC that promised to defeat candidates who questioned the integrity of our elections. He raised a whole bunch of money. And turns out all the expenditures went toward defeating just one "election-denying" candidate:

yours truly. The top political goal of the two men running Maricopa County elections was to defeat the candidate at the top-of-the-ballot they controlled.

The gang of five Board of Supervisors (Gates, Hickman, Sellers, Galvin, Gallardo) run the elections in Maricopa County. The Maricopa County Recorder (Stephen Richer) counts the votes, and all of them report to the Secretary of State of Arizona, who oversees elections statewide.

During the 2022 election the Secretary of State was Katie Hobbs. She was also my Democrat opponent for governor. I spent over eighteen months asking her to recuse herself from running an election where she was on the ballot. She refused.

There's your "gallery of rogues." These were the people in charge of the 2022 election in Arizona.

For the candidate, Election Day is relatively simple. There are no more voters left to convince, no more policies left to explain, you tell the press where you intend to vote so there can be a smiling photo-op, they can take a few pictures of you, and then you retreat to your headquarters and wait for the votes to come.

At least that's how it's *supposed* to work.

On Tuesday, November 8, 2022, I had the wind at my back, a 3.5 lead in the polling average according to Real Clear Politics,[4] our internal polls showed me up 10 points. The goal for the last few weeks of my campaign had been pulling far enough ahead of my opponent to help carry the rest of the Republican ticket over the top. Arizona First was going to become a reality. It was going to be an incredible day. The energy and excitement in Arizona about this was electric.

I hung up the call with President Trump and noticed I had about forty text messages. Seemed like a lot to start the day. As I started going through them my jaw dropped.

One message after the next saying *Holy crap! Are you seeing this! The long lines. Broken equipment. Frustrated voters walking away.* Friends sending me videos from different vote centers. Total chaos. I opened up Twitter.

My eyes scanned my Twitter timeline as, with growing horror, a million tragic stories hit me at once.

And that's how what should have been one of the best days of my life started off weird, got good, immediately became bad, and got even worse. When the first thing you hear after waking up on Election Day morning is that the voting machines in Maricopa County don't work, that tabulators aren't tabulating, printers are out of toner and not functioning, and people are walking away not having voted, your plans change.

So much of Tuesday turned out to be about damage control, about sticking your thumb in a dam hoping to plug the hole long enough to lessen the inevitable crushing impact.

The poll workers announced to frustrated voters, "We've got problems. The machines aren't working. The tabulators aren't accepting the ballots. If you want, you can get out of line and go to a second location and vote from there."

And people did leave. Thousands of them. An untold number left the comfort of the line and headed to uncertain and unfamiliar destinations.

For me, the reality of the situation sunk in FAST. I was furious.

"Okay. *This* is how they do it. We thought we had covered every base. This is HOW they do it."

I picked up the phone and called Colton Duncan. This began one of the worst phone calls of my life—replete with frustration and profanity. Apologies to my readers, but I was left with few words truly expressed my anger boiling inside me. Arizona voters were *once again* victims of mass election crime. I was *livid*!

Colton and I frantically scrambled to make sense of what was happening while simultaneously brainstorming ideas on what to do next to get out in front of it.

ME: "Colton, There's problems with the voting centers. Are you hearing about this? None of the tabulators are working. Anthem, Arcadia, Elliott Road, East Mesa, all of these areas are Republican Areas. The f**king tabulators aren't working. People are being told to vote and put their ballot in a locked box and they'll take it and hand-count it downtown."

COLTON: "What the f**k!?"

ME: "It's happening all over. We've got video of it. I think we need to tell people to show up in the Democrat areas and vote there. Literally, there's *huge* lines. And the people are being told that 'the tabulators don't work, and we're trying to fix it. You can put your vote in this box and we'll send it downtown. It'll be adjudicated.' I'm so pissed right now. I knew they had something planned. I knew it!"

COLTON: "And right at the beginning of the day too."

ME: "We gotta get out ahead of this and say—this is out-freaking-rageous. What do we do?"

COLTON: "Let's call Harmeet [Dhillon—the attorney we hired to oversee Election Day issues and a national Republican Party official]. Let's get Tom Van Flein on the phone too [my Senior Campaign Advisor, also Chief of Staff for Congressman Paul Gosar]."

ME: "Let's get Caroline [staff member] on the phone too, to figure out what our plan is. We don't want to keep people from voting. We want them to show up. Let's find the bluest parts of town, and I'll tell everybody to go there where the machines are working."

COLTON: [having added Tom Van Flein] "Hey, Kari. Got Tom on."

ME: "Hey, Tom. I'm so pissed off! I *knew* they had something up their sleeve."

TOM: "We have the group of lawyers in the Election War Room sending out our investigators to get statements and document this. Then we're just going to have to go to court at this point."

ME: "You know what? Documents and statements, my ass! That takes time. We don't have time. We're losing voters. These assholes! I heard fifteen locations are down."

TOM: "Yeah, it's unreal. And I saw that one video with the woman walking away in frustration. You know, that's a disenfranchised voter. That's completely unacceptable."

ME: "I feel like we need to get ahead of this and go on TV with it and maybe have a press conference. We'll find out *where* the tabulators are working. I'm sure it's in all the liberal parts of town. Tell everyone where to go vote. In Central Phoenix, South Phoenix—where are the liberal parts of town?"

COLTON: "Tom, let's reconvene at 8:10 with the solution."

ME: "It's just unbelievable. I knew they were going to do something. You know what? This shit gives me more resolve that the *first* freaking day in office we're going to call a special session and fix this shit—$100 million on these electronic voting machines."

Tom: "All to be told 'we'll fill it out for you later.'"

Me: "Yeah, 'we'll have somebody *adjudicate* it, decide how you wanted to vote—we'll have Bill Gates and the Board of Supervisors decide who you voted for downtown. And Richer.' Stephen freaking Richer."

Colton: "Do we get to watch when they count those *allegedly*?"

Me: "No, they're already putting up the barriers downtown. They want a freaking war. A civil war. These bastards. They want people so angry that something happens. They—they want that."

Tom: "I'm getting you Harmeet's number, hold on—"

Me: "Brady Smith [Campaign Political Director] just texted. If people reach out, have them go to Maricopa.vote to find a vote center near them. If they've already checked into a polling station. You need to stay in line. You won't be able to vote elsewhere. Let's get this out. And let's put the video of poll workers telling voters the tabulators don't work. I want that to go around the f***ing world. Let's get that video, and then what Brady just said to say, out on Twitter and Truth Social . . . The day started out great, President Trump called and woke me up with the greatest conversation. And then like one second later, people are like—'the voting doesn't work. We can't vote.'"

TOM: "The magnitude of this, Kari. Whether it's deliberate or incompetence . . . Here, I got Harmeet's number. You know, they're supposed to test-run this stuff *for weeks* before today. You know that?? Everything is supposed to be working. So that's what makes me think, is it really incompetence *or worse*—"

ME: "It's *malice*. Yeah. Wait, so who would be in charge of this? Is it Katie Hobbs? Is it Richer?"

TOM: "It's Richer at this level. It's Katie Hobbs later on, the recounts and stuff like that. But it's at this level."

ME: "They also know everyone's going. They'll get these fixed finally, but they know everyone's going in early to vote and they're going to hand-count all these early ones. I am so mad, Tom. God, please step in."

TOM: "You *should* be mad. I mean, we should all be *furious*."

ME: "And will the media even cover this? Colton, we gotta be on this. We gotta get tweets out."

COLTON: "So I'll get off the phone and go."

ME: "OK, let's figure it out. Then stay on top of it . . . Wait, Colton, they're saying the machines for the disabled are working. People could demand using those. At every location. People could demand it. Is that where you just put the ballot through? Tweet it out."

COLTON: "It just sucks. Yeah, we can put this stuff on Twitter—which we're going to—but that's maybe 4% of the electorate will see it. Maybe 2%."

TOM: "Yeah. Push the app too, push everything. We should be pressuring Maricopa County to put the word out as well through their, you know, online site. They're in charge of this."

ME: "Yeah, Tom, let's. You work with the team and have them at each location where these aren't working, explaining what the options are. 'You vote and put it in this box or you use an accessible machine.'"

COLTON: "I'm going to get on with it."

ME: "Alright, bye, guys. This is unbelievable."

Still physically exhausted from the intense campaigning and rallies the night before, mentally, my mind was going in a million directions. I was about to blow a gasket. I chose coffee instead.

Seventy-five percent of the people who showed up to vote on Election Day in Arizona were Republicans—voting for me and a decent chunk of the 25 percent who were Democrats and Independents were also voting for me. We had galvanized Arizonans who were ready for common-sense solutions. And we watched as their sacred vote was trampled.

Those were MY VOTERS. These were people who had watched Maricopa County destroy the integrity of the mail-in ballot system in 2020, and decided to vote in person in 2022.

And they were punished for it.

Our lawyers offered a remedy. We requested that Maricopa County extend voting hours by a few hours to give the people in line more time to vote. But Mark Kelly's attorneys and the County fought this request tooth and nail. They claimed they didn't have a method to get the message out to all voting centers, and that this would cause confusion. Inexplicably, Judge Ryan agreed with them. Our remedy was rejected.

From the minute the polls opened, chaos ensued. From 6 a.m. to 8 p.m., the tabulators' system logs show an average of 7,000 ballot rejections EVERY half hour. That's over a quarter-million times that ballots were spit out of the tabulators on Election Day. None of the poll workers knew how to respond. They weren't trained on what to do when the Election Day operations were sabotaged. The technicians the county sent to fix the problem were equally baffled.

Sixty-one percent of the machines in Maricopa County simply refused to accept the ballots.[5]

While this was happening, Bill Gates and Stephen Richer had the brilliant idea to post a Twitter video via the official Maricopa County account telling people they could simply go vote at a different location.[6]

This was terrible advice. Proper election procedure meant that people had to CHECK OUT of one location before going to another.

Everyone who took Dumb and Dumber's advice were either told they could not vote or forced to use a provisional ballot, which Maricopa County then refused to count.

Worse still was the alternative. The people who refused to go to a second location were presented with the option of depositing their ballot in a box called "Door 3." They were assured that the ballots would be collected and transferred to a separate location where they would be counted. But those assurances meant nothing. To this day, we still have no idea how many ballots were put into this magic box, or if ANY of them actually got counted.

So the lines got longer, and the chaos grew to a frenzy. All of this happened in broad daylight in Maricopa County.

I knew I had to do something. People were panicking and leaving the lines en masse. No voter, whether they be Republican or Democrat, should ever be denied the right to vote.

The plan had been for me to vote in one of two Republican-heavy voting centers near my house. But I was told those were a disaster. Long lines, broken machines, etc. So I informed my staff there would be a change of plans.

Accompanied by my family, my Attorney-on-the-Ground, Harmeet Dhillon, and a small group of staffers, I headed to Phoenix.

The historic post office was a voting center smack-dab in the heart of metro Phoenix. Driving past it, you saw no signs of the panicked multitudes who were desperately trying to cast their votes across other parts of Maricopa County. The only crowd I could see was a massive swarm of reporters ready to pick my brain on how exactly I was feeling about this shit show.

I walked into the voting center and experienced no problems at all. The staff was cordial and professional. When I asked them if they were experiencing any problems, they shook their heads, "no." Are all your printers working? Yes. No issues. How about the tabulators? No problems. Everything running smoothly.

I was so proud to walk in with my husband, Jeff, who had given so much to this campaign. He was my constant companion, my security, my advisor, my rock. I was elated to be voting with my two children: Ruby, nineteen, and Leo, eighteen—both voting for the first time and casting a vote for their mom. So many times after getting home at 11 p.m. or midnight from the campaign trail, they would see how tired I was and how hard I was working. They would tell me how proud they were of what I was doing for Arizona. God blessed me with the most incredible family. We voted TOGETHER. President Trump called me as I waited in line for my ballot to be printed out.

He heard of all the troubles and wanted to see how I was holding up. I told him I was voting and we were doing what we could to tell people to stay in line to vote. He was working his social media to get the word out and even put out a video telling voters to stay in line and cast their vote.[7]

My family walked out of the liberal vote center and walked toward the press from all across the world. Harmeet Dhillon was holding court, giving a statement about the unfolding chaos. She was calm and cool. I wanted to rip their heads off, but did not act on that desire. So I took a deep breath, collected myself, and walked into the belly of the beast.

Stephanie Tsai from PBS Newshour asked me if I thought the Maricopa County tabulation situation was just an unfortunate problem or if I saw something deeper in it.

My response:

"Do you think this is normal, guys? My question is: Do you think what is happening here in Maricopa County is normal? We have had problems after problems, and there's a reason we decided to change locations. We were going to go to a Republican area, but I woke up this morning and within minutes of the polls opening up, I started getting people calling, voters in tears calling my personal number, saying, 'What's going on—the tabulators aren't working! They told me to put my ballot into a box and they would drive it downtown to count it.'

This is not normal stuff. We don't have to have elections run this way. We switched from a Republican area to vote. We came right down into the heart of liberal Phoenix to vote because we wanted to make sure that we had good machines. And guess what? They've had zero problems with their machines today. Not one machine spit out a ballot here today. . . . So we were right to come and vote in a liberal area. They've got to fix this problem. This is incompetency. I hope it's not malice, but we're going to fix it. We're going to win. And when we win there's going to be a 'Come to Jesus' for elections in Arizona. There's going to be a 'Come to Jesus.'"[8]

I took questions for a few more minutes and then broke away from the press who ran after me and followed me to my car.

It was 1:00 p.m. Seven more hours until polls closed. And I intended to make the most of them.

We spent the next few hours going to the locations that we had heard had been hit the worst by the ballot printer and tabulator issues. At every stop, I would pop out of the car and encourage people to stay in line no matter what. Everywhere I went I saw a look of steely determination. These people were going to walk through hot coals if that's what it took to cast their votes. I was so proud of them. They were sacrificing hours of their days standing in the Arizona heat, because they wanted me to represent them. I was so thankful for that.

I tried to stay positive. But treacherous thoughts lingered in the back of my mind. By now, it was around 3:00 in the afternoon, and the madness had been going on for over nine hours. How many people had given up and left? Long lines, parking lots that were full. How many drove around and then took off when they couldn't find a space to park and saw four-hour lines?

Tragically, a statistical analysis would later suggest that approximately 25,000 to 40,000 voters walked away without voting that day.[9] But I didn't know that at the time.

So I pushed those fears to the back of my mind and kept up the cheerleading until it was time to head over to the resort in Scottsdale where the Arizona GOP victory party would be held. Sitting in the back of the car, a feeling of incredible powerlessness washed over me. By all rights, I should have been taking a victory lap, everyone knew we headed for an historic victory, but instead I just felt a slow slip and slide toward the abyss.

I kept thinking back to a question the press had persistently asked me over the last four weeks of the campaign.

"Kari, if you LOSE, are you going to accept the results of the elections?"

At the time I had wondered why they were all asking me that question in unison. Where was it coming from? Why now? I recalled how during the latter stages of President Trump's 2020 campaign, this was the same question he was being asked over and over. Did they know something we candidates did not know? Was the fix in? Were they in on it?

A familiar tingle came across the back of my neck.

The first returns on election night were brutal. Our model said that the worst-case scenario was a -13-point deficit. We hit that exactly. But we knew the night would only get more favorable from there. Just as had been the case in the primary, the counties were deliberately front-loading unfavorable returns to put their unfavored Republican candidates in a panic.

And boy was it working . . . The atmosphere at the victory party felt like a funeral home. As the returns slowly came in, we would send surrogates out to pump up the crowd. They all did their best. But nothing felt right. There was a feeling of existential dread surrounding what should have been a joyous event.

With 52 percent of the vote counted, and Katie Hobbs in the lead, I decided it was time to address the crowd. Walking onto the stage I was almost blinded by the lights coming from the back of the room. I had never seen more reporters in my life.

They had reluctantly come here for a coronation. Now, they were licking their lips hoping for a public execution. I wasn't going to give the vultures in the press what they wanted. I was furious. I wanted to scream and lash out. I was furious they were taking away another election night victory celebration. The corrupt Swamp Creature running the rigged Arizona elections are disgusting, treasonous heathens. I had to get them out of my mind and give my amazing supporters who had done so much for me and the Karizona movement some love.

I prayed before I took the stage. *Heavenly Father, Please fill me with the Holy Spirit. Give me the right words for this moment. I'm tired and, frankly, angry—and that's a bad combination. I need Your help. Get me through this. Get us through this. Bless us all in the name of our Savior Jesus Christ.*

There were so many people backstage and I frankly wanted to be standing alone. Making small talk was excruciating. I really needed a punching bag at that moment. The announcer called my name, music came up loud, and I ran up the steps onto the stage. The crowd was beautiful. Faces from supporters who had become good friends. Moms, dads, ranchers, cops, teachers, doctors, construction workers, computer programmers. We drew support from every walk of life and I wish I could have given each person there a big hug. The crowd was energized and ecstatic. I walked the stage for a bit while the song "American Woman" played loudly. Then I pulled the microphone toward my face and started speaking.[10]

> "We had a big day today. And do not let those cheaters and crooks think differently. . . . We have a movement. We have a movement and we know it. Did you feel that movement? I did a lot of praying to God. I have been praying to God all day today and I said to Him, 'You make this victory come

whatever way You want it. If it comes decisive on election day, bring it to us that way.' If we have to fight through the BS and the garbage, then we will fight through the BS and the garbage.

"But how do you get there—get fair and free elections? You have to fight and win to make them free and fair. We needed another stark reminder that we have incompetent people running the show in Arizona. Who is ready for a change?"

The crowd erupted! There was the ENERGY we needed!

"We had great Patriots around this state show up today. It was so amazing. They showed up at the polls early this morning only to be told the election equipment didn't work. Two minutes into the voting, we had people being told, 'Well, you have to put your ballot over here into another box.' Guys, the fake media back there tried to tell us we were wrong for asking questions about our elections. Guess what? We are going to win this. We are going to win this.

"How many of you remember a couple months ago, August 2? The primary election. It wasn't that long ago we came out . . . and the Fake News was asking us to concede. We kept climbing. We turned fifteen points around and we won by five points. I just want you to know that it is early. It is very early. And if we have to take this fight through, we will. If it takes hours or days, we will. But the great news is that every single drop of election ballots that have come in the last three drops have shown us up 85%, 87%, 81%. I just want the propagandists back there to know, don't embarrass yourselves, don't embarrass yourselves. Don't do it again. You have done it too many times.

"But I want you to know that it is the same movement we had last night at the rally in Prescott. The same movement that we had at that rally in Scottsdale. The same movement that we had at the rallies before with record people, is the same movement we have right this second. Nothing has changed.

"I want you to know we are going to monitor the ballots. We have got to work in the system we have right now, and as they continue to come in and our numbers go up, up, up, like they did last time. When we win, the first line of action is to restore honesty to Arizona elections."

Another pop from the crowd. ENERGY!

"Now, God did not put us in this fight because it was going to be easy. Not one thing we've had to go through has been easy. We beat back a billionaire in the Establishment. Let's just be frank. We have had everyone come against us. Tens of millions in spending has come against us. Nothing has been easy. When corruption has risen to the level that it's at right now, it takes tough, strong people. Are you tough and strong? Are you willing to continue this fight? Are you willing for incompetency to play itself out and the victory to come at us? I'm willing to wait for that and when we win—and I think it will be within hours, I think it will be within hours—we will declare victory and we will get to work turning this around. No more incompetency and no more corruption in Arizona elections. I love you."

KARI, KARI, KARI!

"I kind of feel like it's *Groundhog Day*. We had November 3, 2020, that was called Incompetency 101. Then we had August 2, 2022, Incompetency in Elections 202. Now we are at Incompetency in Elections 303. We need honest elections and we're going to bring them to you, Arizona, I assure you of that. This system we have right now does not work. We, the people, deserve to know on election night, the winner and the loser. . . ."

I LOVE YOU.

"I love you too. I'm looking out—guys, I am looking out here at these beautiful faces of children. Put your hand up if you are a young one in this audience. This is what it is about. We got involved for our children, and we will not stop fighting until we have every legal vote counted. So we're going to be patient. We're going to be patient, guys. We're going to wait. Right now, I told you, the votes that are coming in are going our way, 81%, 85%, and 87%, and we will take the victory when it comes and we will turn this around. Thank you, everybody. Let the partying begin! We know this movement is just beginning. I love you, Arizona. I love you, Arizona."

My voice cracked. The emotions of the moment were crashing down at me.

"I love you. Thank you, Arizona."

I walked off the stage to the roar of the crowd and "We're Not Gonna Take It" by Twisted Sister. It was 12:10 a.m.

I didn't know it at the time, but this would be the high-watermark of the campaign. It was all downhill from there.

Here's a question: How do you count more ballots than you recorded receiving?

On November 10, Maricopa County reported a vote figure that was 25,000 more than what they reported on November 9, period. You read that right. Between November 9 and November 10, the totals changed—25,000 more ballots showed up. Maricopa County has no idea how many ballots they received at their Ballot Tabulation Center in downtown Phoenix.

They then took these ballots to Runbeck, a third-party ballot processor. Runbeck claims they received 263,000 ballots on Election Day. But they reported they counted 298,942. This means Runbeck scanned 35,000 more ballots than they say they received.[11]

In the days following the election, multiple whistleblowers from Runbeck came forward telling horror stories about what they saw. They describe trucks coming in with no corresponding documentation. They saw seals being removed from the transparent containers without the ballots inside being counted. They describe approximately 300,000 ballots illegally inserted into the tally, ballots not coming from drop boxes, not confirming polling locations, but just being brought in by employees.[12]

In this facility, ballots were commingled, injected into the system, or simply not counted at all. But, the most disturbing stories came from the signature verification process.

Three brave whistleblowers came forward to address this issue directly. They recalled how they were rejecting tens of thousands of signatures to a total of up to 130,000 ballots being rejected. These Level 1 reviewers would send the ballots to the Level 2 reviewers, who would then override their judgments and push out and approve ballots with signatures that clearly didn't match. The mismatches were as plain as day. None of the signatures passed the eye test. Shapes, lines, chicken scratches.

And the math just didn't make sense. According to their own numbers, if they had actually gone through and done the signature verifications they claimed, it would have required them to verify a signature every eight seconds working overtime. This is humanly impossible to do.

Runbeck is a nightmare. No sane county would delegate their election procedures to them, which is exactly why Maricopa Country gave them the job in the first place. Runbeck is where the chain of custody for Arizona ballots Arizona goes to die.

But this is what we KNOW now.

All I knew when I woke up on the morning of November 9 was that NOTHING was going the way we thought it would. I would keep checking in with my two data guys, Brady Smith and Landon Wall, for the latest numbers. Without fail, the numbers that the Arizona counties ended up reporting were always significantly lower than we needed.

The days dragged on and the news got worse. I did interview after interview talking about my path to victory, because there *was* a path. And every time there would be another bad batch, another blow. It became very clear to me that this tortured method of reporting the numbers was deliberate. They wanted to bleed me out.

I had a War Room of attorneys working around the clock, calling the counties trying to figure out what the hell was going on. Where were they getting these numbers? And all we were met with was stonewalling and vitriol.

On November 15, 2022—A WEEK after Election Day—they called the race for Katie Hobbs. Statewide, the margin between Katie and me was 17,117 votes. That's only 0.667% of Maricopa County votes.[13] There were 1.3 million votes cast. This is what I'm saying about "Widespread voter fraud." Sometimes it doesn't have to be all that widespread.

Conveniently, this 0.6% margin was just over 0.1% away from requiring a statutory recount. They REALLY didn't want us inspecting those ballots. And in the weeks that followed, my team and I found out EXACTLY why that was.

By now the War Room at the resort was a ghost town. What only a few days earlier had been packed with the hustle and bustle of an army of lawyers and staff members was now down to a skeleton crew of my inner circle.

This was where I had MY "Come to Jesus" moment. Around 10:30 p.m., I had a call with my legal team and closest advisors. It was all laid out before me. And it was a familiar story to some of them. A couple of people on my team advised me that it was in my political interest NOT to contest the election result.

They said, Yes, the election WAS probably stolen. But it would probably be impossible to prove.

I had two choices:

1. Gracefully say that while there were obvious problems in the election, I begrudgingly would concede.
2. Or go full "Stop the Steal" and fight like hell. It was made very clear to me that option two would likely lead to political suicide.

I would like to tell you that I tortured myself choosing between these two possibilities. But I didn't hesitate for a moment. I reflected back on a lesson I learned from my father from his high school football coaching days. He taught me that if you lose fair and square, you shake hands with your opponent and walk away. But that's not what happened in this election.

Game day was rigged. The fix was in before the referees even blew the whistle. And they wanted me to shrug my shoulders and walk away. The people were the victims of a crime—Maricopa County perpetrated that offense and if I don't stand up and fight like hell right now, the people of Arizona will lose their voice. I had made a promise to the people of Arizona that I would fight for election integrity, that I would never abandon them when they needed me, so my political future be damned—I would see this through.

So I set about assembling a legal team and getting evidence. Over the next few days, we received thousands of signed affidavits, videos, witness impact statements from disenfranchised voters, all sworn under penalty of perjury.

While this was going on, the crooks were hard at work codifying the steal. Secretary of State Katie Hobbs threatened to jail ANY county official who sought to investigate the election prior to certification.

Bill Gates, his supervisors, and Stephen Richer held a public hearing where their constituents BEGGED them not to certify the election. "It was a clean election." they responded. "We're proud of it."[14]

And they went ahead and certified it anyway. While this was going on, the news leaked that Stephen Gallardo, one of the Maricopa County Board of Supervisors, had already joined Katie's transition team.[15] (So too did Andy Kunasek, Karrin Taylor Robson's brother.)

While this was happening, damning information was coming from disclosures from Elon Musk's Twitter acquisition. Information revealed that Katie Hobbs and Stephen Richer had been working with the federal government and Big Tech to censor information that they disagreed with and considered election denial.[16]

Mind-blowing revelations were coming in fast. The dam was breaking.

At this point, I was spending more time with attorneys than my actual family. Day after day I spent talking on the phone with lawyers. If there was a hell on earth, I felt like I was in it. Still, I found the voice of my attorney Kurt Olsen incredibly reassuring. Nothing—I really mean NOTHING—rattles to him. It all made sense when I found out he is a former Navy Seal. If I could give you guys a piece of advice: always hire a Navy Seal attorney whenever possible.

Olsen was one of the primary drafters of the *Texas v. Pennsylvania* et al. court case that made it to the US Supreme Court. The suit began with Kurt's eloquent opening statement:

> *Our Country stands at an important crossroads. Either the Constitution matters and must be followed, even when some officials consider it inconvenient or out of date, or it is simply a piece of parchment on display at the National Archives. We ask the Court to choose the former.*
>
> *Lawful elections are at the heart of our constitutional democracy. The public, and indeed the candidates themselves, have a compelling interest in ensuring that the selection of a President— any President—is legitimate. If that trust is lost, the American Experiment will founder. A dark cloud hangs over the 2020 Presidential election.*

Kurt was (and is) unflappable. He is also brilliant and patriotic. Clean cut, gray hair, always impeccably groomed and measured. Like at any moment he could be called back into the Seals and if that day comes, he will be ready, willing and able for duty. Kurt is someone I'd march into battle with and take a bullet for, and trust me . . . this feels like a battle.

It was Kurt who was tasked to relay to me the latest discovery from our investigation into the election. We found a cyber expert named Clay Parikh, whose credentials were unassailable. A man who was familiar with the innermost workings of the machine. He had been consulted on the tabulator failures that had occurred on Election Day, and Clay concluded that the errors could not have occurred without intentional misconduct.

It was a staggering revelation. In the early days, we had been willing to write off the Election Day problems as Hanlon's razor (incompetence, not malice), but Clay's conclusions left no doubt that these "errors" were the result of deliberate actions and could have been prevented.

A voting machine is like any other machine: you program it to do something and it does it.

We would go on to select Clay to be our observer for our court-approved inspection of a sample of Election Day ballots. What he found was another game-changer.

The tabulators were designed to read a 20-inch image, on 20-inch ballot paper, but on Election Day a change was made, the ballot-on-demand printers started printing a shrunken image, a 19-inch image on the 20-inch ballot paper. This caused the tabulators to read the ballot as a paper jam.

During Clay's inspection, he found that 48 of 113 ballots, or 42.5% of all ballots inspected, were printed with the wrong image size. This caused the machines to spit out ballots in nearly 60 percent of all polling locations. This one-inch discrepancy caused chaos on Election Day—ballots were rejected from tabulators 250,000 times! And it led to the mass rejection of votes and the disenfranchisement of thousands of voters.[17]

We would later find out that Maricopa County Tabulation and Election Center had a "heat map" in their central count showing "Republican Voter Dot Density."[18]

When we overlaid that heat map with a map of the locations impacted by the Election Day tabulator failures, the results were shocking . . . It was nearly a perfect overlap. This was a targeted attack on Republican voters.

During our trial, Maricopa County Co-Elections Director, Scott Jarrett, would perjure himself trying to explain away the ballot-size discrepancy. On Day One of the trial, he claimed such an error was impossible. But following a night's coaching with the Maricopa County Attorney's office, he returned to the stand on Day Two, a changed man. He amended his story and was now claiming it was a "shrink to fit" issue. Not just that, but that it was one that had occurred in three prior elections and they were in the process of performing a root cause analysis.

This led to a *Perry Mason* moment from Kurt, where he caught Jarrett in his lie and got him to admit that they had moved forward with the certification of a sham election.

OLSEN: "You did not mention this in your testimony yesterday, did you?"

JARRETT: "I did not."

OLSEN: "You did not publish anywhere that there was a 'shrink-to-fit issue' after the election?"

JARRETT: "I did not."[19]

In a sane world, that would have been the ballgame. But we live in a banana republic where the judges are more afraid of bad press than bad rulings.

By Arizona law, and legal precedent, all that is required for a successful contest of an election is to prove uncertainty. There are at LEAST two historical legal precedents, in Arizona alone, that have led to the overturn of elections:

The 1917 Arizona Gubernatorial election with *Hunt v. Campbell*.

And a 1997 Yuma Board of Supervisors Race with *Reyes v. Cuming*.

We brought over 270 exhibits of evidence before the court in the form of ten claims. Judge Peter Thompson dismissed eight of them (including our damning signature verification evidence) and only allowed us to talk about the machines and the chain of custody.[20] Unfortunately, rather than rule according to the law, the judge set an impossible legal standard in proving intentionality, an entirely arbitrary burden to have to reach.

Still, I'm incredibly proud of my attorneys, and I believe that in spite of this challenge, not only did they meet this nigh impossible burden, they knocked it out of the park.

Joining Kurt Olsen in the courtroom was Bryan Blehm, a former high-powered attorney, who had left his lucrative career behind to rediscover his purpose in life in the Alaskan wilderness. He's incredibly sharp and enlightened, and he's quite good at grilling witnesses on the stand. He, too, is a veteran, a Patriot, and an expert on election integrity after getting involved as an attorney for Arizona's Forensic Audit.

It takes a lot of courage for attorneys to challenge a crooked election, knowing that it could cost them their careers. I had multiple lawyers quit my team telling me that they feared disbarment. I'm incredibly blessed to have found two of the bravest attorneys there are. These men were given an impossible standard, five hours and two days to expose the systemic rot at the heart of the Maricopa County Elections, and they did it.

We wanted to call Katie Hobbs, and put her under oath, but we didn't have the time. We did get to call Stephen Richer who testified over Skype, perjuring himself on the stand, when he denied starting a Super PAC with the sole purpose of taking me down.

We had so many gotcha moments. My lawyers did a hell of a job. They're not the problem. The system is.

Regardless of how the judge ruled, or how any subsequent rulings are adjudicated, I know we have the truth on our side. And I will never regret getting it out there.

I am the lawful Governor of Arizona. The current occupant of the Governor's Office is just a squatter.

I am committed to restoring honesty and integrity to Arizona elections. This is a hill that we *cannot* sacrifice. If the American people are no longer in charge of choosing which officials get to represent them, this whole system falls apart.

I truly don't care what they call me. I've been labeled an "election denier" so much that I might as well tattoo it to my body and save journalists the trouble. Actually, I consider myself an ELECTION INTEGRITY REFORM ADVOCATE.

If I have to, I'll spend the rest of my life traveling throughout his country, talking till I lose my voice, about how we need to fix the elections and prevent madness like what happened to me from happening ever again. I refuse to be a victim, and I refuse to let anyone else be victimized. I will keep fighting. And I believe I will be vindicated. The truth is on my side.

Every day is a new battle. When I wake up, I pray to the Lord above. I tell Him, "I'm Yours. Do with me what You will." And I don't know what comes next but I have faith that God didn't take me so far to leave me here. I wonder what He has freed me up for. I believe it will be SOMETHING GOOD.

The nightmare has to end sometime. And I've always been one to dream big.

EPILOGUE

A Safe Landing

"IF THEY THOUGHT that they could take me down, they should know that they messed with the wrong woman."

That was my thought as I sat in the back of an SUV traveling to Scottsdale for my Save Arizona Rally on January 29, 2023.

It was a wild idea. State Senator Wendy Rogers had talked me into it. My lawsuit challenging the rigged election was now in the Appellate Court, but the Fake News refused to cover it. So Wendy recommended I do something to help keep the people of Arizona updated on the status of my case, and to remind them I was still fighting for them.

A video or a tweet wasn't going to cut it. My strength was always in connecting directly with the people of Arizona. So, with only a week's notice, we put together a rally and did our best to get the word out.

Despite the rally being the same day as two NFL Championship games, I was floored at the massive turnout . . . About 4,000 people showed up to see me! They had put America First and American Football second.

I saw the familiar faces of my coalition leaders, staff members, volunteers, friends and family—all of the people who had been through absolute hell fighting alongside me. One new face was Jeff Dewit, who only a day before had been elected the new Chair of the Arizona GOP. I had endorsed him and helped secure President Trump's endorsement for him. The energy at the Orange Tree Golf Resort, even an hour before the doors opened, was palpable. Like it or not, Jeff was going to get the full Karizona experience.

I turned and saw my friend Floyd Brown, the founder and former publisher of the website *The Western Journal*. Floyd is a good man of tremendous integrity. We need more independent journalists like him. The truth matters. And the truth-tellers have never mattered more.

Beside Floyd and his lovely wife, Mary Beth, stood Wendy Rogers. Wendy, the self-described "Sweet Grandma with a Shotgun" had been with me since Day One. There are few greater champions for America and Arizona First than Wendy. She had come to almost all of the events during the campaign, and I was grateful to see she hadn't broken the tradition.

It was time to step out into the spotlight and talk to the people of Arizona again. The room went dark. A video began playing on one of the screens that flanked the stage. Tom Petty's "I Won't Back Down." His estate was absolutely furious over this turn of events, but it had become one of the anthems of the campaign.

I had taken Tom's advice. I had stood my ground against the political machine, even as they tried to drag me and the state of Arizona down to hell. And here we all were, still standing, battling back. NEVER backing down—not *one damn inch*.

Standing in front of my faithful supporters, about to encourage and rally them around our never-wavering movement, Colton handed me a cellphone with none other than President Trump on the phone. *The crowd roared!*

Putting the phone up to the microphone, we listened in:

"Well, hello everybody! And I wish I was there with you. Because Kari is a fantastic person. It's a shame what happened. They had the machines quote 'broken,' OK? A lot of these Republican area machines were broken. It's a disgrace, and ultimately she's going to be victorious. But I just want to thank everybody for being there. I love you all."

The crowd was energized—happy that Trump, who knows more than anyone what election fraud feels like, was calling in to tell us he's with us in this fight, still.

I spent the next forty minutes methodically going over my election case and urging the array of Fake News in the back to do THEIR jobs, and tell the truth.

"I love this quote. 'We always pray for God to take our stress away, make things easier,' John F. Kennedy said, 'Do not pray for easy lives, pray to be stronger men.' Right? That's what I pray for. God is strengthening us right now with what we're going through. . . .

"Now I'm gonna ask you to do something that some of you might not wanna do. Let's pray for our Fake News media, that they have a change of heart. I've really, really started at this time to start praying for my enemies, because sometimes your enemies teach you something and we need them to soften. . . .

"We're going to restore faith and honesty in our elections here in Arizona, and We the People will take our government back. I know if I've got you on my side, that we're gonna win this. We're gonna save Arizona. We're gonna save America!"[1]

———

Ten days later in early February, I was on a plane above the clouds and soaring over the Midwest. From my seat by the window, I could see familiar sights of the American heartland: rural country homes, red barns, schoolhouses, and frozen-over fields that in just a few short months would be filled with rows of corn.

And I wondered for a moment if somewhere down there was maybe a young girl, staring up at wondering what her future holds. Experiencing that divine bit of KNOWING that big things waited for her somewhere across the sky.

I had grown up in Iowa, and while Arizona was my home, the Hawkeye State would always be a part of me. Besides, Iowans had a tremendous task before them. Their 2024 Caucuses were just around the corner, and they would be tasked with vetting the next president of the United States. The people of Iowa understand history. They understand where we came from; that this country was built on hard-working men and women, and if we got complacent, we stood to lose it all.

I told my fellow Iowans to make sure they don't ignore the most important issue of our time—election integrity. If *any* state is running fraudulent elections, it hurts voters in *all* states. Due to corrupt elections, we ended up with an incompetent fool who is compromised by our enemies in the White House leading us to the edge of complete destruction. Time to reform elections and save our country.

And I know this for sure. This country is worth fighting for! Iowans agree.

The day before, we had an overflow group of 650 Patriots in my hometown in Scott County, Iowa. Then we had another massive event near Des Moines. Traveling further, I stood on stage in front of a packed room of about 300 Patriots in Ankeny, Iowa, and—like I have tried to do in these pages—I did my best to sum up how we save our country. How we fight back for our kids. And how fighters come in all shapes and sizes, because fight is measured not in the size of one's muscles . . . it's found in the heart.

"They picked a fight with the wrong woman. I have just enough Arizona in me. And just enough Iowa in me. And I'm not going to let them win. No way!"

I didn't have my sledgehammer that day. But I think I got my point across. I am up for the battle, and I am UNAFRAID. And every day our movement grows as more and more Americans are standing shoulder-to-shoulder right beside me.

ACKNOWLEDGMENTS

TO MY SUPPORTIVE husband, Jeff, who has been there every step of the way. To my most precious children, Ruby and Leo. Thank you for your patience and support during this roller coaster ride.

To my seven sisters and one brother: Vicki, Jill, Kim, Lori, Jack, Lisa, Susan, and Jennifer—thank you for showing me the ropes in this world.

To Winning Team Publishing, especially Sergio Gor, Donald Trump Jr., Connor Hickey, and Sean Gantwerker. Thank you for bringing this book to life.

To every Arizonan who got involved, knocked doors, showed up for rallies, helped energize this movement—I know you will not give up and together we will take our nation back.

To the mama bears, dads, grandparents, students, every Arizonan who cared enough about our great state to step forward and get involved to make sure our children and grandchildren and future generations enjoy the freedoms and liberties we've enjoyed.

To my entire campaign team—the best in the business—to the donors, supporters, volunteers, and fighters. Thank you for standing up, giving your time, money, and energy to save our great state.

To President Donald J. Trump, thank you for fighting for us. We've got your back because you always have ours.

Finally, to those who don't support our mission. We are fighting for your future too. I know you will eventually come around and join us in MAKING AMERICA GREAT AGAIN!

NOTES

Chapter 1: The Red Pill Generation

[1] Elaine Kamarck, "The Iranian hostage crisis and its effect on American politics," Brookings, November 4, 2019, https://www.brookings.edu/blog/order-from-chaos/2019/11/04/the-iranian-hostage-crisis-and-its-effect-on-american-politics/.

[2] "Goldwater's 1964 Acceptance Speech," Washington Post Archives, https://www.washingtonpost.com/wp-srv/politics/daily/may98/goldwaterspeech.htm.

[3] "A Time for Choosing Speech, October 27, 1964," Ronald Reagan Presidential Library & Museum, https://www.reaganlibrary.gov/reagans/ronald-reagan/time-choosing-speech-october-27-1964.

Also see "Ronald Reagan, A Time for Choosing (a.k.a. 'The Speech,'" American Rhetoric, Air date, October 27, 1964, Los Angeles, https://www.americanrhetoric.com/speeches/ronaldreaganatimeforchoosing.htm.

[4] "Here are the worst slogans in the history of U.S. political campaigning," *Business Insider India*, January 7, 2020, https://www.businessinsider.in/slideshows/miscellaneous/here-are-the-worst-slogans-in-the-history-of-us-political-campaigning/slidelist/73141253.cms.

[5] "Ronald Reagan, 1962," *Time*, https://content.time.com/time/specials/packages/article/0,28804,1894529_1894528_1894518,00.html.

Chapter 2: A Modern-Day Persecution

[1] "Kari Lake, Republican candidate for Arizona governor, drops F-bomb live," YouTube, https://www.youtube.com/watch?v=2DCqP2I5icw.

[2] Sarah N. Lynch and Lisa Lambert, "Sex ads website Backpage shut down by U.S. authorities," Reuters, April 6, 2018, https://www.reuters.com /article/us-usa-backpage-justice/sex-ads-website-backpage-shut-down-by -u-s-authorities-idUSKCN1HD2QP.

[3] Tyler Olsen, "Fauci's mixed messages, inconsistencies about COVID-19, vaccines and reopenings come under scrutiny," Fox News, February 23, 2021, https://www.foxnews.com/politics/faucis-mixed-messages -inconsistencies-about-covid-19-masks-vaccines-and-reopenings-come -under-scrutiny.

Chapter 3: Take This Job and Shove It

[1] John Tierney, "Unlearned AIDS Lessons for Covid," *Wall Street Journal*, October 3, 2021, https://www.wsj.com/articles/aids-panic-covid -19-coronavirus-pandemic-experts-politicized-fauci-follow-science -11633290650.

[2] Emma-Jo Morris and Gabrielle Fonrouge, "Smoking-gun email reveals how Hunter Biden introduced Ukrainian businessman to VP dad," *New York Post*, October 14, 2020, https://nypost.com/2020/10/14/email-reveals -how-hunter-biden-introduced-ukrainian-biz-man-to-dad/.

[3] KariLake, "AZ Gov Candidate Kari Lake's Election Reform Rally Honoring Grassroots Volunteers," Rumble, https://rumble.com/vosjfs -watch-and-share-az-gov-candidate-kari-lakes-election-reform-rally -honoring-.html.

[4] Arizona Governor Debate, C-SPAN, September 1, 2020, https://www .c-span.org/video/?295287-1/arizona-governor-debate.

[5] "Jan Brewer, Former Arizona Governor," *The Gaydos and Chad Show*, August 31, 2022, https://omny.fm/shows/the-gaydos-and-chad-show /jan-brewer-former-arizona-governor-81.

Chapter 4: The Ride to the Big Stage: CPAC

[1] Internal polling

[2] Internal polling

[3] KariLake, "Kari Lake Stares Down the Fake News in Her Epic CPAC 2022 Speech," Rumble, https://rumble.com/vw1y4s-kari-lake-stares -down-the-fake-news-in-her-epic-cpac-2022-speech.html.

Chapter 5: The Californication of America

[1] Louis Casiano, "Nonbinary former Biden official Sam Brinton accused of serial luggage theft released without bail," Fox News, February 15, 2023, https://www.foxnews.com/politics/nonbinary-former-biden-official-sam -brinton-accused-serial-luggage-theft-released-without-bail.

[2] Andy Puzder, "Lockdowns Starve Mom and Pop," *Washington Journal*, January 4, 2021, https://www.wsj.com/articles/lockdowns-starve-mom -and-pop-11609802683.

[3] Danielle Wiener-Bronner, "Why thousands of restaurants are open, but not allowed inside," KSBW Action News, November 23, 2021, https:// www.ksbw.com/article/thousands-restaurants-open-but-youre-not -allowed-inside/38338501.

[4] Grace Dickinson, "How to wear a mask at the beach (properly)," *Philadelphia Inquirer*, May 22, 2020, https://www.inquirer.com/things-to- do/jersey-shore/coronavirus-covid-19-beaches-masks-20200522.html.

[5] Samirah Majumdar, "How COVID-19 Restrictions Affected Religious Groups Around the World in 2020, Pew Research Center, November 29, 2022, https://www.pewresearch.org/religion/2022/11/29/how-covid-19-restrictions-affected-religious-groups-around-the-world-in-2020/.

[6] "Letter to the Editor: Unruly protests are OK, but outdoor church services are not?" *Los Angeles Times*, July 29, 2020, https://www.latimes.com/opinion/story/2020-07-29/unruly-protests-are-ok-but-outdoor-church-services-are-not.

[7] Nick Givas, "Over 16K US inmates have been released as coronavirus crisis has progressed," Fox News, April 16, 2020, https://www.foxnews.com/us/here-is-how-many-prisoners-have-been-released-covid-19.

[8] "Tucker Carlson speaks to Kyle Rittenhouse about Kenosha shootings," Fox News, November 24, 2021, https://www.foxnews.com/transcript/tucker-kyle-rittenhouse-after-his-acquittal.

[9] "Revolver's Jan. 6th Reporting Changed the Game: Read Our Top Jan. 6 Investigative Stories Here," Revolver, June 18, 2021, https://www.revolver.news/2021/06/revolver-january-6th-investigative-series-summary/.

[10] Lia Eustachewich, "Man twice bailed out by Kamala Harris-backed fund—gets arrested again," *New York Post*, February 3, 2021, https://nypost.com/2021/02/03/man-twice-bailed-out-by-harris-supported-fund-arrested-again/.

Chapter 6: America First

[1] Don Gonyea, "Jesting, McCain Sings: 'Bomb, Bomb, Bomb' Iran," NPR, April 20, 2007 https://www.npr.org/templates/story/story.php?storyId=9688222.

[2] "John McCain 'Complete the Danged Fence,' Campaign 2010," *Washington Post*, June 10, 2015, https://www.washingtonpost.com/video

/video/politics/john-mccain-complete-the-danged-fence--campaign
-2010/2015/06/10/a0f87e4a-0fbb-11e5-a0fe-dccfea4653ee_video
.html?itid=lk_inline_manual_30.

[3] Karl Rove, "The President's Apology Tour," *Wall Street Journal*, April 23, 2009, https://www.wsj.com/articles/SB124044156269345357.

[4] Ben Smith, "Obama on small-town Pa.: Clinging to religion, guns, xenophobia," *Politico*, April 11, 2008, https://www.politico.com/blogs/ben-smith/2008/04/obama-on-small-town-pa-clinging-to-religion
-guns-xenophobia-007737.

[5] "Here's Donald Trump's Presidential Announcement Speech," *Time*, June 16, 2015, https://time.com/3923128/donald-trump-announcement
-speech/.

[6] Bill Chappell, Tamara Keith, Merrit Kennedy, "'A Nation without Borders Is Not a Nation': Trump Moves Forward with U.S.-Mexico Wall," NPR, January 25, 2017, https://www.npr.org/sections/thetwo
-way/2017/01/25/511565740/trump-expected-to-order-building-of-u-s
-mexico-wall-wednesday.

Chapter 7: Inside the Fake News

[1] Morgan Gstalter, "Trump: 'Fake news media' didn't cover when Obama said '57 states' in 2008," *The Hill*, September 15, 2018, https://thehill.com
/homenews/administration/406825-trump-fake-news-media-didnt-cover
-when-obama-accidentally-said-57/.

[2] "November 2, 2022, Barack Obama: 'Kari Lake Actually Interviewed Me Back in 2016,'" Forbes Breaking News, YouTube, https://www.youtube
.com/watch?v=qsWgcBYjw5M.

[3] "The Liberals Who Saw Through Russiagate," *Wall Street Journal*, May 18, 2022, https://www.wsj.com/articles/harpers-mag-russiagate-steele -dossier-holman-jenkins-cockburn-clinton-trump-putin-11652827839.

[4] Rich Noyes, "Study: The Dangerous Partisanship of Midterm Coverage," November 1, 2022, https://www.newsbusters.org/blogs/nb/rich-noyes /2022/11/01/study-dangerous-partisanship-tvs-midterm-coverage.

[5] Megan Brenan, "Media Confidence Ratings at Record Lows," Gallup, July 18, 2022, https://news.gallup.com/poll/394817/media-confidence -ratings-record-lows.aspx.

[6] Khaleda Rahman, "Katie Hobbs Blames Kari Lake as HQ Break-In Spark Watergate Comparisons," *Newsweek*, October 27, 2022, https:// www.newsweek.com/katie-hobbs-kari-lake-office-break-watergate -comparisons-1755047.

[7] Danielle Miller et al., "2022 Election: Arrest made in connection to burglary at Katie Hobbs' Phoenix campaign office," Fox 10 Phoenix, Updated November 2, 2022, https://www.fox10phoenix.com/news/2022 -election-hobbs-campaign-confirms-break-in-at-phoenix-headquarters.

[8] Elias Weiss, "Kari Lake Turns Burglary into Kinda Clever Kentucky-Fried Campaign Prank," *Phoenix New Times*, October 28, 2022, https:// www.phoenixnewtimes.com/news/kari-lake-turns-burglary-into-kentucky -fried-campaign-prank-14782780.

[9] Jared Gans, "Zuckerberg tells Rogan Facebook suppressed Hunter Biden laptop story after FBI warning," *The Hill*, August 26, 2022, https://thehill .com/policy/technology/3616579-zuckerberg-tells-rogan-that-facebook -suppressed-hunter-biden-laptop-story-after-fbi-warning-defends-agency -as-legitimate-institution/.

[10] KariLake, "Top-rated Arizona news anchor resigns," Rumble, March 1, 2021, https://rumble.com/vea79d-top-rated-arizona-news-anchor-resigns -i-longer-want-to-do-this-job.html.

Chapter 8: Flipping the Script on the Enemy of the People

[1] All excerpts from the June 15, 2021 Lake/Welch interview are from Lake's Rumble account, https://rumble.com/vikyqh-10-minutes-of-pure-discomfort-as-candidate-for-az-governor-kari-lake-torche.html.

Chapter 9: Trump in Heels

[1] @KariLake, Facebook, June 29, 2022, https://www.facebook.com/watch/?v=599298598165208.

[2] Julian Hattem, "Trump to Jeb: Your brother gave us Obama," *The Hill*, September 16, 2015, https://thehill.com/blogs/ballot-box/gop-primaries/253976-trump-tells-bush-your-brother-gave-us-obama/.

[3] KariLake, "AZ Gov Candidate, Kari Lake, Brings Down the House at Trump Rally," Rumble, https://rumble.com/vkebfx-az-gov-candidate-kari-lake-brings-down-the-house-at-trump-rally.html.

[4] Stacey Barchenger, "Kari Lake gets coveted endorsement from former President Trump in Arizona governor's race," *AZCentral*, September 28, 2021, https://www.azcentral.com/story/news/politics/arizona/2021/09/28/donald-trump-endorses-kari-lake-arizona-governor/5837690001/.

Chapter 10: Draining the Desert Swamp

[1] @KariLake, "Sledgehammer to Media Lies" Ad, Facebook, July 22, 2021, https://www.facebook.com/watch/?v=322618936226365.

[2] George F. Will, "The Cheerful Malcontent," *Washington Post*, May 31, 1988, https://www.washingtonpost.com/wp-srv/politics/daily/may98/will31.htm.

[3] Laura Meckler, "Goldwater Legacy Echoes in McCain Run, Despite Differences," *Wall Street Journal*, May 20, 2008, https://www.wsj.com/articles/SB121124793915505799.

[4] Amy Silverman and Jeremy Voas, "Opiate for the Mrs.," *Phoenix New Times*, September 8, 1994, https://www.phoenixnewtimes.com/news/opiate-for-the-mrs-6432986.

[5] "Cindy McCain admits that she and others knew about Epstein's trafficking," C-SPAN, January 24, 2020, https://www.c-span.org/video/?c4849210/user-clip-cindy-mccain-admits-knew-epsteins-trafficking.

[6] Maeve Sheehey, "Biden nominates Cindy McCain for U.N. food agency ambassadorship," *Politico*, June 23, 2021, https://www.politico.com/news/2021/06/23/cindy-mccain-un-ambassadorship-495752.

[7] @Alexander Soros tweet, Twitter, February 17, 2023, https://twitter.com/AlexanderSoros/status/1626619665848885251.

[8] Cliff Schecter, *The Real McCain: Why Conservatives Don't Trust Him and Why Independents Shouldn't Either* (Sausalito, CA: PoliPoint Press, 2008), 49–50.

[9] Nick Gass, "McCain: Trump 'fired up the crazies,'" *Politico*, July 16, 2015, https://www.politico.com/story/2015/07/john-mccain-donald-trump-immigration-phoenix-120216.

[10] See full interview at "Road to the White House 2016," C-SPAN, July 18, 2015, https://www.c-span.org/video/?327045-5/presidential-candidate-donald-trump-family-leadership-summit&event=327045&playEvent.

[11] John Haltiwanger, "John McCain described how he received the Steele dossier," *Business Insider*, March 22, 2019, https://www.businessinsider.com/how-john-mccain-received-steele-dossier-trump-russia-2018-5.

[12] Madeline Conway, "McCain: Mexico won't pay for the wall," *Politico*, February 3, 2017, https://www.politico.com/story/2017/02/trump-border -wall-mexico-john-mccain-234612.

[13] "McCain rival suggests he should resign after brain cancer diagnosis," CBS News, July 21, 2017, https://www.cbsnews.com/news/kelli-ward -john-mccain-brain-cancer-diagnosis/.

[14] Associated Press, "Thumb Down, McCain Votes No on 'Skinny Repeal,'" YouTube, July 28, 2017, https://www.youtube.com/watch ?v=DWeayFHsH90.

[15] @KariLake tweet, Twitter, August 25, 2018, https://twitter.com/Kari Lake/status/1033512364979642368.

Chapter 11: The Great Debates and the Debate Denier

[1] Reagan Library, "First Presidential Debate with President Reagan and Walter Mondale, October 7. 1984," YouTube, https://www.youtube.com /watch?v=ZH2NgqA3CVY.

[2] Peter Baker and Susan Glasser, *The Man Who Ran Washington: The Life and Times of James A. Baker III* (New York: Doubleday, 2020), 239.

[3] "Debate Between the President and Former Vice President Walter F. Mondale in Kansas City, Missouri," October, 21, 1984, Ronald Reagan Presidential Library & Museum, https://www.reaganlibrary.gov/archives /speech/debate-between-president-and-former-vice-president-walter-f -mondale-kansas-city.

[4] "Debate Between the President and Mondale."

[5] 1984 Statistics, The American Presidency Project, https://www .presidency.ucsb.edu/statistics/elections/1984.

[6] "Transcript and Audio: First Obama-Romney Debate," NPR, October 3, 2012, https://www.npr.org/2012/10/03/162258551/transcript-first-obama-romney-presidential-debate.

[7] "Transcript and Audio: Second Presidential Debate," NPR, October 16, 2012, https://www.npr.org/2012/10/16/163050988/transcript-obama-romney-2nd-presidential-debate.

[8] "Transcript of the Second Debate," *New York Times*, October 10, 2016, https://www.nytimes.com/2016/10/10/us/politics/transcript-second-debate.html.

[9] Hannah Getahun, "The Trump-backed frontrunner in Arizona's gubernatorial race said the GOP primary debate felt "like a spoof," *Business Insider*, July 1, 2022, https://www.businessinsider.com/arizona-gop-governor-candidates-debate-feels-like-a-spoof-2022-7.

[10] "Cut the Fat Off Government," YouTube, June 28, 2022, https://www.youtube.com/watch?v=BHb0V1SfyxM.

[11] All quotes from the debate can be found at "6-29-2022 Republican Candidates for Governor," PBS, Episode 126, https://www.pbs.org/video/6-29-2022-republican-candidates-for-governor-foqv5z/.

[12] Chance Townsend, "Twitter reacts to the pure insanity that was Arizona's Republican primary for governor debate," Mashable, July 2, 2022, https://mashable.com/article/arizona-republican-primary-debate.

[13] Brahm Resnik, "4 questions about Arizona TV debate for governor as Hobbs seeks changes in format," 12 News, August 23, 2022, https://www.12news.com/article/news/politics/sunday-square-off/will-katie-hobbs-debate-kari-lake-for-arizona-governor-four-things-you-need-to-know/75-03897e99-4b2a-455a-b110-616b70ed48eb.

[14] Phil Boas, "Katie Hobbs tells Arizona she is a coward—and it's Kari Lake's fault," *AZ Central*, September 6, 2022, https://www.azcentral

.com/story/opinion/op-ed/philboas/2022/09/06/katie-hobbs-not
-debate-kari-lake-why-run-arizona-governor/8002816001/.

[15] Brad Dress, "Democrat Hobbs refuses to debate 'conspiracy theorist'
Lake in Arizona governor race," *The Hill*, September 11, 2022, https://
thehill.com/homenews/campaign/3638395-democrat-hobbs-refuses-to
-debate-conspiracy-theorist-lake-in-arizona-governor-race/.

[16] @KariLake, Twitter, September 8, 2022, https://twitter.com/KariLake
/status/1568001280827596801?s=20&t=ol7Yy_PVtoiVQK57jlmcRg.

[17] @KariLakeWarRoom, Twitter, September 11, 2022, https://twitter.com
/KariLakeWarRoom/status/1569071110108631040.

[18] Andrea Mitchell, "Katie Hobbs: Debating Kari Lake 'doesn't do any
service to the voters,'" MSNBC, October 12, 2022, https://www.msnbc
.com/andrea-mitchell-reports/watch/katie-hobbs-debating-kari-lake
-doesn-t-do-any-service-to-the-voters-150486085867.

[19] Jordan Conradson, "Arizona PBS to Defy the Arizona Clean
Elections Commission, Allow Katie Hobbs One-on-One Interview
in Place of Debate," Gateway Pundit, October 12, 2022, https://www
.thegatewaypundit.com/2022/10/breaking-arizona-pbs-defy-arizona
-clean-elections-commission-allow-katie-hobbs-one-one-interview-place
-debate-kari-lake-releases-statement-pbs-betrayal/.

[20] Irene Snyder et al., "2022 Election: Debacle continues over debate
between Arizona gubernatorial candidates," Fox 10 Phoenix, Updated
October 23, 2022, https://www.fox10phoenix.com/news/2022-election
-arizona-clean-elections-commission-postpones-interview-with-kari-lake.

[21] Nick Gilbertson, "Republican Kari Lake's Q&A Postponed
after Arizona PBS Grants Democrat Katie Hobbs Underserved
Interview," Breitbart, October 12, 2022, https://www.breitbart.com
/politics/2022/10/12/republican-kari-lakes-qa-postponed-after-arizona
-pbs-grants-democrat-katie-hobbs-undeserved-interview/?utm_source

=facebook&utm_medium=social&fbclid=IwAR3jMHO0C-tQKGob42dy
DsdRZc9SBj0MYE9PIg1r8MTVX_TE_q0h-wWj52g.

[22] "Arizona Governor – Lake vs. Hobbs," Real Clear Politics, https://www.
realclearpolitics.com/epolls/2022/governor/az/arizona_governor_lake_vs_
hobbs-7842.html.

Chapter 12: David vs. Goliath

[1] KariLake, "Kari Lake is the CLEAR winner in the first AZ Gov
Debate," Rumble, https://rumble.com/vvg944-kari-lake-is-the-clear
-winner-in-the-first-az-gov-debate.-watch-her-respons.html.

[2] Matthew Foldi, "Watch GOP Ad Yanked from Airwaves Due to Images
of Illegal Border Crossings," Free Beacon, February 8, 2022, https://
freebeacon.com/elections/watch-gop-ad-yanked-from-airwaves-due-to
-images-of-illegal-border-crossings/.

[3] @clegg1776 tweet, Twitter, January 18, 2022, https://twitter.com/clegg
1776/status/1483662426528616448?s=42&t=uaPrxJ4BqVgDXhXdWjf
aIw.

[4] Kalyn Stralaw, "Karrin Taylor Robson spent more money than any other
Republican statewide candidate or officeholder in Arizona," Ballotpedia
News, August 31, 2022, https://news.ballotpedia.org/2022/08/31/
karrin-taylor-robson-spent-more-than-any-other-republican-statewide
-candidate-or-officeholder-in-arizona/

[5] @Karrin4Arizona tweet, Twitter, July 8, 2022, https://twitter.com/karrin
4arizona/status/1545482157908340736.

[6] Kevin Stone, "On the fence? Border union leader likes Lake's plan but
prefers Taylor Robson for governor," KTAR News, July 13, 2022, https://
ktar.com/story/5151461/border-union-leader-prefers-lakes-plan-but
-endorses-taylor-robson-for-governor/.

[7] Dareh Gregorian, "Drag queen blasts Arizona governor candidate as a 'hypocrite' for drag digs," NBC News, June 21, 2022, https://www.nbcnews.com/politics/2022-election/drag-queen-blasts-arizona-governor-candidate-hypocrite-drag-digs-rcna34534.

[8] KariLake, "Kari Lake Exposes Her Opponent's Disgusting Fundraising Tactic," Rumble, https://rumble.com/v1diivp-kari-lake-exposes-her-opponents-disgusting-fundraising-tactic.html.

[9] KariLake, "Kari Lake Calls Out RINO Opponent for Predatory Fundraising Scheme," https://rumble.com/v1cvt85-kari-lake-calls-out-rino-opponent-for-predatory-fundraising-scheme.html.

[10] Nick Sanchez, "High campaign spending keeps Karrin Taylor Robson competitive with more popular Kari Lake," KJZZ, updated August 1, 2022, https://kjzz.org/content/1798966/high-campaign-spending-keeps-karrin-taylor-robson-competitive-more-popular-kari-lake.

[11] @TheKariLake, "Our First TV Ad dropped today," Facebook, February 21, 2022, https://www.facebook.com/watch/?v=3126574544290318.

[12] "Kari Lake delivers late-night speech to supporters after taking the lead," Arizona's Family, August 3, 2022, https://www.azfamily.com/video/2022/08/03/kari-lake-delivers-late-night-speech-supporters-after-taking-lead/.

Chapter 14: Moving America Forward

[1] "A City upon a Hill: Winthrop's 'Modell of Christian Charity,' 1630," Bill of Rights Institute, https://billofrightsinstitute.org/activities/a-city-upon-a-hill-winthrops-modell-of-christian-charity-1630.

[2] "Remarks by President Obama at Strasbourg Town Hall," The White House, April 3, 2009, https://obamawhitehouse.archives.gov/the-press-office/remarks-president-obama-strasbourg-town-hall.

[3] "Tenth Amendment," Constitution Annotated, https://constitution
.congress.gov/constitution/amendment-10/#:~:text=The%20powers
https://constitution.congress.gov/constitution/amendment-10/ - :~:
text=The powers not delegated to,respectively, or to the people.%20
not%20delegated%20to,respectively%2C%20or%20to%20the%20people.

[4] "Democrats Still Believe Russia Changed 2016 Election,"
Rasmussen Reports, April 21, 2022, https://www.rasmussenreports
.com/public_content/politics/general_politics/april_2022/democrats
_still_believe_russia_changed_2016_election.

[5] Mark Murray, "Poll: 61% of Republicans still believe Biden didn't win
fair and square in 2020," NBC News, September 27, 2022, https://www
.nbcnews.com/meet-the-press/meetthepressblog/poll-61-republicans-
still-believe-biden-didnt-win-fair-square-2020-rcna49630https://www.
nbcnews.com/meet-the-press/meetthepressblog
/poll-61-republicans-still-believe-biden-didnt-win-fair-square-2020-.

[6] "Most Voters Share GOP Concerns about 'Botched' Arizona Election,"
Rasmussen Reports, November 30, 2022, https://www.rasmussenreports
.com/public_content/politics/biden_administration/most_voters_
share_gop_concerns_about_botched_arizona_election#:~:text=The%20
latest%20Rasmussen%20Reports%20national%20telephone%20and%20
online,the%20outcome%20of%20the%20Senate%.

Chapter 15: A Dream Becomes a Nightmare

[1] Maricopa County Quick Facts, https://www.maricopa.gov/3598/County
-Quick-Facts.

[2] Jordan Conradson, "EXCLUSIVE: Maricopa County Supervisor
Steve Chucri on 2020 Election in Leaked Recording," *Gateway Pundit*,
September 21, 2021, https://www.thegatewaypundit.com/2021/09
/exclusive-maricopa-county-supervisor-steve-chucri-2020-election-leaked

-recording-think-done-dead-people-voting-think-multifaceted-ballot
-harvesting-audio/.

3 "Arizona Republican Party Election Audit, Preliminary Report" by
Stephen Richer, January 25, 2019, https://s3.documentcloud.org
/documents/5699777/AZGOP-Preliminary-Audit-Findings.pdf. Also see
Jeremy Duda, "AZGOP audit says Fontes actions questionable, not illegal,"
AZ Mirror, January 31, 2019, https://www.azmirror.com/2019/01/31
/azgop-audit-says-fontes-actionshttps://www.azmirror.com/2019/01/31
/azgop-audit-says-fontes-actions-questionable-not-illegal/-questionable
-not-illegal/.

4 Arizona Governor – Lake vs Hobbs, https://www.realclearpolitics.com
/epolls/2022/governor/az/arizona_governor_lake_vs_hobbs-7842.html.

5 Tracy Beanz, "Kari Lake Takes Election Case to AZ Supreme Court,"
Uncover DC, March 5, 2023, https://www.uncoverdc.com/2023/03/05
/analysis-kari-lake-takes-election-case-to-az-supreme-court/.

6 @MaricopaVote tweet, Twitter, November 8, 2022, https://twitter.com
/MaricopaVote/status/1590009384377384961.

7 @Kari Lake tweet, Twitter, November 8, 2022, https://twitter.com/Kari
Lake/status/1590088202408189952?s=20.

8 @theblaze tweet, Twitter, November 8, 2022, https://twitter.com/the
blaze/status/1590072053033406464.

9 Caitlin Sievers, "Day 2 of Kari Lake election trial marked by competing
'expert' testimony," *Tucson Sentinel*, December 23, 2022, https://www
.tucsonsentinel.com/local/report/122322_lake_election_trial/day
-2-kari-lake-election-trial-marked-by-competing-expert-testimony/.

10 All quotes from election night in Scottsdale are from Fox 10, "2022
Election: Arizona governor candidate Kari Lake addresses supporters,"
YouTube, November 8, 2022, https://www.youtube.com/watch?v
=quSu1EAEZI8.

[11] Arizona Supreme Court Case of *Kari Lake v. Katie Hobbs*, https://savearizonafund.com/ArizonaSupremeCourt/.

[12] Tracy Beanz, "Fraud in the Arizona Election: There's No Evidence!" Uncover DC, February 23, 2023, https://www.uncoverdc.com/2023/02/23/fraud-in-the-arizona-election-theres-no-evidence/.

[13] Erick Wikum, "A Decidedly Insufficient Statistical Analysis," Informs, February 16, 2023, https://pubsonline.informs.org/do/10.1287/orms.2023.01.05/full/.

[14] "Residents Blast Maricopa County Bord of Supervisors for Disenfranchising Voters, Gross Incompetence," *Arizona Daily Independent*, November 16, 2022, https://arizonadailyindependent.com/2022/11/16/residents-blast-maricopa-county-board-of-supervisors-for-disenfranchising-voters-gross-incompetence/.

[15] Neil Jones, "Republican Maricopa County Board Supervisor Steve Gallardo Serving on Katie Hobbs Transition Team," *Arizona Sun Times*, November 28, 2022, https://arizonasuntimes.com/news/republican-maricopa-county-board-supervisor-steve-gallardo-serving-on-katie-hobbs-transition-team/njones/2022/11/28/.

[16] Kari Donavan, "'Censorship Regime!' Lake Lawyer Kurt Olsen Slams AZ Hobbs and Richer in Historic Election Lawsuit," Frontline America, December 10, 2022, https://frontlineamerica.com/censorship-regime-lake-lawyer-kurt-olsen-slams-az-hobbs-and-richer-in-historic-election-lawsuit/.

[17] "Kari Lake Election Lawsuit Trial Underway, Day 2, Pt. 1," YouTube, December 22, 2022, https://www.youtube.com/watch?v=vx3NxaVvP1s.

[18] Adam Carter/Tracy Beanz, "Maricopa Heat Maps: The Story Keeps Getting Worse," UncoverDC, February 8, 2023, https://www.uncoverdc.com/2023/02/08/maricopa-heat-maps-the-story-keeps-getting-worse/.

[19] @KariLakeWarRoom tweet, Twitter, December 26, 2022, https://twitter.com/KariLakeWarRoom/status/1607519675528904704?lang=en.

[20] Caitlin Sievers, "Lake election suit will go to trial: Judge dismisses eight of 10 counts," *AZ Mirror*, December 20, 2022, https://www.azmirror.com/2022/12/20/lake-election-suit-will-go-to-trial-judge-dismisses-seven-of-nine-counts/.

Epilogue: A Safe Landing

[1] KariLake, "Save Arizona Rally featuring Kari Lake," Rumble, January 29, 2023, https://rumble.com/v27mq3w-save-arizona-rally-featuring-kari-lake.html.

Visit WinningPublishing.com for our newest books!

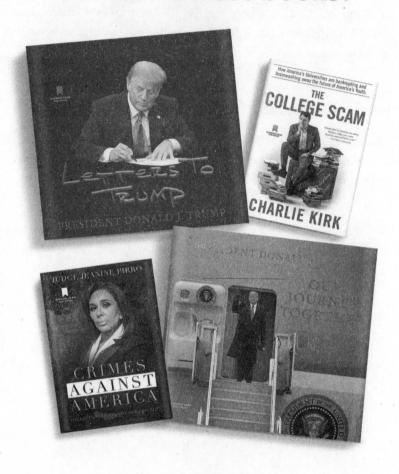